'A gripping and exciting book for all explorers, whether the armchair or real variety' *Geographical*

'The emotional highs and lows are always the lifeblood of these explorers' accounts, not the altitude of the mountains they climb. Hempleman-Adams and his collaborator Ian Stafford have grasped this. There is a lot of talk about missing the absent family, and much gnashing of teeth when equipment or weather foils progress. *Toughing It Out* is an excellent read, too, if you are interested in the nitty-gritty: how heavy the sledge was, why the crampon snapped . . . there are some exhilarating accounts of exceptionally hard slogs and some nice moments back at home' *Daily Telegraph*

'Compulsive reading, real gut-churning, seat-of-the-pants escapism for a long grey winter' *Birmingham Post*

'Over 20 years of death-defying adventures, bringing us closer to understanding the strength of character needed to survive hostile conditions . . . a must for teatray travellers everywhere' *Maxim*

David Hempleman-Adams has become one of the world's greatest living explorers by climbing the highest mountain on each continent and reaching the North and South geographic and magnetic poles. His recent conquest of the North Pole ended an 18-year odyssey that has dominated his life and written him into the history books as the first person to complete the Adventurer's Grand Slam. David Hempleman-Adams was born in Swindon, Wiltshire, in 1956. His interest in adventuring was inspired by the Duke of Edinburgh Award Scheme, of which he is a gold medallist. A businessman by profession, he lives in Wiltshire with his wife and children.

By the same author
Walking on Thin Ice

Ian Stafford, who has collaborated with David Hempleman-Adams in writing this book, is a prolific writer, journalist and broadcaster. A former chief sports reporter for the *Mail on Sunday*, he was voted best National Sports Reporter of the Year in 1990, and Magazine Sports Writer of the Year in 1995. He was commended for his work as a magazine writer in 1994 and 1997. He lives in Kent with his wife and children.

TOUGHING IT OUT
The Adventures of
A Polar Explorer and Mountaineer

DAVID HEMPLEMAN-ADAMS

ORION

An Orion Paperback
First published in Great Britain by Orion in 1997
This paperback edition published in 1998 by
Orion Books Ltd,
Orion House, 5 Upper St Martin's Lane,
London WC2H 9EA

A CIP catalogue record for this book
is available from the British Library.

ISBN: 0 75281 740 X

Typeset by Selwood Systems, Midsomer Norton
Printed and bound in Great Britain by
Clays Ltd, St Ives plc

To my girls, and friends lost
For times past, and times to come

CONTENTS

Foreword by H.R.H. The Prince of Wales   ix
Acknowledgements   xi

PART ONE

1   The Start of an Obsession   3

2   A Cold Reality
    The Geographical North Pole Trip, 1983   21

3   Close Call
    The Magnetic North Pole Trip, 1984   40

4   Journey to the Unknown
    The Geomagnetic North Pole Trip, 1992   56

5   On Top of the World
    Mount Everest   79

6   The Magnificent Seven
    The Completion of the Seven Summits   104

PART TWO

7   Attention to Detail
    The South Pole Trip, 1995–6   121

8   Thank You, Mrs T   138

9   Close to the Abyss   159

10 'Can Anyone Hear Me?'   176

CONTENTS

PART THREE

11   A New Danger
The Magnetic South Pole Trip,
February–March 1996   197

12   Success in the Night   216

13   Breaking Ice
The Ultimate Challenge, April–May 1996   233

14   In the Nick of Time   251

15   Unlucky for Some
The North Pole Expedition, 1997   272

Maps   295

Index   303

ST. JAMES'S PALACE

I first became associated with David Hempleman-Adams in 1996 when he introduced me to an intrepid group of novice adventurers who were about to embark on a North Magnetic Pole Expedition.

That expedition proved to be hugely successful. They were the largest ski group to reach the Magnetic Pole and David became the first person to visit both the North and South Magnetic Poles in the same year. In addition, they served the cause of science by recording the most accurate position yet of the North Magnetic Pole.

As President of The Prince's Trust, I was delighted that it was the beneficiary of this latest, unsupported expedition, by David and his Norwegian partner, Rune Gjeldnes, to reach the Geographical North Pole. Sadly, this attempt was thwarted by ill luck when much of the work had been completed.

This book is about an extraordinary man, whose love for adventure has inspired many others throughout the world, not only to discover the planet we live on, but also the limits of their own endurance. David Hempleman-Adams has carried the torch in the best tradition of the gloriously mad adventurers of this country, embodying so well the human spirit of determination, courage and sheer will power.

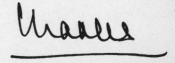

ACKNOWLEDGEMENTS

After nearly thirty expeditions around the world, I am very conscious that I have not got enough space to thank everyone who has helped me over the years, and while people may be omitted, they certainly have not been forgotten. I thank each and every one of you.

I would, however, like to take this opportunity to mention a few people. Firstly, Ian Stafford, who put in an immense amount of time, skill and patience helping me to write this book. I would also like to thank my teachers, who started me on my journey of discovery: Mansell James, Roy Knight and John Price.

To a thousand and one sponsors, and many who have become good friends, people like Jim May and family, John Nelligan, Clive Mann, Rikki Hunt, Bill Tidy, Rajiv Wahi, Peter McPhillips, Mike Boon, Jeremy Lang, Malcolm Wallace, Franz la Rosee, Sir Graham Kirkham, Eric Worrall of the Duke of Edinburgh Award, and Tom Shebbeare of the Prince's Trust.

To friends who have helped and joined me: Steve, Mitch, Neill, Jock, Geoff, Anne, Brian, Clive, Jules, Becks, Stud, Blue, Borge, Rune, Feodore, Bernard, Thierry, Mac, George, Paul, Phil, Ron, Eric, Stewart, Mags, Tony, Duncan, Quint, Jerry, Sue and Charles.

To my office, who sort my mess out for me: Norman, Mark, Sue, Lynn, Rachel, Christine, Dot and Adrian.

And last, but most important of all, my girls – Claire, Alicia, Camilla and Amelia – for being there.

PART ONE

"I SUPPOSE WE'RE LUCKY TO BE ALIVE!"

THE START OF AN
OBSESSION

Waiting is the worst part. As I lay in my tent, knowing that a recovery plane was on its way to collect me and my partner and take us away from the icy ravages, I knew that the long journey home had already begun. I could not quite believe that the Arctic had defeated me again. Fourteen years before, the North Pole had given me a sound beating for having the temerity to attempt to reach it, supported but solo, and with next to no experience. I paid a heavy mental and physical price back then; this time it was totally different. We had survived the hardest part of the expedition and I fully expected to be standing at the Pole within four weeks. As ever, it would have depended on our luck holding out, and the weather, the ice and nature itself being kind to us. This time I fell short in the luck department.

So much has happened to me since I first decided I wanted to be an adventurer. As I fidgeted in my tent, with the wind howling outside and the snow swirling around reducing visibility almost to nil, I realised, despite this huge set-back, how lucky I had been in the past, not only in conquering the highest and reaching the furthest – indeed the top and the bottom of the world – but also in staying alive. I felt tired and hungry. Fourteen years after my first polar adventure, eighteen years after climbing the highest mountain in North America, I was still in one piece in one of the most barren and unwelcome places on the planet. As I closed my eyes and drifted into a deep, deep sleep, I saw a young schoolboy in Wales discovering, for the first time in his life, the lure of the mountains, the outside, and the dangers of the natural world. That boy had since come a long way.

I was born David Kim Hempleman, back in October 1956, in Swindon. When I was nine my parents were divorced, a terribly messy business made worse because, even in the mid-sixties, at least in the West Country, divorce was still rather taboo. I was faced with a difficult decision: should I go with my father, or my mother? I plumped for my mother, deciding for my five-year-old brother Mark in the process. This was partly because my father was often abroad on business.

We moved to a small village outside Bath called Stoney Littleton where, shortly afterwards, my mother remarried, changing my name to Adams. My mother did not want anyone to know she had been divorced and tried very hard to keep it a secret. It got to the point where everyone called me Kim instead of my first Christian name, David, which I shared with my father. For the first year I hated my stepfather. I didn't blame him for the split, I just resented the fact that he had become a replacement father. As I grew older I began to respect the fact that at least he looked after us all. This did not alter my affection for my father, however, and when I was twenty-four I decided to reintroduce the name Hempleman, placing it before Adams.

By the time I was eleven I had already developed a love of the outdoors. Where we lived felt as if it was in the middle of absolutely nowhere; it was a mile's walk just to the bus stop in order to catch the bus for school. I was allowed to work during my school holiday around the local farms, driving tractors and combine harvesters, and gathering vegetables and cereals. I worked through all seasons, in shirtsleeves during the summer sitting on top of tractors, and in the raw cold of winter, pulling sheep out of snowdrifts. Even then I knew I would never want to work in the smoke of a big city. I had been transformed from a boy from a railway town to a country lad. I loved getting dirty, working hard, and forever being in the fresh country air.

My love affair with adventure followed shortly afterwards. I went to Writhlington Comprehensive near Bath where there was a PE teacher called Mansell James. 'Jesse', as we all called him behind his back, was universally feared. If for any reason you were unable to play sport, he would make sure you still carried out some kind of chore, from rolling the cricket pitch to cleaning the batting pads. At the time he was in his late thirties, and spoke with a deep, resounding Welsh accent. For some reason he took an early shine to me. He used to sit down and talk to me, which he never seemed to do with anyone else. Mind you, I was the only kid with divorced parents in the whole school, so maybe that was the initial reason. It was his guidance and encouragement which led me into adventure through the Duke of Edinburgh Award scheme, which the school eagerly offered to its pupils.

I was thirteen when I first became involved in the scheme. In July 1969, a group of kids from the school were bussed out to the Brecon Beacons and housed in a big army tent. It was the first time I had been away from home. I had never been on a mountain before and I had never seen stars so bright, nor so near. I tried a bit of rock climbing and instantly loved it. I recall vividly the mist and the solitude of that trip up my first mountain. It was the unspoilt, untarnished beauty of the terrain that hit me like a boxer's punch. I seemed to strike up an immediate affinity with the wilderness, and with the solitude. Maybe that was it. Although I did not feel at the time that I was particularly affected by my parents' divorce, perhaps it was the peace and calm, in direct contrast to the personal turmoil I had previously experienced, that drew me, like a magnet, to the mountains. When it was time to go home, the kid who had never been away from home before did not want to go back. I had just discovered something totally wonderful, and it was obvious, even at such an age, that the outdoors and adventure would have to play a major part in my life.

The following year I was awarded with the Duke of Edinburgh bronze award after performing a series of skills. These, in my case, were first aid, physical fitness, a hobby (for which I chose badminton), and an expedition which, for me, was the highlight. I returned to the same camp in the Brecon Beacons and, together with four companions, had to reach a checkpoint thirty miles away using maps and compasses. We were supposed to reach Jesse by six o'clock that evening, but as the day went on it became clear that we would struggle to make the appointed time. There was no way I was going to fail so, because I was the cockiest in the group, I said I would go on ahead at my faster speed, reach Jesse, and tell him that the rest were just coming over the hill. I shot off and succeeded in finding Jesse by the appointed time. I naturally thought that Jesse would think I was the bee's knees for doing this; instead, he gave me a smack around the head and told me never to leave a group again. He said either you all get there, or none of you, because this was supposed to be about teamwork. It was an early lesson that was to prove important time and time again in later years.

Still, I had done enough to claim my bronze. Before trying for my next goal, the silver award, I went on my first school skiing trip. This was the first time I had ever been skiing. Within a couple of days I felt quite comfortable on skis; by the end of the week I was reaching the bottom of the mountain, wondering why the teachers were so far behind.

For my silver award I more or less repeated the skills carried out for the bronze award. When it came to the expedition I returned once more to the Brecon Beacons. I was older and more mature, so I was, therefore, physically stronger, more confident, better at map reading, and more of a team player.

With this latest award under my belt I began to go off and do my own things. For example, I hitched a lift to Snowdonia with a few mates during the following Easter holidays, and we scrambled our way up Snowdon and other mountains. For my gold award I had to complete a seventy-mile expedition, this time on Dartmoor. I was sixteen by that time, and enjoyed it as much as my bronze award.

Mountaineering had, in a very short space of time, become my life. I very quickly came to the conclusion that I was at my happiest half-way up a mountain. I seemed particularly to enjoy meeting stiffer climbing challenges, and in proving to myself that I was good in this area. The proving part may have stemmed from the insecurity of the broken home; I just felt compelled to prove that I was as good, if not better, than anyone else. I never bothered to analyse this urge at the time – I was too young, and probably still too hurt – but looking back, at a time when I must have seemed a novelty to my classmates at school who went home to both parents, the divorce clearly must have affected me more than I realised. To this day I still feel at my most relaxed when climbing a mountain. Some things never change.

I literally lived and breathed mountaineering, devouring books and magazines on the subject, desperate for as much information as I could obtain. I remember attending a lecture at the Colston Hall in Bristol in 1972 conducted by members of Chris Bonington's team which had just failed to reach the summit of Mount Everest using the difficult south-west face. Bonington was, at the time, Mr Mountaineering, at least as far as Britain was concerned. He was the face of the sport, partly through his books, but also because he was the only real professional mountaineer in Britain, and it was his efforts that paved the way for the financial rewards mountaineers can obtain today. My heroes were, however, Dougal Haston, who reminded me of my Uncle Peter on my father's side, and Doug Scott, who back then wore John Lennon-style glasses, a bandanna, and had long hair. I had posters of Che Guevara and Steve McQueen on my bedroom wall at the time, so I saw Scott as the epitome of anti-establishment. At the end of the lecture I queued up with an Everest poster. I wanted to ask Scott and Haston a stack of questions, but when it came to my turn I froze, and I just ended up thanking them for signing my poster.

Later I recalled them mentioning how Bonington used numerous porters to help the team reach base camp which, at Everest, is still higher than anywhere in the Alps. When I looked at some of their slides I noticed how they used everyone and everything to help them get to base, from women and (seemingly) kids to yaks and dogs. I decided to write to Bonington. I told him I was sixteen, was midway through my Duke of Edinburgh award, and had enjoyed his lecture. I added that I noticed how he had used young people as porters and, if I paid for myself, wondered if I could be a porter on his next Everest trip, which was pencilled in for the following year. I was so determined to get to Everest I would have left home and my school if given the chance.

Bonington replied within a week. He thanked me for the letter, and said how well I was doing with my Duke of Edinburgh awards, but that I was too young to join him on the next trip. The overriding message of the letter, however, was to hang in there and keep on aiming to fulfil my dreams. Everyone should have their own Everest to climb in life, although it does not actually have to be the mountain itself. Although he rejected me, Chris Bonington gave me a tremendous boost with this letter by not just telling me to sod off.

Funnily enough, though, Everest was my own particular mountain to climb at the time. I thought I was becoming quite accomplished as a climber, and it was therefore natural to dream of reaching the summit of the world's highest mountain. Polar adventures just did not come into my reckoning at all as a teenager. I knew every route on Everest, everything about every trip that had ever been made on the mountain and about every person who had summited.

I was still living at home when I first obtained a place at Hollings College in Manchester to specialise in business studies, and then, almost immediately after hearing this news, I was selected to partake in a student exchange trip to America. I headed straight off to a summer camp in New York State. On arriving in New York City I was told that I would be at Camp Ranger in upper New York State beside a lake named Swan Lake. The kids attending this summer camp were aged between six and seventeen. It turned out to be a school of excellence, light years ahead of anything Britain could offer at the time. Specialists were flown in from all corners of the country to provide the best tuition. It turned out that I had been chosen as the specialist in rock climbing. The only other British specialist out there was another eighteen-year-old called Steve Vincent, who would be teaching sub-aqua diving.

I made a point of introducing myself to Steve. We went out for a burger one night and I discovered that he, too, came from Swindon. By the end of the evening we had hit it off in a big way. As the weeks passed Steve and I spent more and more time together. We used to drive the kids up into the Catskill Mountains, famous as a favoured training venue for American heavyweight boxers, and teach them to hill climb and rock climb. After the eight weeks were up Steve and I spent a further five weeks by ourselves climbing first in Newpalz, and then out in Wyoming and California.

The following Easter, after two terms at college, I joined Steve on a climbing expedition in the Alps. He was study-ing geography at Queen Mary College in London. In order to finance myself I raised £250 through sponsorship which, back in the late 1970s, was a huge amount of money. I achieved this by finding ten pubs in the Bath area telephone directory called The Red Lion. I took a sheet off my mother's bed and painted a red lion on it. I then telephoned the pubs individually and told them I would take a photograph of me holding out the sheet with the pub's name on top of a mountain called Monta Rosa which, at 15,000 feet, is the highest in Switzerland. Each pub thought it was The Red Lion depicted in the picture.

We became close climbing partners, building up a rapport which meant that we could understand each other without even speaking. We were soon shooting up moun-tains like the Matterhorn as if they were the Sussex Downs. If there was any doubt left in my mind about mountains, the Alps settled the issue once and for all. Their sheer beauty, size and grandeur converted me completely to the cause. I knew that ahead of me lay a host of wonderful challenges. I also recognised that I had been lucky enough to discover my vocation in life. How many people can honestly say the same thing? I came to the conclusion that I had a chance to do what I really wanted to in my life, and that I owed it to myself to grasp the opportunity with both hands. Steve, at least for a while, felt the same way. I had a better technical knowledge, but he was undoubtedly the bolder climber. We continued to obtain local sponsorship and set out to climb as many well-known peaks in the Alps as possible. By the time we were twenty-two years old we had climbed Mont Blanc, Monta Rosa, the Eiger and the Weisshorn, among many, many others.

It was on the Weisshorn that we both had our first brush with death. We found ourselves half-way up the mountain as dawn broke, when a fierce electric storm suddenly hit us from nowhere. A combination of wind and powdered snow began to pile into our faces and we reached a quick decision to give up on our attempt to reach the summit and return to our base hut. It took us twenty hours to get back. During this time I slipped on a couple of occasions and was saved by Steve's instinctive hands. I remember looking across at him and seeing some of his protection ping out of the rock. It was a time to pray that at least some of the nuts would hold on and remain in the rock; with a steep drop below, the alternative was too much even to consider.

There are thousands of stories concerning climbers who have died a hundred yards or so from their hut, or at least from safety. Our hut on the Weisshorn was close to the bottom of the mountain on a ledge. It had got to four o'clock in the morning and we had somehow managed to get off the main mountain and on to the path back, which was on the snowy bottom of the mountain. The conditions were still horrendous, and we were both exhausted. We had not eaten or drunk anything for over a day and felt completely dehydrated. We were both young, strong and fit guys, but to this day I have never again been in such a state. It is likely that we would not have survived another hour.

Steve sat down and told me he was finished, and that he wanted me to cut the rope and leave him. I pulled the rope in an attempt to drag him with me, which prompted him, rather bizarrely, to say that he would kill me if I didn't do what he had asked. I don't know how much further we could have got away with it but, after staggering another fifty yards, our hut suddenly appeared from within the snowstorm. That same night a fellow British climber, a young man called Dave Allcock who had worked with me at Plas-y-Brenin, died in the same storm on the Breithorn.

For the next couple of years Steve and I spent our holidays travelling the world on a shoestring budget and feeding our voracious appetite for climbing and skiing. Yet still I yearned to see Everest. In 1979 my chance, or so I thought, came. A German and a Yugoslav team were attempting to climb the mountain. I wrote to both of them saying that I was coming out and would like to join up. Steve, who was earning some extra cash at college dispatch riding, had just broken his leg in an accident and could not travel with me, but I was determined to go. I managed to save up just enough money to obtain all the necessary equipment. I was hoping that one of the teams would let me climb with them up the ice fall, or at least carry some of their load for them.

Having arrived at base camp – Everest – I managed to pay for a trekking permit, but not a climbing permit, which cost far too much for my resources. Still, at least I was looking at Everest for the first time in my life, albeit from base camp at 18,000 feet. It was as impressive as I had imagined it to be. I remember sitting down looking up towards the peak and thinking that maybe one day I would get to the top. For the time being, however, I had to make do with climbing around the base camp. Unable to go with either of the Everest trips because of my lack of climbing permit, I set off alone towards the gateway between Nepal and Tibet. The further I climbed the worse I felt until I suddenly realised that, although it hardly seemed mountainous, I was higher than I had ever been in my life and, as a result, was experiencing mild altitude sickness. On reaching a loose, shaly part of the climb, and without the use of ropes, I began to slip and slide. It took the rest of the day to return the short route back, stumbling my way while feeling light-headed and nauseous. I had been incredibly irresponsible to have gone out by myself in the first place.

On returning to England I completed my business studies course before obtaining a postgraduate place at what was then called Bristol Polytechnic in order to take the equivalent of a Master of Business Administration. The work was hard, but I also had a great deal of free time, which meant that Steve and I could carry on with our adventures. Our next aim was Mount McKinley in Alaska which, at 20,320 feet, is the highest mountain in North America. At the time I never gave the idea of climbing the seven highest summits in the world's seven continents a moment's thought, but we both had an affinity with America, and McKinley was considered both hard – because it is one of the coldest mountains in the world, being in the north of Alaska – and dangerous – because its mixture of snow and rock meant possible avalanches and crevasses.

Having obtained £1000 in sponsorship, mainly through a company called Euro Pleasure, courtesy of managing director Colin Fuller, we flew to New York and then caught the Greyhound bus first to Anchorage, and then on to a tiny hicksville town called Talkeetna. From there we were flown in a Cessna to McKinley, landing at the base camp in the Kahilitna Glacier. It was now August 1980, which was late in the year to climb McKinley. As a result only Steve and I and a Japanese team would be attempting the summit. At base camp there is a shack where a meteorologist provides weather reports for those in Talkeetna; the climbing fraternity has christened this shack the Talkeetna Hilton. We stayed at base camp acclimatising and climbing around the foot of the mountain for a week until we decided we were ready.

Looking back, two aspects of the climb still amaze me: by reaching the summit in just over four days we achieved our goal in incredibly quick time, but we were also extremely fortunate, and lucky in our arrogance and naivety, to survive. A little knowledge can sometimes be very dangerous, and I reckoned I could recognise an avalanche path when I saw one. The truth was, once out on the slopes of McKinley, we crossed over a series of avalanche paths, all of which could at any time have provoked a snowfall which would have swept us to our deaths.

One night, while in our tent, the ground started to shake. This went on for three minutes while Steve and I tried to keep still, absolutely petrified. Once the shaking stopped the rumbling began. Even we could tell what was going on outside: a minor earthquake, not uncommon in Alaska, had sparked off a series of avalanches, and the rumbling represented the sound of ice and snow cascading down the mountain. I stuck my head out of the tent to try to see if any was coming our way, but the weather conditions, the earthquake and the distant avalanches had created a total white-out, a situation where the ground and the sky are indefinable, resulting in visibility of less than five yards through a pea-soup fog of white.

I withdrew my head and confirmed what Steve was fearing. We then just sat staring at each other, scared witless and mute, waiting to see if we would suddenly be eaten up by an avalanche. Eventually the rumbling died down and, exhausted through our climbing efforts and fear, we both fell asleep. In the morning we emerged from our tent to discover that an avalanche had ground to a halt just fifty yards from our tent. To this day I do not know why the avalanche stopped where it did, but I do know that I would not be writing this book if it had decided to roar on a little further.

After this scare we flew up the mountain, following the bamboo-cane-marked route as we neared the summit. On reaching the top we shook hands, took photographs and got the hell out of there. It was not a time for emotions. We were both scared, homesick, and very tired, and all we wanted to do was get back down to base camp. The weather remained atrocious as we groped our way back down the mountain. I remember, out in front of Steve, trying to retrace our steps and find our tent. It was another white-out and I started to veer off to the left.

At this point Steve shouted out to me that I was wrong. Tired and short-fused, I turned round and yelled back, 'Bollocks. This is the route.' It's probably the only cross word I have ever exchanged with Steve. He repeated his claim that I was wrong. By that time he had grown a thick Mexican moustache, which was crusted up with ice. My eyelids, meanwhile, were freezing up, the wind was howling all around us, and we really were in a dangerous situation. Bearing in mind that we could barely see anything, I asked him what made him so sure; he said he just had a gut feeling that the tent was fifty yards away in a totally opposite direction. I stared at him for some time, but he seemed so full of conviction that eventually I decided to do it his way. Turning 180 degrees we came to the tent within a couple of minutes of walking. I reckoned, with me saving his neck on the Weisshorn, we were quits.

On completing McKinley we made our way down through the United States, climbing in the Yosemite

National Park, and through to Mexico and Central America, ascending 19,000-foot volcanoes, before finally making our way into South America and the Andes. In all we were away for six months. We had both finished our college courses and, in short, we had little to do and wished for nothing more than to climb.

During this time we bummed our way through Ecuador, Peru, Chile and Argentina before finally landing in Rio de Janeiro where, within a few days, all our gear was stolen. On obtaining more money from the British Consulate we were told that Ronnie Biggs could be found in a nearby bar so, with nothing better to do, we went down and met the man. It sounds strange moaning about how some bastard had just stolen our gear to a former train robber, but he bought us a drink, listened to us for a few minutes, and was probably glad to see the back of us.

Once we arrived back in Britain Steve and I got hold of student railcards and managed to visit twenty-one different European countries in just one week. We might have gone on like this for ever had we then not decided it might be sensible to start looking at making a living. Together with a mutual friend, Jerry Scriven, who went to Bristol Poly with me and who joined us on one of our Mont Blanc climbs, Steve and I decided to set up a company importing ski and mountaineering clothing and equipment, making New York our base. But before we settled down a bit and grew up, we wanted one last binge. We plumped for Mount Kilimanjaro, the highest peak in Africa.

Just before leaving Steve and I met the girls we were later to marry. I went for a drink in the student union bar at Bristol Poly with a former professor of mine and saw Claire standing in the corner with some friends. She was a first year law student and, for some strange reason, I seemed to know at first sight that this would be the girl for me. We started talking, got on really well, and met a couple of times more. I gave her my address in Nairobi, where I would be mainly based, and she agreed to write. Steve, meanwhile, had met a young doctor called Cathy.

Like everything else in those days, the trip had to be done on the cheap, so we jumped on various buses in August 1981 and weaved our way through Greece, Israel, and down through Egypt until we reached the border with north-west Sudan, closed due to civil war. We returned to Cairo and caught a cheap flight to Nairobi in order to climb Mount Kenya. This was a simple climb and was achieved in a couple of days with little hardship and no mishaps. The bigger test would be Kilimanjaro on the border between Kenya and Tanzania.

On reaching the foot of Kilimanjaro, we started to make our way round the mountain and, subsequently, over the border to Tanzania. As soon as we set foot across the border the Tanzanian police picked us up, chucked us in some grotty police cells and supplied us, for some reason, with *Playboy* magazines. For a couple of hours we were uncertain what fate awaited us. They would not even let us telephone the nearest British Consulate. I started to have visions of them taking us round the back and blowing our heads off, but eventually the police kicked us back over the border. We then discovered a different route to our destination. Catching a local flight we landed at Entebbe airport in Uganda, where in 1976 Israeli commandos had rescued the hostages on board a French aircraft hijacked by a Palestinian liberation group. It was an empty, scary place to be. There was nobody around, and the walls were scarred with bullet holes. I was amazed that a flight was leaving for Tanzania at all. Paying the equivalent of five pounds, the airline cashiers had no change, so we each accepted a bunch of bananas instead.

Kilimanjaro proved to be a difficult mountain to climb,

not because it was particularly dangerous, but because the volcanic ash under our feet turned it into a hard slog. Looking back, with all seven summits now under my belt, I would say that for all the wonderful wildlife and jungle at the base, Kilimanjaro was probably the most disappointing of the lot. Still, the flip side was that it was also comparatively the safest to climb.

The trick was to climb the mountain as quickly as possible. For each day spent on Kilimanjaro you have to pay a certain amount to the Tanzanian National Park, and as we had next to no money we knew we could expect more time inside some cells unless we delivered the goods sharpish. The environment is very lush and green at the base of the mountain. You actually begin your climb through jungle, with monkeys swinging from tree to tree beside you. As the sun comes up each morning across the Masai Mara and the National Park you instantly recognise that you are in the very heart of Africa.

Eventually, past 10,000 feet or so, you rise above the tree belt and come across a lunar landscape of volcanic rock across a plateau. It was only as we neared the 18,000-foot summit that the ice began to appear. Having spent the best part of two months travelling to Kilimanjaro, and with both of us missing the new-found loves of our lives, we were desperate to get the trip over with. Much of the ascent was hiking rather than climbing, and even as we neared the summit we seemed to be running up the mountain.

At the summit we back-slapped and took more pictures. There is a small plaque confirming that Kilimanjaro is the highest peak on the continent, and a route of bamboo wands leading climbers to and from the summit. As I sat on top of Africa I compared the climb to others I had completed, like McKinley, and reckoned this was, in comparison, like a walk in the park.

I may have been away from home, and from Claire, for too long, but whatever the reason I suddenly started to feel dissatisfied, yearning for something else to do apart from just climbing. On my return to England I stumbled across a copy of *National Geographic* magazine which ran an article about a Japanese adventurer called Naomi Uemura. He had just returned from a successful trip to the Geographical North Pole using a dog team and air supplies. My first reaction was, why bother with dogs?

At the same time Ranulph Fiennes was organising his epic trans-global expedition, while Reinhold Messner had just climbed Mount Everest solo and without oxygen. I reckoned this was just about the ultimate in mountaineering. To do it solo was amazing enough, but without oxygen was just incredible. Although I still dreamed of climbing Everest, and to continue climbing elsewhere, I realised there was nothing left to do in mountaineering. Focusing on the North Pole trips I had read about, I reasoned that the extra cost and load of using dogs or snowmobiles, plus the awkwardness of trying to take them across Arctic terrain, quite possibly outweighed any advantages of using them. Why not do a Messner and just go in a straight line? This is how the idea was first born. I wanted to become the first man ever to walk solo to the North Pole, without the use of either dogs or snowmobiles.

I told Steve, who immediately volunteered to come out and be my main man at base camp. It was all rather embryonic at this stage, however, and I put it to the back of my mind while Steve, Jerry and I flew off to New York, a city we all loved and knew well, to set up the company, which we called Vascon. We lived in an apartment in a town named Far Rockaway on Long Island and worked hard to make the company a minor success. In our spare time we sold T-shirts at rock concerts. I also took advantage of New York's facilities by carrying out extensive research on the Arctic and the North Pole at the city's central library.

We had been going for six months when Steve suddenly announced, during a walk down Fifth Avenue, that he would be returning to England to marry Cathy. He assured me he would still accompany me on the North Pole trip, and asked if I would be his best man. I was missing Claire like mad by now, and Steve's news was the excuse I needed to return home. We ceased trading and made our way back to England.

As I sat on the long flight home I sized up my situation. I had little money to my name, no job, and no real ambition to do anything except be an adventurer. But, in my youthful naivety, I did not care one iota. I would be going to the North Pole, and from the moment I made the decision it became an obsession.

A COLD REALITY
The Geographical North Pole Trip, 1983

Once back in England Claire and I found a flat in Bristol, where she was studying law. Her parents were incredibly understanding and brave to let her do this, bearing in mind she was only eighteen and shacking up with some guy who wanted to spend all his time setting up a fool-hardy trek to the North Pole.

For the next year I used the flat as my office, and carried out more research in Bristol's main city library. Steve Vincent was married but was still determined to be with me, at least at base camp, for the trip ahead. Another friend of mine, Giorgio Matranga, who had been at school with me since the age of ten, was also brought in to the expedition. He had left college and become a radio operator for Portishead Radio in Bristol, which was extremely convenient for my purposes.

My next move was to meet Sir Ranulph Fiennes. He was the most experienced polar explorer in Britain, having been to both the North and South Poles (although neither solo nor unsupported), and had just returned from his trans-global expedition which saw him travel around the globe following the zero meridian from Greenwich. After a quick telephone call we arranged to meet at Chelsea Barracks. Fiennes proved to be extremely helpful. I pep-pered him with questions about equipment, radios, food and so on, and he was very forthcoming in his advice. He told me to take some Valium with me, so that I could sleep a little better, but I chose to ignore this. As I left he wished me the best of luck and told me that he had every confidence in the attempt.

I also made a point of contacting Wally Herbert. He traversed the North Pole with dogs, and probably knew the Arctic better than anyone in Britain. He was in his early fifties back in 1982, and never quite received the recognition he deserved, partly because the day he arrived at the North Pole a certain Neil Armstrong made a giant leap for mankind on the moon.

I then went off to meet the Royal Geographical Society in order to obtain official recognition and approval for the ensuing trip. I do not want to sound as if I have a chip on my shoulder about being educated at a comprehensive, but it was clear within minutes of meeting a small group of RGS committee members that I was frowned upon. They all seemed to look me up and down as we sat around a table. One of them started talking about changing a valve on a radio. I thought to myself that people had not been using valves on radios for many years, but politely explained that I was using an experienced radio operator. Another one asked if I would be wearing string vests. It was patently obvious that these old gentlemen had been on some kind of trip twenty or thirty years before and, consequently, saw themselves as experts. It was not the biggest shock to be told by the RGS that they were unable to rubber stamp the trip.

Much of my time was spent finding manufacturers and sponsors. I wrote nearly three thousand letters, bashing furiously away on an old typewriter in the flat. Most were in vain. I either received polite rejections or, in many cases, no response at all, but the sheer volume of letters sent out to people proved just about enough for my purposes. Over the next few months equipment started arriving at the offices of my father's epoxy resins company in Swindon,

Robnor. Because the rented flat in Bristol was already bursting at the seams with polar equipment, I started to use some warehouse space at Robnor. Each week jumpers from Pringle, or radios from Plessey, or sleeping bags from somewhere else would turn up at the door unannounced, and then be dumped in the warehouse. If my father minded, he never made it known to me.

I needed to raise £40,000 for the trip which, in polar expedition terms, is almost a shoestring budget. The most helpful sponsors were Gestetner, the photocopiers and stationery firm. They must have provided me with half of the required total. The rest came from local businesses, many of whom had helped me out on previous mountaineering trips.

The final piece in the jigsaw before leaving for the Arctic was to court publicity. I had no money, we were living in a small flat, and Claire was a student, so the only way to get sponsorship was to be publicised. In general I quite enjoyed the exposure and the experience of talking, for the first time in my life, to the media. In fact, some of my best friends now work in the media. I felt genuinely sorry for the BBC reporter whose mouth very nearly seized up while he was trying to interview me in a deep freeze. There were also some questions so fatuous that they almost hurt. One guy asked me if I would suffer from altitude sickness on reaching the North Pole; another asked why I would be flying back when it was an easy downhill ski ride.

By January 1983 I was just about ready. My research had been extensive, and I genuinely believed I stood a decent chance of making it to the Pole. But before leaving for Canada, I went through everything once more with meticulous detail. The goal was not only to reach the Pole, but to beat the existing record of forty-two days from Cape Columbia, the best starting point, to the North Pole.

I settled for an expedition base at the Eureka Weather

Station, from where I would be flown to my starting point at Cape Columbia. The journey would then fall into three stages, with each stage carrying a vital time deadline and each bringing its own brand of danger. From Cape Columbia I would face 200 miles of iced rubble. Here the terrain would forever be moving: when pack ice does not groan it is cracking, splitting and powdering, making a noise like a barrage of guns. Occasionally, the pressure of the ocean under the ice forces a massive fountain through the surface which drenches everything nearby in freezing water.

On other occasions icequakes take place. The surface is constantly uneven, with a series of pressure ridges, some as high as twenty-five feet, stretching in a series of batches over thirty miles or so. These pressure-ridge fields are littered with blocks of ice and debris left scattered for miles.

The Japanese adventurer Naomi Uemura wasted too much time and energy hacking away at the ice with picks and crowbars to allow his dog team to get past these ridges. Fiennes, during his trans-global expedition, navigated his way round the ridges in snowmobiles, also using up crucial time. As a result, both men needed constant air drops of food and fuel, at enormous cost. I, rather simplistically, believed it would be easier to do away with dogs and snowmobiles and just climb over these ridges. Why not just don a pair of crampons and go over them in a straight line northwards?

Speed would be of the essence here. The Arctic summer begins at the start of March. By the end of April the Baltic and Siberian giral currents start to meet the ice between the 85th Parallel and the 88th Parallel, making the whole area impassable. I therefore had to be at the 85th by the end of March to begin the next stage of the expedition, which would be the most dangerous. It would involve crossing 100 miles of constantly moving ice floes which vary in depth from ten feet right up to a centimetre or so. I would have to be extremely wary of not plunging through the ice which, with my clothing and the pack on my back, would almost certainly result in my death. The other concern here was the danger of floating away on one of these ice floes; the current could divert me twenty miles from my intended route. The third, and final, stage from the 88th Parallel to the Pole was, in theory, the easiest. I would be able to make a ski dash over firm ice to the Pole, before radioing in and being picked up by a plane.

On writing all the above information down I realised that it must seem a great deal easier sitting in a warm flat in Bristol. What I had not yet given much thought to were the cold and biting winds which would produce temperatures as low as − 70°C windchill. Neither had I seriously considered the thin ice. The Eskimos, through years of experience, have the ability to determine the thickness by the depth of the colour and subtleties of shade; I, in contrast, lived in the West Country of England.

Then there would be the polar bears. There would be plenty of them about, and all would present a very real danger. A polar bear can scent a human from five miles away, and is difficult to see against the snow and ice, especially in white-out conditions. Both Wally Herbert and Naomi Uemura were close to being torn to shreds by bears which, despite their size, can move incredibly quickly across the ice.

My initial intention was to try to make the trip as pure as possible. I wanted to walk to the Pole using a sextant, the stars and the sun to chart my way, but the Canadian authorities were also against this for safety reasons. Consequently, the expedition would be using advanced navigational equipment. I would be able to plot my position at any time using a lightweight satellite navigation system. Another system would bleep my position via a fixed polar satellite to France, and the technicians there would then radio it to base camp.

Food would be another important consideration. I would need to take in about 6000 calories a day, the amount I would be expending through my efforts on the ice. Breakfast would consist of muesli with a ton of sugar and milk made from powder and melted snow water. A mug of cocoa would follow, with a dollop of a foul-tasting, high-protein powder. While walking I would be sucking small squares of Mars bars, plus the occasional glucose tablet. Once back in the tent at night time, I would eat the one cooked meal of the day, courtesy of my stove. This would be one of a variation of packet, boil-in-the-bag foods such as pasta, chilli con carne and beef or chicken stew.

I read all these details over and over again. Everything seemed to be ready. Saying goodbye to Claire was very hard. We had grown incredibly close to each other since moving in to the flat, and I knew that she would be taking her law exams while I was away facing constant dangers. But nothing would stop me from attempting this trip, not even many of my friends, who kept telling me I was crazy and that I would never make the Pole. I was determined to prove them wrong.

As one of my sponsors was the now defunct Canadian Pacific Airlines, they flew Steve, Giorgio and myself to Montreal first class at the end of January 1983. We were met at the airport by a stretch limousine and taken to the Champlain Hotel, one of the best hotels in the city. We could not quite believe our luck. Steve and I had spent the previous four years bumming around the world with barely two pennies to rub against each other, but now we were drinking complimentary champagne in first class accommodation.

We stayed in Montreal for five days, picking up extra bits of equipment like a rifle, which then had to be used in practice, and last items of clothing and food. I also collected my Argos transmitter which, back then, was a great deal larger than it is now. Old habits, however, die hard, and we also nicked the nice soft toilet rolls from our hotel bathrooms for use further up north. We then flew to Frobisher Bay in the North-West Territories. This would be a mere stopover, but as we got out of the aircraft the biting cold hit us full in the face. It was no colder than the temperatures I had grown used to by sitting in deep freezers back in England, but for some reason it felt a lot colder.

From Frobisher Bay the plane took us on to Resolute, the last town, as such, before the Pole. Well inside the Arctic Circle, Resolute back then boasted around 1000 inhabitants, a number that has since decreased to 200 because the cash-strapped Canadians have cut back on the civil servants and weather technologists who stay up there. It was the last frontier in the north and, long before the days of glasnost and the collapse of communism, the Canadians were wary of the Russians attempting to claim some of the further North-West Territory islands for themselves.

Although I was the only polar trip taking place at the time, the Canadians were engaged in 'Operation Caesar', which planned to make a floating island on the Lomonosov Ridge. They would then take samples from the sea bed and take various measurements to see if it was part of the continental shelf. We stayed in a small shack at Resolute for two weeks, acclimatising to the freezing weather conditions and checking all our equipment. One day we decided to take out the champagne we had brought with us to celebrate the fact that the three of us had at least made it to the Arctic Circle. We discovered that all the champagne had frozen and the bottles had shattered. To this day I have never repeated the mistake. Besides, although I tried to dismiss it at the time, I saw this as an omen.

We finally flew to Eureka. Ten people inhabited the weather station, situated next to a long aircraft strip. We were to set up a small base hut two miles away, in $-40°C$ conditions. Steve and I were a little more used to the conditions than Giorgio, or 'Mac' as we called him, who used every opportunity to wander down to the weather station for a meal, some warmth, and a spot of television. Even inside the hut the temperature was well below freezing. A BBC crew came up to stay at Eureka for my trip: a young reporter called Clive Ferguson, cameraman Steve Morris, and Bill Norman, the sound man. Martin White, from the Press Association, also made the trip. I remember the horrified look on their faces when they first emerged from the plane.

All of them turned out to be extremely professional under adverse conditions. Typically, there was a lot of droll humour. We all found it funny when Steve Morris was convinced, during filming, that he had just shat himself. In fact what really happened was that through his hard work he had been sweating under his clothing and, around his backside, the sweat had frozen. Mac, Danny DeVito's doppelganger, went ballistic with the rest of us after we removed the fur seat from the toilet in the dark. Within seconds of sitting down Mac's arse had frozen to the bare seat. He emerged with it literally hanging off him, and it took a pot of boiling tea to remove it. Bill Norman used to wear Brylcreem, and within a day of arriving at Eureka he could snap parts of his hair off. All these incidents were funny, but they also had a flip side to them. As I laughed, I could not believe that I would soon be going out there on my own.

After a week at Eureka disaster very nearly struck. Steve Vincent almost died, and I would have had to blame myself, purely because I had dragged him away from his wife to join me in this hell-hole. I woke up one morning in the small room within the hut in which I slept. I shouted across to the next room where Steve was sleeping for him to get the tea ready. There was no reply. As I tried to get up I suddenly felt drugged. I was sleeping in a top bunk, and I remember not having the strength to climb down. Now extremely worried, about myself and especially about Steve, I fell out of the bunk on to the floor, my fall partly cushioned by the sleeping bag I was still wrapped in. Crawling on my knees into the next room I found Steve asleep on the floor, his face literally blue and seemingly lifeless. I could also smell gas. Steve, and to a lesser extent myself, had been poisoned by carbon monoxide from the stove in his room. Although barely able to do anything myself, I managed to radio down to the weather station for help and then, placing Steve on my knees, I carried him like a baby, crawled out of the hut, and flung us both outside into the snow for fresh air.

Back at the weather station the medic checked us both and diagnosed Steve to be suffering from severe carbon monoxide poisoning. The BBC filmed all this and put it out on the news back home, which is how Steve's wife first got to hear about it. They pumped oxygen into Steve, who took two days to fully recover. I felt terribly guilty about the whole affair, but Steve just wanted to get on with it, and did not want to be the one person to delay the trip.

In the first week of March we finally piled on to another plane which took us up to Cape Columbia on the northern tip of Ellesmere Island. Even the flight was scary. I sat in the front with the pilot who circled round and round trying to find a suitably large area of flat ice. We were hovering just twenty feet or so above the ridges, with the aircraft's instruments buzzing and flashing because we were close to stalling. The landing has to be one of the bumpiest of my life, and we all breathed a great sigh of relief when we finally came to a standstill. There was a famous incident not too long before when a Twin Otter, packed with tourists visiting the North Pole, landed on the ice and plunged straight through.

Cape Columbia was my starting point. Steve and Mac came up just to see me off, while the BBC crew were also there to film the moment. Looking back, years later, at the BBC film, where Clive Ferguson interviewed me, I looked like a startled rabbit. I knew that I was about to be left out there on my own, and there would be no turning back. It was pretty obvious I was very scared. We must have stood on the ice for half an hour. The BBC crew were flying back home after this, which clearly delighted them, while Steve and Mac, who both gave me a huge bear hug and told me to look after myself, were returning to the base hut at Eureka.

I stood for ages watching the disappearing plane turn into a tiny speck. Then I turned around and surveyed the scene. It was a beautiful sunset, and the ice glistened all around. The view was dangerously deceiving, like a Christmas card depicting a snowy scene, and there was little to suggest the dangers that lay ahead. It was desperately cold, and quite easily the most solitary place I had been to in my life. For all I knew, a nuclear war could have been taking place throughout the rest of the world. Here, it was as if time had stood still for hundreds, indeed thousands, of years. Strangely, the peace and solitude I normally craved frightened me here. It was almost too much of a good thing. I was the loneliest man, literally, on the whole planet. Pitting my physical and mental strength on a mountain was one thing, but facing a whole frozen ocean suddenly made me feel extremely small and inferior.

There was no point in starting my walk so late in the day, so I erected my tent and prepared myself for my first night out, alone in the High Arctic. Even though I was petrified, and ever on the look-out for polar bears who may have been disturbed by the plane, I also felt proud that, after all the work put in, I was now here and on my way to the North Pole. This would prove to be my most positive moment. From this point onwards my mood, and my fortune, would spiral downwards.

In the morning it took me a ridiculous three hours to have my breakfast and load up the sledge. This was purely down to working in the extreme cold. I had planned to walk the 476 miles in forty-one days, at just over eleven miles a day. The reality was that, after my first day of walking, I had covered just one mile. Although the sledge, at just over 100lb, was not particularly heavy to pull, it was the effort of climbing up and over the ridges and the rubble that half killed me. There was absolutely no respite from it at all. From the moment I began walking to the end of the day, when I slowly put the tent back up, I found no more than a few yards of flat ice.

The immediate message from all this was that there is nowhere in the world you can simulate Arctic conditions to prepare and train for a trip to the North Pole except in the Arctic itself. There is simply no place like it. The deep freeze back in England did not provide the windchill, and the mountains of Switzerland did not provide the rubble, the ridges, or the cold.

The next couple of days turned out to be exactly the same. By the end of day three I should have covered around thirty miles; instead, I had not even managed five miles. I was physically knackered despite my excellent fitness, and growing increasingly worried about the time factor and the advent of the Arctic summer. Each day a salutary lesson took place. One night I cooked up a boil-in-a-bag meal using what later turned out to be first year ice. After a year the salt water in the ice filters through so that the top layer becomes fresh water, whereas first year is frozen salt water. I had to spit out my first mouthful of dinner because it was mixed with pure salt water. The rest of the dinner was ruined.

After a week I was still faring appallingly. I was woken up from a deep sleep one night to find the whole tent shaking as if in an earthquake. This was my initial thought, until I realised that I was in fact on top of shaking, shuddering ice. In the distance I could hear the sound of running water, and it seemed to be getting louder, and therefore nearer. This has to be one of the scariest moments of my life. It was pitch black, I was moving around without any say in the matter, there was a terrifying noise outside alternating between groaning and squealing, and water was evidently close by. I became convinced I was going to die; I would be eaten up by the ocean, forming all around me, and my body would probably never be dis-covered. I got fully dressed and packed everything into my rucksack and then on to the sledge in readiness, should I be required to move quickly. Then I crouched in a corner, with my sleeping bag wrapped around me, and waited.

Eventually I dropped off to sleep again. As soon as I woke up in the morning I shot my head outside the tent to investigate. I had been camping on a flat pan of ice, approximately half a mile across in every direction. During the night a pressure ridge had been formed by the move-ment. I could see exactly where the ice pan had chunked into the next one, forming a massive ridge. This was no more than fifty yards from my tent. As I prepared for another hard day's slog, I tried not to dwell too much on what would have happened if the ridge had formed fifty yards further on in my direction.

On day ten I was to receive my first supplies. By that time I had crept up to an average of five miles a day, which was better than my initial performances but still woefully short of the plan. I spent most of the day trying to find an area suitable enough for a small runway before calling them in. After a while I could hear the plane so I let off a smoke flare. Unfortunately, I was standing downwind and promptly got smothered in orange smoke. Steve and Mac, together with the pilot, emerged from the Twin Otter, smiling and waving. It was good to see them again, even if it had only been ten days. Apart from new food, fuel and a sleeping bag, they also brought with them luxuries such as chocolate chip cookies and newspapers, even news of who won the University Boat Race.

Beneath my smiles, however, I remained concerned. We only had money for three drops, and this first one should have taken place a great deal further north. But they remained positive, filling me with encouragement, and telling me that during the flight they had sussed out the area and could see no open water at all. This, if nothing else, was good news.

It was clear within the following few days that any thoughts of beating the record to the Pole were ridiculous. Now all I was bothered about was just getting there. The work remained far harder than I had ever imaged. I ached so much each night as I zipped myself up in my sleeping bag, knowing that another day of climbing and hauling awaited me. By day seventeen I ran into further trouble: my Plessey radio suddenly packed up due to the extreme cold weather conditions. Normally it was a superb radio used by the British army, but now, just when I needed it to deliver, it was no longer functioning. This was perhaps understandable because the radio was not as advanced as it is today; nevertheless, it was a serious situation because it meant I had no form of contact with Mac at Eureka, save for my Argos which had one emergency button, to be used only if I wanted to abort the mission. I also knew we had agreed that if Eureka heard nothing from me for two days then they would automatically come and pick me up.

Sure enough, the following night a Twin Otter suddenly appeared and landed close by. The pilot was supposed to be supplying Operation Caesar but was re-routed to pick me up. I discussed the situation with the pilot, a man called Paddy, and as he had no spare radio on him he felt the best bet was to fly to Alert, the forward missile warning base on the Lincoln Sea. After an hour's flight we arrived at this top secret base. It was so hush-hush I was even escorted by an armed guard to the toilet. They then kept us waiting in the plane on the runway until Steve and Mac, whom Paddy had contacted back at Eureka, joined us. Although they brought a spare radio with them, we decided that we should all go back to Eureka to work out what had gone wrong with the first radio. With the huge expense of air supplies, the last thing we wanted was for the spare radio to conk out as well.

On arriving at Eureka I noticed how there seemed to be less snow, and that the temperature had risen from – 40°C to around – 20°C which, believe me, is a noticeable difference. The guys had made their hut much more hospitable, although I gathered Mac was still sneaking down to the weather station as often as possible. Mac got to work on the radio and discovered that moisture was getting into the mouthpiece. To counteract this, we covered the new radio up in a plastic bag. After four days, with some new equipment and clean clothes, I was lifted back to the exact spot where I had been picked up to continue my trek to the Pole.

I was criticised later for this brief sojourn during my journey. The adventuring world argued that I should have started from the beginning again; I may as well have enjoyed a fortnight's holiday in the Caribbean midway through my walk before starting out again. On my return to England this hurt me terribly, but now I say this was valid criticism.

The rubble and the ridges began to ease off, at least in terms of quantity. I was walking over more and more pans of ice, which meant that there was the occasional day when I managed to walk ten miles. But as the days passed I just could not see how I could possibly walk the whole distance to the Pole. After three weeks I was beginning to act strangely. I started calling my sledge Sybil, after Basil Fawlty's long-suffering wife in BBC TV's *Fawlty Towers*. I even began to 'feed' it with Mars bars. I would find myself saying things like: 'You must be hungry, Sybil, have a Mars bar.' I knew what I was doing and, out in such conditions, considered it an acceptable way to help beat the misery of solitude. It is a method I have repeated in other polar conditions, but when I analyse it back in the warmth of England it does strike me as possibly the first signs of insanity.

I knew the trip was over on day thirty-two, on the 87th Parallel, and still over 200 miles to the North Pole. I was climbing up a high pressure ridge, straining to drag my sledge behind me. I reached the top of the ridge some fifteen feet above the flat ice around it when the ridge suddenly collapsed beneath my feet. I landed on my side with a heavy bump and immediately doubled up in pain. I did not know it at the time, but I had just cracked two ribs.

I tried to catch my breath, hoping against hope that I had just badly winded myself, and waited for the pangs to ease. They did not. In excruciating pain, it took me two hours to erect the tent, an exercise that normally took me ten minutes, now that I was well-practised. I then remembered something the picture editor of the *Sunday Express* magazine, to whom I was relaying the story of the trip, told me before I left, that the best pictures in the world are often the ones you do not want to take. I set up the camera, slumped back on my sledge, and took a photo, thinking that this might be the last picture of me alive.

I waited three hours to make sure that it really was the end, and then contacted Eureka. Mac said stop mucking about, but I told him I was badly injured and needed to get out. Steve radioed down to a doctor in Resolute, and then began to relay a series of questions back up to me. The main question, to see if I had punctured a lung, was whether I was coughing up blood. I was taking pain killers, but they seemed to have no effect. Lying down flat and straight was especially painful, so I stayed fixed in a foetal position during the radio call and after.

The nearest plane was at Resolute, but a storm had set in down there and they would not be able to move for two days. If there was a danger of me dying out there, then they might be able to use a military plane, but as they reckoned everything was relatively okay I would have to wait. Everything was not okay. I was in complete agony. I was also utterly dejected, missed home and Claire terribly, and just wanted to return to warmth and comfort. Instead, I knew that I would be stuck out there alone, the most northerly man on earth, for at least the next two days. Still, I tried to reason, it was better to be a living failure than a dead hero.

The storm at Resolute moved on, as predicted, after two days, but straight up to Eureka where the plane was scheduled to stop in order to refuel. The message that crackled over the radio was not what I wanted to hear: 'Hang in there, we've got to wait for the storm at Eureka to clear.' I was beginning to run out of food and fuel now, and I could feel the ice beginning to drift. A cold fear began to creep back inside me: if my radio batteries went flat I would not be able to give the pilot a weather report from where I was, which could result in him flying all the way up to me, only to turn back again in storm conditions. At £10,000 a flight, I would have to pocket the bill, knowing that I had no money at home. If the batteries went down on the Argos then they would have to find me blind. It would be like trying to find the proverbial needle in a haystack. Then, of course, there was a very clear danger that the ice around me would break up.

Outside the wind began to whip up until, in a very short space of time, I found myself in storm conditions. The radio blasted out that the weather was fine now at Eureka, and a plane would be coming to get me shortly. I had to radio them back telling them to forget it because the howling storm was now with me. This was to last for four days. The wind tugged incessantly at the tent's flysheet, producing spindrift so fine that it was blasting into my tent through the sewing-needle holes in the fabric. Now I began to pray for the storm to stop. My life, I reckoned, was now completely in the lap of the gods.

When the storm eventually died down I heard the depressing news that another storm had arrived at Eureka. Now I was seriously worried. My food supplies had just about gone, I was rapidly losing weight, still suffering from enormous pain from my ribs which prevented me from moving, and growing increasingly colder. It was clear that unless I was rescued immediately I would die out there, in the frozen wastes of the Arctic Ocean.

After ten days out in the wilderness, Steve and Mac managed to persuade Operation Caesar to lend their plane, which happened to be only sixty miles away out on the floating ice station on the polar shelf. Mac's voice told me the reassuring news over the radio. Half an hour later he returned over the airwaves: 'A plane should be over you at any moment now.' Even as he said this, I could hear the wonderful hum of an aircraft engine. I crawled out of my tent and saw a Twin Otter landing close by. To say it was an emotional moment would be an understatement. Barely able to stand up, a lump appeared in my throat and the tears began to pour from my eyes. My nightmare was almost over. I was going to survive the ordeal.

The pilot jumped out of the plane, walked over to me, shook my hand and said, 'Congratulations.'

'What on earth for?' I asked, surprised by his response. As far as I was concerned, I had been a total failure.

'Well, you've walked two hundred and thirty miles and spent forty-two days out here on your own and lived,' he said. 'That's success to me.'

I remember muttering: 'I'll be back.' The pilot then lifted all my gear on to the plane, while I slowly climbed in. They took me back to the Operation Caesar base where I was met by a Dr Webber who found me a bunk and then took me to the kitchen. I must have eaten everything I could lay my hands on. The scientists there were all very kind to me. They seemed to appreciate what I had just been through and could relate to me. After a brief stop I was then flown back to Resolute, to join up with Steve and Mac who had come down from Eureka. They were pleased to see me, and although disappointed that the trip did not work out, seemed eager to get back home.

The doctor at Resolute had a good look at me and diagnosed two cracked ribs. Steve watched all this and laughed as I was bandaged up. 'No pain, no gain,' he smirked. I then took a series of telephone calls from the press. One reporter asked me what it was like to be a failure. This question obviously hurt, but I replied by repeating what I had told myself back in the tent out on the ice: 'At least I'm a living failure.'

It was good just to be getting out of the ice and cold of the Arctic. On arriving at Montreal airport we discovered that, having been flown out to Canada first class by Canadian Pacific, the airline had decided to return us to Britain in economy. The eventual flight was half empty, but we were still made to wait at the back of the queue until they were sure they had three stand-by tickets. Nobody likes a loser.

During the long flight back to London I began to tell myself a few home truths. I was immensely inexperienced in polar travel, and had been completely foolhardy even to have attempted the walk. Much of the equipment was wrong, and the very best I could say about the trip was that it proved to be a valuable training exercise. It was a warm May evening as I arrived at Stansted airport. It was so good to be back, away from the cold, and to see the lush green fields of England. It was even better to see Claire.

Over the next few days I received a complete pasting from the mountaineering press in particular, but also from the world of adventuring. The final straw was when I was interviewed by BBC South-West. 'Was it not just the case that you simply were not man enough to complete the trek?' asked the reporter. This was probably true, although being 'man enough' had much less to do with the failure of the trip than just the simple, but crucial, factor that I was not experienced or prepared enough for what the North Pole was going to throw at me. Despite the living hell I had experienced over the past couple of months, I was not finished. I vowed to myself that I would return to the Arctic and, one day, would make it to the North Pole itself.

CLOSE CALL

The Magnetic North Pole Trip, 1984

It took me a couple of months to get over my experiences in the Arctic. I was physically weak and tired, and mentally shattered and scared. The reception in England hardly helped matters either. I can listen to constructive criticism all day, but what annoyed me was the false reporting I read, particularly in the mountaineering press, who clearly felt I should have stuck to climbing. I needed the media coverage prior to leaving to please my sponsors, but I ended up promoting a failure.

After a while the enormity of the failure to reach the North Pole lessened. As I actually thought about it, I began to identify clear reasons why I fell some way short of achieving my goals. I wrote down a check-list and identified numerous ways in which I could have improved my chances. I should, for example, have taken a bigger sledge, with a canopy as opposed to a rucksack. I needed to have a better stove system. I had to have a thicker insulation mat for the floor in the tent. I needed better food, and a faster way of wrapping the tent. I should have screwed the skins on my skis; they kept coming off in low temperatures because I could not afford the time spent re-applying them. There was a multitude of mistakes. Recognising this made me feel a great deal better. Besides, in the end it was an injury that stopped me.

I began to set my sights, however, on the Magnetic North Pole. To be honest, I think I was probably scared of attempting the Geographical North Pole again so soon, and failing for a second time. Instead, I focused on walking to the Magnetic Pole, solo and unsupported. Unlike the geographical poles, on which the earth's axis rotates, the magnetic pole (or dip pole) in both hemispheres is the point to which all magnetic compasses point. In theory the magnetic dip should be ninety degrees down at the magnetic pole, but in reality this pole is a moving target. The extent of its movement depends on various factors such as the magnetism of the earth's core and solar flares, both of which determine the size of the pole's circumference.

The Magnetic North Pole is undoubtedly easier to reach than the Geographical North Pole, simply because it involves a shorter walk, but the difference, which evened up the balance, was that I would be attempting it without the aid of additional food supplies and the help of an aeroplane. Instead, it would just be me and my sledge. This would mean a far heavier load to haul, and having to cope with the psychological test of being on my own, without any of those important food and 'goody' visits.

I went to visit Mansell James. Over a couple of beers I expressed my thoughts to him. After careful consideration he suggested, in his deep Welsh accent, that the North Pole might still be the easier trip to take. That proved to be the final bait. I told him I would be going for the Magnetic North Pole. In truth I just did not fancy the North Pole again, but Mansell knew me too well and deliberately steered my decision by suggesting that the Magnetic Pole would be harder.

The other important factor behind my decision was that it would prove far cheaper to go solo and unsupported. The companies who sponsored me for the North Pole trip all came back to me as well, which was a nice surprise. They felt, despite my failure, that it had been a good effort, and they wanted to back me once more. The equipment – and this time it was the right equipment – started to arrive again, and all I had to do was find myself a small back-up team.

I first turned to Steve Vincent, but within a few months of returning with me from the Arctic in 1983 he had settled down with Cathy and wanted it to remain that way. He had just secured a good job in the city, and did not need a freezing cold disruption. There was no way Mac was coming back either. He was glad he had experienced the Arctic, but had no wish to return to such conditions again. Besides, his mum wouldn't let him go.

I did manage, however, to persuade Steve Morris, the BBC cameraman, to join me. 'How about another cold holiday, Steve?' I said, plying him with a succession of pints in the BBC bar at White City. It seemed to do the trick. Steve agreed to come up to film, working during his spare time. Unlike the North Pole trip, I was not looking for any pre-publicity this time. I had learned my lesson the hard way.

I then asked John Burgess to be my base camp operator. John was in his fifties, a typical, to-the-point Yorkshireman. He lectured at Taunton Technical College, and also made rucksacks, which is how I first got to know him. He had supplied me with a rucksack for the North Pole trip, and also helped to modify my sledge. He leapt at the chance to go to the Arctic.

Claire was still studying for her law degree and, secure in the knowledge that this trip should be far safer than my attempt to reach the North Pole, she was relatively happy to let me go off on my travels again. Neither of us could have anticipated the dangers that awaited me. Finally, after rechecking all my equipment and making last-minute modifications to eliminate any possibility of error, I was ready.

It was February 1984, almost exactly a year since leaving for the North Pole on my first trip. Steve, John and I met up at Stansted airport where we could catch a flight to Montreal courtesy, once again, of Canadian Pacific. This time, however, we would be leaving Britain in economy class. With a support team comprising just two members, and with less than 250lb of equipment to load on to the plane, as opposed to 2000lb the previous year, I already felt in a much happier frame of mind.

Two days later we arrived back at Resolute to the same friendly faces I had seen just twelve months previously. We grabbed a room at the back of a maintenance shed and made it our home for the next few days while I carried out some more testing of my equipment, and trained. I was ready to leave within five days, compared to the two months it took us to prepare at Resolute and Eureka the year before. Experience had taught me a great deal. Everything was checked once more, from the radio to the rifle, the Argos satellite system – which would provide irrefutable evidence if I reached the Magnetic North Pole – to the tent, stove, sleeping bags and sledge.

On the morning of my first day, Steve had arranged for a Mountie to see me off. I felt distinctly sorry for the young man. Normally he would have been dressed like me, kitted out for −40°C conditions, but to add to the occasion he appeared in the official and instantly recognisable red uniform of the Royal Canadian Mounted Police. It turned into quite an amusing few minutes. He would jump in and out of his truck, posing for a few seconds for photographs with me, before leaping back into the vehicle to get warm again.

Then I was off, walking down towards the iced-over beach, and out into, or rather on to, the frozen sea. I was undoubtedly scared of failing again, but also felt confident that this time I had prepared as well as possible. The only other concern was whether my navigation would be up to scratch. Although there would not be tons of barrier ice and pressure ridges like there were en route to the North Pole, at least with that trip all you had to do, in simplistic terms, was just keep heading north. This time I had to vary my course on a number of occasions, turning east here and west there, following the coastline of this island and avoiding other islands.

If I could do all this, then I felt pretty sure I could make it to the Magnetic North Pole, and by doing so I would become the first man ever to have reached the spot solo and unsupported. There is no doubt that Inuits have migrated near or even over the site of the ever-changing Magnetic Pole, but I am certain none has ever walked solo there. It simply is not in their nature. They go out into the Arctic wastes to hunt, not to enter the record books.

The first night's camp was still in sight of Resolute. I could see the steam rising from afar, which was a comforting thought as I prepared for my first sleep. I had covered seven miles during the day, and although I found the sledge – at nearly 200lb double the weight of my North Pole sledge – hard work, I was delighted with my start. I radioed Steve and John in Resolute, and their voices boomed back over the airwaves so loudly that they might as well have been standing outside my tent. So far, so good.

Still, as I settled for the night, the fears stayed with me. I knew that potential dangers lay ahead, notably from wandering polar bears, open water and polyanas, which were areas of open water surrounded by thick ice, proving to be favourite haunts for seals coming up for air. I also knew that I had to walk something in the region of 280 miles completely by myself.

The next few days seemed to go well. My mileage was perfectly acceptable, I seemed to have quickly got myself into a well-organised routine and, although it was always hard work, I felt relatively comfortable. The days and the nights passed, incident free, and as I ventured further and further away from Resolute, so my mood became more and more upbeat.

Everything was to change during the sixth night of my adventure. I had been walking that day round a headland called Stanley Head, which can be found at the southern tip of Cornwallis Island. I was tracking around here because I wanted to get a bearing across the bay and then head straight towards the Polaris Mine. I had been warned that a storm was coming my way so I made doubly sure that everything was secure inside my tent that night. A final look up at the sky confirmed fast-moving clouds gathering ominously. Having battened down the hatches, I fell asleep.

I woke up at around two a.m. Outside the wind was howling. The twenty-four-hour sunlight had been smothered by white-out conditions, and the only place to be was inside my tent. But it wasn't the weather that had stirred me: I could distinctly hear the sound of first scratching and then sniffing, right outside my tent. I shot up like a bolt on to my knees. I could now quite clearly see the shape of a nose protruding through the tent's flysheet. I was petrified. I was being visited by a polar bear and unless I did something pretty quickly, he would be joining me inside my tent, and it would not have been for a friendly chat. As I reached for the rifle, a Winchester 306, I started to scream out as loud as I could. This was partly designed to scare the bear, but the main reason was because I was shitting myself. I cocked the gun and, still yelling, fired a bullet into the ground. The scratching immediately stopped, the indent in the tent's fabric disappeared, and the bear ran off.

A few moments later I plucked up enough courage to

open up the tent's zip and peek outside. To my absolute horror the bear was standing twenty-five yards away staring right at me. Now my heart really was in my mouth. I fired another warning shot into the snow. He lumbered off for a few more yards, half disguised by the white-out conditions. The wind was bitter, and the visibility very poor. Suddenly the bear swivelled round and, facing me, started to plod back towards the tent. After a few more steps the plod turned into a steady canter. In my fear it took a few more seconds to register what was happening. When the penny dropped, and I realised that the bear was attacking me, I started to scream 'you bastard'.

Prior to setting off I had listened to advice about what I should do if ever I came across a situation like this. I was supposed to kneel down, breathe slowly and exhale while squeezing the trigger. I was not to pull the trigger, and I was supposed to aim at the bear's body, as the bullet could ricochet off its skull. Well, this is all very well while sitting in a nice warm room at Resolute, but all the advice goes out of the window when confronted with the real thing. It was not so much of an aim, more a spray of bullets. I hit him when he was twenty yards from the tent; he stopped, then continued for a few more yards before crashing to the ground. I was still pumped up to my eyeballs with fear and adrenalin so, still screaming and shouting at the top of my voice, I pumped the bear with two more bullets. The animal lay motionless, but still I was not finished. Throwing on some clothes, I ventured outside and, a little closer to the creature, reloaded and emptied a further five rounds into the huge body mass.

In my frenzy I had completely forgotten about the cold. When finally convinced that I had killed the bear, I dashed back into my tent to avoid frostbite. I was also worried that the dead bear had not been alone. In any case, I had to make contact with base. If you shoot a polar bear in the High Arctic, you have to arrange for the carcass to be collected and provide the wildlife authorities with a damn good reason for killing the animal. Polar bears are far from endangered in the Arctic, but you cannot go around shooting them.

The dismal weather conditions meant that I was unable to radio back to base. The next best thing was to press the emergency button on the Argos. During the course of the next hour I slowly regained my composure. I even began to feel guilty for what I had just done. I had to shoot the bear or I would have ended up as his breakfast; it really was either him or me, but I also knew that if I had not been there in the first place, trying to fulfil my own aims, the bear would still be alive.

After an hour I realised that although I had pressed the emergency button on the Argos, it was not really an emergency. I stepped down the signal to the next message: 'Pick up requested, ASAP.' In no time a Twin Otter appeared and came down close to my tent. Bruce Jonasson, the Bradley base manager, and the pilot took one look at the closeness of the dead bear to my tent, and laughed: 'Christ, that was close.' I showed Bruce and the co-pilot the scratch marks next to my tent on the ice, took photographs, and then filled in a statement for the Canadian wildlife authorities. We then attempted to lift the bear on to the plane, an event that turned into farce. The plane did not have any ramps, and the loading bay was quite high, especially when trying to place 500lb of animal on to it. The three of us lifted a leg each, and then recoiled in disgust as the bear, in a final act of defiance, managed a post-mortem bowel movement. After that we somehow found renewed strength to haul the bear aboard.

I was not to know this at the time but, due to my encounter with the bear, I instantly became world news. Having tried to keep the whole attempt quiet through fear of publicising another failure, I had now alerted everyone to my whereabouts, and to my purpose. I expected a great deal of flak for the incident, but seemed to escape with virtually none. Each village has a quota of bears, and this one came from the Resolute quota. At that time the Inuits were allowed to kill ten bears a year for meat and skin; the number has since increased to thirty-eight. This particular bear came off the Inuits' ten, and the bear was thus delivered to the Inuit village. I am not proud of the fact that I had to kill one of the world's most dangerous, but undoubtedly most beautiful, animals.

I made my way up to the Polaris Mine and camped down in the bay. Steve and John had flown up to the mine to see what all the fuss was about. They came out to meet me, still none the wiser as to the reasons why I had pushed the emergency button. Both fell silent as I told them the whole story. After half an hour they returned to their plane and flew back to Resolute. I turned in the opposite direction and headed towards Bathurst Island.

Nobody needed to tell me that my route led me straight through the middle of an area commonly known as 'Polar Bear Pass', thus named because the area supposedly boasted more polar bears than anywhere else in the world. A couple of days later I saw another bear in the distance. He must have been half a mile away from me, but after my experience he was close enough. I knew that bears tend to appear from out of the wind so that they cannot be smelled, so I made sure my tent door was away from the wind with the zip undone on my sleeping bag and the tent door. I also left my sledge twenty yards in front of the tent with food lying on top, in the hope that any subsequent bears would go for the food on the sledge rather than the human food in the tent, giving me valuable time to prepare for a confrontation.

Just over a week had passed since the polar bear incident, and I was getting my confidence back again. I was in a good routine, I was coping with the weather, the hardship and the solitude, and the prospects of reaching the Magnetic North Pole seemed good. Then disaster almost struck.

As I made my way up the coast of Bathurst Island I encountered some sticky brown ice, and the more I progressed the more I was drawn into this mushy area. I felt that this could only lead me to open water, so I made a large detour over to the actual coast and Cape Kitson. I must have been three hundred yards from the shore when my right leg and ski suddenly plunged through the ice into the freezing ocean. Water immediately shot up my leg to my thigh, and the rest of my body lurched drunkenly over to my right.

In what I can only describe as sheer blind panic, I scrambled furiously on to the ice, pulling my leg from out of the water and clawing my way on to what proved to be stronger ice close by. If my heart had thumped any more it would have burst out of my chest. My only intention then was to get myself on to the shore as quickly as possible. Shaking with fear, I sprinted as quickly as I could across the ice before flinging myself, like a shipwreck survivor, on to the safety of iced-over land. At this point I knelt down and began to throw up uncontrollably until, with nothing left to give, I retched. I was in a complete state of panic. I knew that I had just been extremely lucky. For a start the ice around my right leg stayed firm, enabling me to drag the leg out of the water and haul the rest of my body and the sledge to safety. If any more ice had given way, then that would have been it. I also knew that, once my whole body lurched in a downward direction towards the water, I was lucky that the sledge had not dived down below the ice. If it had done, it would have taken me with it. I wasn't even injured by the experience, at least not physically.

Mentally, however, I was finished. I erected the tent, still in a complete state of shock, set the radio up and contacted Steve Morris. 'I've gone through the water,' I told him in a frightened tone. 'That's it. Come and get me. I've had it. I don't care if it's another failure. Just get me out of here.' My bottle had completely gone.

Steve remained calm. 'Look, there's no problem,' he said. 'We're more than happy to get you out. But get some tea down you first, with a lot of sugar, relax and we'll talk again in half an hour.'

Thirty minutes later Steve radioed back. My sentiments remained the same. 'Steve,' I said, 'I've calmed down a bit, I've had my tea, and I'm telling you I've had enough.' Steve reaffirmed that there would be no problem, but it would take a little time to get the aeroplane ready to fly. He would therefore radio back in a further half an hour.

When he next contacted me I was beginning to grow angry. Steve started to tell me to keep calm and to wait a bit longer. I interrupted him. 'Look, Steve, stop fucking about and just pick me up.'

I then heard a slight commotion over the radio airwaves before John Burgess suddenly started to talk to me. 'I hear you want to give up,' he began.

'That's right. When can you get me?' I said.

There then followed a Yorkshire tirade, laced liberally with expletives. 'If you think you're going to get me and Steve all the way up here in the Arctic just to return home again because some fucking sissy doesn't like water, you've got another think coming. You get walking in the morning and you fucking get on with it.'

John was a clever man. He knew exactly how to deal with people. Steve had tried the soft, sympathetic approach with me; John tried the short, sharp treatment. It did the trick. I was so taken aback by the force and tone of John's words that I was instantly shaken into a determined adventurer again. Besides, who the hell was he to talk to me like that? 'Right then,' I shouted back down the radio. 'If that's the way you feel, I'm carrying on. I'll fucking show you, you bastard.' I slammed the radio down, oblivious to the fact that back at Resolute Steve and John were laughing at their success. John had undoubtedly saved the whole expedition.

The next day, in a bullish rather than paranoid mood, and swearing under my breath all the time about what I would do to John Burgess when I next saw him, I came across the site of some ancient stone igloos. They must have been hundreds of years old. Now in need of some repair, they would have housed wandering Inuits centuries before the rest of the world even knew of their existence. It was a strange feeling that I was not the only person to have been to such ice-ravaged wastes of land. I then had to climb over a small mountain to a place called Kew Bay. Standing on the tip of land, the scenery in front of me was truly stunning. Across the bay I saw an Arctic fox and, above, the first bird since my trip had begun, a sure sign that summer, and yet more open water, was coming. The bird – I think it was a storm petrel – followed me for three days. It almost became a companion of mine. I found myself leaving flapjacks for it on my sledge, food that I might well need myself in later days. The bird occasionally swooped down, plucked up a large crumb, and flew back skywards to its domain.

The sledge was getting lighter as my supplies lessened, but the physical effort was beginning to take its toll. I was feeling increasingly tired and weak, while bleeding piles made each step painful. In the end I resorted to stuffing a sanitary towel, which I brought with me in case of such a condition, up between the cheeks of my buttocks. It certainly helped to lessen the pain.

By the time I reached pack ice I knew I was close to the outer rim of the Magnetic North Pole, having been given its position by the Geological Survey. My aim was to walk to the very centre of the Pole's oval area, just to make doubly sure that I had actually reached my intended destination. I could only navigate, however, by using a sun compass; the standard magnetic compass was rendered useless because, being so close to the Magnetic North Pole, it just pointed downwards. The problem with a sun compass was that you needed the sun. On this morning, during my fourth week in the High Arctic, I faced yet more white-out conditions. Sometimes you can still see the faint outer rim of the sun, but not on this day. I knew I was very close to the Pole, and felt it was important to keep on making some distance.

I then came up with what I thought was a clever idea. By circling for a full 360 degrees using the light meter on my camera, the largest deflection would occur at the brightest spot which, in theory, should be pointing at the sun. I was pleased that I had worked all this out by myself. That, after all, is what being an adventurer is all about: when you are faced with a problem, you have to use ingenuity to get out of it. By now, knowing where the sun was, I could create my own shadow and walk in the right direction.

After four solid hours of walking I came across some ski tracks. I stopped, looked at them over and over again, and then sat down on my sledge to think. Nobody had told me that someone else was out there. I chewed on some Mars bar chunks. The day was coming to a close so I put my tent up, switched on my Argos to give out my position, and then radioed back to base camp. I was mystified about the tracks, but also excited because I knew

I was now just a matter of two or three days away from the Pole.

I could not believe it when base reported that my position had barely changed from the previous evening. I had been walking all day, and must have covered at least ten miles. I asked them to confirm if anyone else was skiing close by. When they denied this, the penny finally dropped. My expert navigation had resulted in my walking a full circle. Those tracks in the snow were my own. I was only twenty miles from the Pole, but that night I felt thoroughly dejected. The whole day had been a complete waste of time and strenuous effort. Steve advised me to stay put in my tent until the weather cleared a little and I could once more see the sun.

The next morning the sun poked its head around the clouds. I needed no further invitation. I shot off like a runaway express train, anxious to make up for some of the lost time the day before. The weight of my sledge was down to just 40lb now, making the going far easier, and although my piles and my generally tired condition still made life hard, I was too close to my goal to let it bother me. That evening my Argos reported that I had made excellent progress.

As I woke the next morning I fancied it to be my last day. I thought about ditching almost everything to make the final twelve miles an easy stroll, and then thought twice about it. What if a storm broke during the day, creating impossible conditions to walk in? I could be stranded in my tent for days on end, as I was the previous year half-way to the Geographical North Pole. If this happened, without my supplies I would have to abandon the trip, just a few miles from the finish. It was just not worth the risk.

Four hours into walking I radioed camp to see how much further I needed to go. 'You've gone two miles,' Steve reported back. Two miles! I couldn't believe it. By my reckoning, walking at three miles an hour by this stage, I should have just about been standing at the epicentre of the Magnetic North Pole. 'Just keep on going,' Steve insisted. A couple of hours later I contacted him again. 'You've covered four miles now,' Steve told me. I was beginning to get tired, angry and more than just a little confused. 'Just another three miles to go,' Steve added. He then said that they were leaving with the Twin Otter to pick me up, so I had better get moving.

I kept the Argos switched permanently on so that they could find me. The thought of going home that night provided an added incentive which initially counteracted my anger, but after a couple more miles the rope began to pull on my shattered body with virtually every step I took. That was it, I was now at the end of my tether. I placed the beacon and flares on top of the sledge, put up the tent and slumped inside. I was past caring.

I could not have been in the tent for more than a couple of minutes when I heard the sound of a Twin Otter approaching. I rushed outside again and let off the flares. The Otter dipped its wings to say it had me in its sights, before landing close by on a flat surface of ice. Jim Merritt, the Canadian pilot who resupplied me during my North Pole trek the previous year, jumped out of the plane first. 'Well done,' he said. 'What took you so long?'

Steve, John and Jack Napper, from Trans Excel, one of the expedition's main sponsors, then appeared. Steve said: 'Why did you walk ten miles further than you needed to?' Now I understood. Steve had made me walk through the epicentre and right out to the other side of the Pole's oval shape, just to make doubly sure that I had, beyond any question, reached the Magnetic North Pole. My anger lasted a couple of seconds, to be replaced by laughter, a few tears and a great deal of hugging. I was so relieved to have done it. After the previous year's experience, I had a lot of doubts about myself. These had now been allayed. After thirty-two days on my own I was tired and hungry, but I was going home. This was a wonderful prospect.

We spent an hour or so at the Pole, drinking champagne and taking photographs. Then we were off again, flying over the ice I had just covered. As soon as I arrived at Resolute I telephoned Claire to tell her that I had made it, and that I was coming home. News of my success spread quickly and, after the North Pole débâcle, I was pleased to receive so much positive press coverage. I think that a British polar success had become a bit of a rarity, so the British media were pleased to report on my story.

On my arrival at Montreal the Canadian Consulate met me at the local airport. A stretch limousine appeared to cart us all off to the international airport across the city. We were booked to fly back on Canadian Pacific in economy class but, unlike the previous year, we suddenly found ourselves upgraded to first class. As we flew above the clouds and headed for Britain I sipped champagne and decided that, given a choice between failure and success, I much preferred the latter.

JOURNEY TO THE UNKNOWN
The Geomagnetic North Pole Trip, 1992

Within a few weeks of returning to England I was off on a badly planned and ill-advised trip to Chile, where I tried to canoe around Cape Horn. I wrongly believed that nobody had ever attempted this solo before and, buoyed by my Arctic success, I fancied giving this a go.

The subsequent fortnight away turned out to be a farce. I discovered in Chile that an American and a German had already achieved my desired feat, and that the Chileans, close to war with Argentina over a squabble concerning the Beagle Channel, refused to allow me to canoe around the Cape without an escort. As soon as I had passed the Cape the ship's crew insisted I should board with my canoe. I returned home with my tail between my legs.

Back in England I started doing the lecture circuit, talking about the Geographical and Magnetic North Poles. I was at Ludgrove, Prince William's future preparatory school, when a young boy came up to me after a lecture and asked, 'What's the difference between the Magnetic North Pole and the Geomagnetic North Pole?'

I gave it a moment's thought and told him they were the same. He insisted there was a difference. Slightly annoyed at his precociousness, I asked what made him so sure. 'Because it's at the back of the *Times Atlas*,' he answered, before running off to prove his point. Within seconds we were both huddled over the book. 'There you are,' he shouted with triumph. 'The Geomagnetic North Pole.'

The Geomagnetic North Pole was distinctly marked just off the west coast of Greenland, in the Kane Basin. A good approximation to the Earth's magnetic field is the field that would be produced by an extremely strong bar magnet placed at the Earth's centre and tilted at an angle of about eleven degrees to the axis of rotation. The place, in the northern hemisphere, where this bar magnet meets the Earth's surface is the Geomagnetic Pole, positioned at 79.12 degrees north, 71.12 degrees west.

That night at home I read Lord Shackleton's account of the Oxford University Ellesmere Island expedition. I then re-read Wally Herbert's *Across the Top of the World*. Neither he nor Shackleton ever mentioned the Geomagnetic Pole. I had never heard of any expedition reaching this point and, in fact, had never even heard anyone mention it before the young boy at Ludgrove.

I then contacted the Geological Survey, the Royal Geographical Society and the Scott Polar Society. There was indeed a Geomagnetic North Pole. Its position had moved into the middle of the Kane Basin, and as far as all concerned knew nobody had ever been there. This was all I needed to know. My next trip had been decided.

After carrying out more research I discovered that I faced a choice of two routes: either to start from Thule in Greenland, taking a shorter route up the Greenland coast and into the Kane Basin, or to go from either Grise Fjord or Eureka, which would mean crossing Ellesmere Island. I had every intention of attempting the trip solo. This initial plan changed after reading Wally Herbert's accounts, and also Otto Sverdrup's traumatic story of his crossing way back in 1899. In particular, I swayed towards taking a group of men after consultations with Dr Geoffrey Hattersley-Smith, a man who had spent much time mapping and travelling across Ellesmere Island. At the end of a very helpful meeting at the RGS, I asked Dr Hattersley-Smith a couple of straight questions: 'What are my chances of doing this solo, and what is the best route to take?' He advised me to forget about a solo trip, and to take a longer, more southerly route through the Sverdrup Pass.

The preparations for the trip were just beginning to get under way when my father suffered a heart attack. There were management problems at Robnor, his company, and in his absence I was asked to join the board of directors. I became the production director at a time when many changes took place within the company, which had been struggling to come to terms with its transition from a small to a large organisation, and with a new set of health and safety regulations recently imposed by the government. It turned into a bureaucratic nightmare, and I discovered that the managers within the existing company soon found themselves out of their depth. Just when my father had recovered from the heart attack he contracted leukaemia. It would be a further five years before he succumbed to this terrible illness. Work at Robnor quickly became too time-consuming to concentrate on polar adventures, and the Geomagnetic project was, if you'll excuse the pun, put on ice.

The months soon turned into years. Apart from my work – something which pleased my grandmother, who always went on about me getting myself a 'proper' job – two other significant events in my life occurred: my marriage to Claire and later, in 1989, the birth of my first daughter, Alicia. Claire and I were married on 4 October 1987 in the village church in Turnditch, Derbyshire. We had been together for six years and I suppose I had been a little wary of marrying her, only because I was scared it would end up the same as my parents' marriage. It felt strange with a ring on my finger, but my uneasiness was lightened by seeing so many of my climbing, student and schoolboy friends at the wedding.

Being present at Alicia's birth was one of the most momentous and emotional events of my life, as I am sure it is for most fathers. As I held a small bundle in my arms I suddenly realised that, for the first time in many years, I was being asked to be a little responsible. I had been far from responsible in my early adulthood, but now I knew that not only did I have myself and Claire to think about, but also a baby daughter. I still went climbing every so often afterwards, just to keep myself fit and interested, but I found myself confined more and more to the office, and to my duties at home as a husband and father.

In late 1989 I received a telephone call from a man called Jock Wishart. He needed my advice and wanted to meet up. Over a couple of drinks in a London pub he explained that he was involved in an idea to try to get a large airship to the North Pole, and needed to pick my brains about Arctic conditions. I agreed to fly up to the Isle of Man to look at a project which was part of his expedition. Once there I was peppered with questions: How cold is the water? What thickness is the ice? How much open water in July? How many calories per day does a person need? What is the minimum weight? And so on. Slowly I was becoming engrossed in the Arctic again.

A friend of mine called Ray Shaw had often suggested doing a polar trip together. When he asked again, shortly after my trip to the Isle of Man, I became interested, especially when he promised to put together the research programme and let me get on with my work. It was January 1990, and the trip to the Geomagnetic North Pole was back on again.

Ray was as good as his word and got to work. I

assembled a team comprising Steve Morris, from the Magnetic North Pole trip, Captain Richard Mitchell – an army officer, fitness fanatic, climbing partner and good friend – and Ray. Jack Napper, our main sponsor from the Magnetic North Pole trip, agreed to come up and man the radio. But within weeks of this the whole project began to fall apart. Jack Napper was selling up his company and retiring, just when we should have been crossing Ellesmere Island. 'Mitch', as I called Richard, was posted to the Gulf as part of the UN forces during the war with Saddam Hussein. Ray was determined to make it work. I went up to join him in January 1991 to have a final look around. The plan was to start shortly afterwards.

On arriving at Yellowknife I bumped into Jim Merritt, the Canadian pilot who picked me up at the Magnetic North Pole. I told him of my plans and, after warning me that there was too much open water, he advised me to catch the next plane home. At Resolute I discussed the situation with Bezal Jesudason. Bezal had started up High Arctic International in Resolute Bay, an organisation similar to a trekking company in the Himalayas. He has since, unfortunately, died, but he happened to have a vast knowledge of the Arctic and its conditions. When he told me that he had just flown over the Kane Basin and it did not look good, I grew seriously worried.

I then went to the Polar Continental Shelf Project and talked to Leif Lundgard. I showed him the thermographics. 'You'll be swimming,' was his to-the-point verdict. Glen Bond at the weather station had the same opinion: 'The Pole will be under water by the time you reach it,' he said. I had no choice. We had just been unlucky with the unusual weather conditions. Mindful of my Chilean canoe fiasco, I told the others that the trip would have to be postponed for a year.

Within a few weeks I was ready to start planning again.

Ray pulled out, but Mitch was back from the Gulf and raring to go. Another army officer, Hugh Ward, whose wife worked for me in the Robnor laboratory, leapt at the chance to join us. I then invited Neill Williams, a business associate and friend, to be part of the team. He was hesitant at first, mainly because of his work commitments as managing director of Polycrown, but he eventually agreed.

The Ice Climatology Unit based in Ottawa sent me monthly photographs and thermographs. This time the ice bridge into the Kane Basin was rock solid. We would be able to have a crack at the Pole in the first week of April 1992 when the weather was not unbearably cold, but while we still had enough time to beat the advent of summer. I then managed to persuade Jim May at Advantek, Robnor's agents in America, to be our major sponsor for the trip. Jim was a friend and business colleague of my father. He even provided his daughter, Elaine, to help out in Resolute. Elaine asked if Shirley Chenoweth could join up as well.

With a sponsor on board we needed the right publicity. I immediately thought of Jock Wishart. 'Jock, this will be a walk in the park for a man like you,' I told him over lunch. He telephoned me the next day to say that he was in, providing the whole trip took no longer than twenty-five days.

Next, I assigned each person to duties. Hugh, because of his previous Arctic experience, would be responsible for cooking and for looking after Neill and Jock, the two novices. Neill and Jock would be responsible for camp administration, while Mitch and I would carry out research projects, set the radio and Argos up, and carry out all the navigation. Jock would look after the public relations.

Finally, on 3 April 1992, we were away. Mitch and I

kissed our wives goodbye at home but, against my advice, Neill, Hugh and Jock all said farewell to theirs at Gatwick. Hugh's wife was crying, Neill's looked like a frightened rabbit, and Jock's just thought we were both being stupid and irresponsible. I suddenly realised that, for the first time, I was responsible for men who had wives and children back home. I also knew that for the past eight years I had been sitting behind a desk. I only hoped I had not lost whatever attributes I possessed for polar adventuring.

We flew to Canada on the Friday, and by Sunday lunchtime the trek had begun. With our business or army commitments, we had three weeks to reach the Geomagnetic North Pole, so there would be no hanging about. As we stood in readiness outside the hut in Eureka I had used back in 1983 for my unsuccessful walk to the North Pole, I delivered a quick speech. 'If we can make it through the first five days, we can hack the trip,' I said. 'We have come here as a team. At times we will be tired, frightened and hungry. We will also get on each other's nerves, but we pass or fail as a team. One for all, and all for one.' We shook each other's hands and started to walk.

The weather was beautiful if, at −40°C, a little on the cold side. After an hour we stopped for coffee and a pee. Mitch and I knew each other well, but the others walked away and turned their backs for solo efforts. This, as the days passed into weeks, would soon change. Still, we were all in good spirits and completed fourteen miles on day one, a very satisfactory effort. We had 286 miles in total to complete, but it was a good start.

The time factor was always uppermost in my mind. Our sledges were relatively light to aid our speed, but this meant that our resources were limited. I had kept the food supplies down to fifteen days, plus an extra five days' emergency rations. Nevertheless, when faced with a severe wind on day two, causing a −55°C windchill factor, I decided we should still be walking. We had to be careful not to expose our skin because in such conditions frostbite would occur within seconds, but with the wind into our backs and safe inside our Sprayway windproof outer jackets, we made such good progress that everybody got too warm and actually started to take some of their layers of clothing off! We were all hungry and tired that night, but I was delighted with the way in which the team had faced up to the conditions. I went to sleep imagining a huge bowl of mussels with French bread, followed by a seafood platter. This, if not precisely the same meal, became a recurrent focus for me each night as I dozed off, especially the longer the trip went on. The following night, for example, all I could think of was steak and kidney pie, chips and baked beans.

On day four I had my first angry word with Hugh. After my experiences with Steve Vincent at Eureka before I started my walk to the North Pole, I told Hugh that it was unwise to cook with the stove with the tent door closed. I had to remind him again the following day, but he insisted he had everything under control. Mitch told me that Hugh might change his mind if he killed someone from carbon monoxide poisoning. Neill seemed a little homesick, while Jock expressed his concern about polar bears. Then Elaine warned us, during our radio call that night, that the ice bridge was beginning to eat its way north, but if we made good progress we still should be okay. The mood of the camp changed for the better, however, when Mitch emerged from his tent with his sunglasses on, and began singing the signature tune from *The Blues Brothers*. Within a few moments we were all joining in, jigging our way round our tents. Later during the trip Mitch would annoy us by singing 'The Birdie Song', which infuriatingly resulted in us humming it to ourselves all day. I found the best revenge was to mention food to Mitch just before he fell asleep each night.

Mitch was more concerned, however, by our still slow progress. During the following day he had worked out that we were one-third into our food, but with under a quarter of the route covered. At this rate we would run out of our emergency supplies as well. This prompted me to make a rallying cry to the troops to pick up our pace. That night Elaine reminded us again that the ice bridge was definitely creeping up north. We were still ten to twelve days from the Kane Basin, but going relatively strongly and, as I settled down for a much-needed sleep and thought about eating fish at the Waterside Inn in Bray, I congratulated Jock and Neill for completing their fifth day and becoming true Arctic explorers.

On the sixth day we all got to meet a polar bear. We were making our way slowly into the Vjessel Fjord when we came across a number of bear prints. These prints were huge and clearly belonged to a large male. Jock, in particular, grew nervous at the sight and shot off like a bullet to check the rifle. That night my sledge acted as a bear decoy, piled up with food and positioned fifty yards from the tent. I was in a deep sleep when I heard Jock shouting, 'David, David, quick. Something's outside.' I grabbed the rifle, started to scream and shout, and looked outside the tent. Standing by the sledge, fifty feet away, a large bear was watching us. It had, according to Jock and Neill, sniffed the sledge, walked right through our camp, pausing only to sniff at Jock's head, and then walked past. I told Mitch that if we had to kill the bear I was not going to be the one to do it after my experience during the Magnetic North Pole trip. After I had fired a warning shot the bear strolled nonchalantly away, seemingly without a care in the world. I tracked it for fifteen minutes before returning to my tent. After another ten minutes I took another look and caught sight of a different bear tracking along the coast. The area was riddled with the animals. Still, we were all so shattered that we took no time to fall asleep.

The following day, detecting Jock's eagerness to get the hell out of the area, we all gently ribbed him about polar bears. My Achilles tendon, thanks to an old running injury, had grown progressively more painful until I started to take painkillers every four hours. Reaching the top of Vjessel Fjord it was time to climb over land. What appeared to be a flat crossing turned out to be a series of undulating hills so that, by night time, we camped on a mountain totally exhausted by our efforts. I started to reappraise the situation. We had now used up a week's food, which was over a third of the total amount, but had not yet covered a third of the expedition distance. We were stuck on the side of the mountain and still had two difficult stages to tackle, the Sverdrup Pass and the Kane Basin. Spreading our maps out, Mitch and I tried to plot optimistically. It didn't look good. We basically needed to increase our average mileage and pray for good weather, yet I remembered Wally Herbert's book. It had taken him just nine days to go through the Sverdrup canyon, let alone the rest of Ellesmere, and I was looking at half this time for the whole crossing of Ellesmere.

The next day we upped our pace. My Achilles was so bad that I started taking painkillers like Smarties. Each of my men took turns to lead our single file group, pushing hard to try to make up for lost time. Late in the day we came across a blow hole. Seeing this persuaded all of us to venture on for a further hour, for where you get seals popping up through the ice, you can bet your life polar bears are not too far away.

Food, as always, became the main topic of conversation that night. Neill suggested we shoot a musk ox and eat it. Mitch wondered if it would taste like beef. I told Jock that Mitch reckoned the little Scot was the meatiest of the group, and warned him not to die. For all the banter there was an underlying sense of frustration and fatigue emerging. It reared its head on the ninth day, after a good day's walk highlighted by a fantastic view of Thumb Mountain, the gateway to the Pass of Ellesmere. The next day we would be on solid land again. Hugh started to dig out the site for the tents. For the past few nights he had become increasingly annoyed with Mitch and me pulling back the powder of snow cover on the ice he had just excavated.

'Why did you ask me to be camp administrator and set up the tents when you both go and kick the snow back into the hole?' he finally asked.

'It's not all the snow, but every night we have had a snow layer for insulation. I'm not stopping you from camping on the ice,' I replied.

Jock, meanwhile, was frantic to get his polar bear story over the wires, after we had failed to get a clear line back to Elaine for three days.

'Bollocks to the PR,' Hugh chipped in.

'Hold on a minute,' Mitch countered. 'You have your duties, and you do them well. Jock just wants to do his duties well, but we're not giving him the opportunity.' I then asked Hugh to warm up the batteries so that Jock could make a good radio call.

'Why don't you just ask me to run back to Resolute with a message for Elaine?' Hugh asked, somewhat heatedly.

I turned round to him and said, 'Why don't you just bloody well grow up?' There then followed a long 'now you've done it' silence before Jock saved the day.

'That's amazing,' he said. 'That's the first bad words on the trip. We ought to celebrate.'

I was annoyed and ashamed with myself. Having given this stirring team talk on the day we left Eureka I had been the first one to break. I immediately apologised to Hugh. 'I've already forgotten about it,' Hugh answered. 'Pass me the batteries, and what soup would you like?'

What was heading for a major argument ended up in laughter thanks to Jock's subsequent radio conversation with Elaine. 'We aroused a polar bear,' he told her.

'Jock, please repeat,' she answered.

'We aroused, A for Alpha, R for Romeo, O, Oscar, U, Uniform, S, Sugar, E, Echo, D, Delta.'

There was a long pause before Elaine enquired, 'Aroused?'

'Roger, roger,' Jock shouted back excitedly.

'Jock,' Elaine eventually asked. 'How do you arouse a polar bear?'

We all collapsed in laughter.

By the end of day ten we had moved up the Sverdrup Pass and beyond. We knew that from now on the going would be tough, and that the next couple of days would determine whether we succeeded or failed on this trip. During the night we were hit by a fearsome storm, but on waking in the morning we were met by a wondrous sight of cliffs and glaciers tumbling down into the valley floor. Mitch blurted out, 'Christ, it looks like *The Valley of the Dinosaurs*.' Indeed it did. This could have been something straight out of Tolkien. It would have surprised none of us if a dragon had suddenly appeared.

After three hours' walking the valley closed in on us, turning a nice wide passage into a tight squeeze in between the mountains and cliffs. We faced no alternative but to heave our sledges over boulder after boulder. No wonder Wally Herbert, with his dog team, took so long. We finally came to a constriction of cliffs about four feet wide with a waterfall of ice pouring through the rocks. If we pushed one sledge at a time through the hundred yards of canyon, we could get through. Just as we reached the top Mitch suddenly announced, 'I think the trip's over. The bottoms of the sledges have been pulled out as we hauled them over the rocks.' We turned every sledge over, and although they had clearly been damaged, I still felt they would stand up to the rigours of the trek. This was a crucial moment of the trip. We all looked up to Mitch and I knew I had to handle the situation very carefully. I suggested that as we were in an impenetrable place for support, we may as well trudge on to Flagler Bay, where we would either double up loads or call for an aeroplane. The whole team agreed, culminating with Neill shouting, 'Well, come on then, let's get going.' Now I knew the team wanted success as much as I did.

An hour later we broke out on to a lake. What had taken Wally Herbert and his dogs twelve hours to do, we had completed in just one hour. As we walked past Witch Mountain I became almost paranoid with anticipation of what to expect in the big canyon that lay ahead. Again, both Sverdrup and Herbert had written graphically of the enormous difficulties they faced in the canyon. The slopes of the hills rose gradually into steep cliff faces, the wind noticeably picked up and began to howl like a demented wolf, and the width of our track was reduced to just ten feet. We came across a pair of bear prints right in the middle of this track which only raised our adrenalin. If we happened to come across a bear here we would have no room to manoeuvre. It would be like Robin Hood facing Little John over the small bridge, and we all know who won that encounter.

We came to a junction where the route divided into two equally impressive canyons. We stared at the choice for quite some time. I decided to venture down one route for half an hour with Hugh, while the other three were to take the other route, before meeting up again in an hour. My upward route was hard going, not helped by the fact that the narrows closed to just four feet in a number of places. I noticed how the bear prints seemed to follow our route and go onwards.

The others reported that their canyon seemed to be all clear. I knew we could not afford to walk two days in the wrong direction. Following my gut I decided, like the beer commercial, to follow the bear. Maybe he knew the easiest way. We made slow progress, heaving our sledges from the front and pushing from behind. God, this work was back-breaking.

The cliffs closed to an impenetrable two-foot gap. I decided to carry out a further reconnaissance. Climbing up the steep cliffs and over until the narrows widened, I eventually came to yet another canyon going into a valley. On my return I suggested that we should try this route. The others would hear none of it. Mitch, who had insisted on pulling a heavier sledge than the rest of us to help out, and Jock were both exhausted. We camped right there for the night.

I could not sleep a wink that night through worry. Surrounded by high cliffs the Argos and radio had no reception. If an avalanche came down, or a rock broke off, we would stand no chance. It would be impossible for a helicopter or aeroplane to find us, and the over-hanging cliffs ruled out the possibility of letting off flares. What if somebody injured himself now? And what if a bear decided to retrace his steps through the pass? His only way down the gorge would be to walk straight through us. As I dozed in semi-consciousness, I knew that this was as tight a spot as any I had ever been in.

We woke the next morning, on day twelve, in bullish mood; ahead of us lay seven vertical lifts and a great deal of hard work. Mitch and Hugh would haul while the rest of us would push. Over the course of the next few hours we used just about every part of our bodies to get our sledges up and over, swearing and cursing, encouraging and shouting until, with our last ounce of breath, we reached the high point where I had stood the day before. A few yards further on by some rocks we suddenly came across the most wonderful sight. Witch Mountain was now behind us, and Flagler Bay lay ahead in the distance. We all started to thump each other on the back. We had beaten the canyon in a day, compared to Wally Herbert's nine days with his dogs, and we were right back on schedule again.

As we made our way down the slopes and to the watershed of Ellesmere we came to a parkall hut that belonged to the Polar Shelf. We shouted from a hundred yards away, just in case there were scientists in there who mistook us for a polar bear. I was reluctant to enter, but the rest of the lads were inquisitive. Eventually curiosity got the better of me. The site had been left by scientists the previous year. There was a log book and a shotgun, but I was eager to leave; it felt strange to come across semi-civilisation in such a barren and lonely place which had, for the past few days, become our home, and our territory. That night it took a matter of seconds for us all to fall into a deep and desperately needed sleep.

It was imperative that, before nightfall the following day, we reached Flagler Bay. The going was initially slow: we had to pick our way cautiously through beds of huge stones in order to avoid damaging our sledges further. As we dropped down to sea level we came across more wildlife, from Arctic foxes to hares and the odd musk ox wandering around. At one point I felt we stood no chance of making the bay when, turning a corner, we discovered a blue road of ice descending as far as we could see. Like children on a toboggan, we were able to skate along at four miles an hour, sometimes even able to sit on top of our sledges and simply slide. Flagler Bay gradually came into view and we pitched up camp on the shoreline.

Now there were just seventy-eight miles to go to the Pole. The previous summer Mitch, myself and my neighbour and trainer, Tony Rolls, had completed the eighty-mile World Trail Championship run in under twenty hours. Just for a moment I thought about ditching all the gear and running. But the madness passed and, instead, I thought of the remaining days ahead of us.

I decided to change our planned route from here. Elaine had told us how, having just flown up to Thule, the ice bridge was still moving north at a fair pace. We were supposed to cross the Bach Peninsula and get into the Kane Basin well north of the bridge, but on listening to Elaine I plumped for a more southerly route, following the coast of the Bach Peninsula to Cape Camperdown, and then head north.

In the morning, two weeks after leaving Eureka, Jock once again said we should go for twenty miles, as he did every morning. This time we shot off as if we meant it, before Neill, who had suddenly begun to hobble, shouted at us all to stop. It transpired that his cartilage had gone. I remembered the lesson I had learnt in the Brecon Beacons while undertaking the Duke of Edinburgh exercises. I had left my party behind and made the intended destination by myself, only to receive a mighty bollocking from my teacher, Mansell James, for forgetting all the aspects of teamwork.

This time we would all be working as a team. Hugh strapped Neill's knee and dosed him with painkillers. I was still knocking them back for my Achilles and, as a result, supplies were now running low. Mitch redistributed much of Neill's load on to our sledges. I told Neill to lead us, so that we could keep to a pace he was comfortable with; if this proved too difficult he would be hauled on a sledge. Failing that, we would bloody well piggy-back him to the Pole.

I studied my team on the following morning. Neill had insisted on taking back all his kit – how he had grown in stature over the past three weeks. He now looked like a beanpole. On 6000 calories a day I had already lost twenty pounds in weight. Mitch's eyes were hollow, and Jock was starving hungry. I was also still concerned about the ice bridge. I prayed that we would make Cape Camperdown before the ice broke away, because a huge detour north would finish us off.

We reached the end of the Knud Peninsula. Polar bear prints were all around us. Ahead lay open water, stretching right across our path except for a thin bridge across the middle. Hugh was all for crossing it, but after going through the ice en route to the Magnetic North Pole back in 1984, I steadfastly refused. I would rather have faced a hungry polar bear than walked across the ice again. Besides, I remembered the scared look on the wives back at Gatwick. It was my responsibility to get everyone back home alive.

We made a huge two-hour detour around the ice, pausing only once to watch a couple of seals pop their heads up in the open water and take a look, like submarine periscopes. We were fast approaching Buchanan Bay, and in the distance we could see the high snow-capped mountains of Greenland. Now we knew we were close to the Kane Basin.

On day twenty we had to reach Cape Camperdown. It would have been a terrible shame to have ventured so far only to be resupplied when so close to the Pole. All of us were quietly concerned, not least because the threat of open water ahead of us was very possible. Progress on an empty stomach only made life harder. Mitch suggested we should see who could suck on a Rolo the longest. I could only manage twenty seconds before swallowing it whole.

The hardship was making us all very homesick. Jock, who had been the main focus of the group's gentle ribbing throughout the trip, sat on his sledge midway through the day and said something that went straight to all of our hearts: 'When I get home, I promise to read a bedtime story to my two children every night, especially the one about the teddy bears.' Nobody said a word after that, deep in their own thoughts.

We passed by Cape Camperdown and could quite clearly see Victoria Head and the mountains to the north of the Kane Basin. Suddenly we hit pack ice. Ahead of us, right the way to the horizon, lay ice rubble. At least we did not have to face open water, but some of the boulders were as big as houses. This would reduce our speed to half pace. That Monday night we camped knowing we were fewer than forty miles from the Pole. Elaine reported some mixed news over the radio: they could only get a ski plane to us on Thursday, a day later than we had hoped. It meant we would be cutting it very close for food, but at least the delay would be better for us in terms of mileage. I went to bed praying that the weather would hold.

This was supposed to be something of a fun jaunt; now I knew that the expedition was as hard as anything I had ever attempted in the past. I wondered whether I should have persuaded my colleagues to join me in the first place, and to have made out it would be a breeze. In the back of my mind I contemplated whether I should cut all of our losses and end the pain by calling for a plane.

Day seventeen began at a frustratingly slow pace thanks to the rubble. We were working our backsides off but making little progress. I sensed that spirits were collectively spiralling downwards; I knew that mine were. My face was burning from the wind, my eyes were sore, my nose was raw from loss of skin frozen to my glasses when I removed them, my backside was sore from walking, I had cold sores on the cheeks of my face, and my Achilles tendon was still playing up. On top of all this, every single bone in my body ached. I never expected to fail on this trip, but as I sized up the situation, I began to feel my eyes welling up.

Mitch, who knew me better than the rest, must have subconsciously known how I felt. He quietly came up to me and, without saying a word, squeezed my shoulder. Neill then came over and said that all the lads were one hundred per cent behind me. My moment of despair then quickly passed, and I responded to this support. By night time we had walked for nine and a half hours, one of our longest days, and yet had completed the shortest distance, just over eight miles. We had less than the distance of a marathon to go. I regularly ran a marathon route at home, and as I slipped into a deep sleep I visualised my route, retracing every step.

The next day the tension boiled over again. I had produced the Douglas protractor and nautical almanac. 'This is a sun compass,' I told the group. I told Neill to lead the day's walking with Hugh backing him up. Mitch and I would keep on checking the compass each hour to provide updated information on the sun shadow that we should follow. We came to a flat pan of ice, but after a while I noticed that Neill and Hugh kept veering off either to the west or east. I was becoming extremely pissed off with this unnecessary zig-zagging. An hour before the end of the day I said my piece. 'Hugh, for Christ's sake, we're going in completely the wrong direction!'

Hugh's reply stunned me. 'You go your way, and we'll go ours and we'll meet you at the Pole.' I felt like punching him, but the patience I had learned since becoming a father taught me now to count to ten and take a long gulp of air.

Half an hour later we called it a day, totally shattered by our exertions. I asked Hugh how many miles he felt we had made towards the Pole. 'Oh, it's definitely our best day,' he replied. 'Twenty-two miles.'

Then I asked Neill. 'Twenty.'

Then Jock. 'Twenty-four, and nearly at the Pole.' That was typical Jock, always the optimist.

Then Mitch. 'Twelve miles.'

Mitch's estimate was met with calls of 'rubbish' from the others. I then predicted just eight miles. We all waited for the Trimble, the apparatus that measured our distance each day, to warm up. Mitch finally made an announcement: 'We have travelled the grand distance of eleven miles.' The other tent remained quiet.

Later I pulled Hugh aside. 'I'm telling you now, either you follow the sun compass tomorrow, or we get picked up tonight.' It took him a few moments to reply. 'I'm sorry,' he said. 'I was well out of order.'

We had eighteen miles to go, with two days' supply of food left. This problem was exacerbated when Elaine's normally reassuring voice sounded over the radio airwaves. They had a problem getting hold of a suitable plane, and we would now be picked up on the Friday. It took Neill and Hugh to placate a ballistic Jock. At least we would be able to make the mileage in this time, but we also knew, as we looked at our dwindling food supplies, that it was now going to be very tight.

Considering our condition, and the still less-than-favourable terrain, we were more than happy with eleven miles by the following night. We were just seven miles from the Pole now, and I got Jock to radio Elaine to ask the plane to pick us up at seven the following evening. This should give us ample time to reach the Pole, and although we were desperate to get out of the Arctic as soon as possible, I wanted to cover for any unforeseen events. After all, with bad luck seven miles is a long way.

I woke up three times during the night, hoping that it would be morning and time to get going. I desperately wanted this to be my last night in a tent in the Arctic. As I lay in a doze I mulled over the trip. I would remember the beauty of the mountains, the teamwork, the hardship and the humour, but most of all I would look back on the care and concern each person had shown for the other team members. We were all strong personalities and, in hindsight, it was amazing there had not been any major wars. If ever a harsh word was spoken – and there had, admittedly, been a few – it was forgotten within minutes. I reckon, to this day, it was the best team I had ever worked with, and the comradeship was absolutely first class. I felt privileged to have been part of such a team.

As we set off on day twenty the sum total of our food supplies was a monster bag and one main meal. It was not enough for the day, especially as we were all starving, but it would have to do. Within fifteen minutes Neill's sledge suddenly split into two. Of all the days for this to happen! Mitch produced some tools from his kit and got to work drilling holes on either side of the split and using helicopter plastic ties to hold it together. If this did not work we decided to ditch the sledge and split the load, which was now down to a mere 30lb. Within another quarter of an hour the repair was completed and we were on our way again.

The going, through yet more ice rubble, was tough. After three and a half hours Mitch, who had been walking with the Trimble down his front to keep it warm, checked on our distance. Three miles had been covered, which meant we had four more to go. The thought of the end, and home, removed all feeling of pain as we trudged on, determined now to finish the job before we completely ran out of food. Another three hours later Mitch checked the Trimble again: two more miles had been covered. For all our eagerness we were moving slowly, but we still had enough time on our side. I began to worry about finding a suitable landing site for the pick-up plane, but I kept the thought of Greenland to myself.

After another two hours the Trimble told us we had to walk just seven-tenths of a mile in a north-easterly direction. At this point, perhaps, the Arctic felt we had passed the test and decided at this late stage to help us out because, after another half an hour's walking, we came across the biggest flat pan of ice in our entire crossing of the Kane Basin. Not only did it make the going easier, it also provided a suitable landing area for the plane. Mitch, who now had the Trimble permanently on, and Neill stopped after a short while. Mitch drew a line in the snow, and at this moment we all knew that we were standing on the exact site of the Geomagnetic North Pole.

'Two hundred and eighty-six miles in twenty days,' I said. 'Thank you all.'

Neill was speechless, but Jock said to me, 'Don't ever ask me again to join you on a holiday which is supposed to be a walk in the park.' He then pulled out a Union Jack, marshalled us into line, and made us all sing the national anthem. As 'God Save the Queen' sounded out across the ice, five grown men cried.

Reluctant to leave the spot we had worked so hard to reach, we nevertheless retraced our steps to our sledges and gear, which we had dumped half a mile away in order to make the final walk to the Pole easier. On reaching the sledges we were about to set up the radio and flares for the plane when we first heard, and then saw, a huge orange bird come into view. The plane was an hour early. It circled and circled round the pan of ice, clearly deciding that the surface was not as flat as we considered. I watched it praying that it would land so that we would be out and away. Finally the pilot's voice reported over the radio that he had found a flat lead point five miles north of us.

A concerned Mitch asked the pilot to repeat the message. 'That is zero point five miles,' the pilot said, much to our collective relief. We packed up and rushed back towards the plane, which had landed fewer than fifty yards from the site of the Pole. Jim May, our chief sponsor, emerged from the plane, smiling and waving. Elaine appeared too, followed by a young man who introduced himself as Jim's son, Jeff. The next half an hour seemed to pass into a blur as we devoured food from the plane, drank champagne and took photographs.

After all the pain, hardship and genuine concern for our safety, I felt strangely reluctant to leave the Arctic when we hauled our gear and our tired bodies on to the Twin Otter and rose up above the ice and into the sky. After all the joy expressed at the Pole, the team now remained quiet, gazing out of the windows and looking down below at the ice and the mountains.

We headed across the Kane Basin, where strips of open water now dotted the icescape, and then on to Cape Camperdown. The open water was now swirling around the shores of the Bach Peninsula. We had succeeded in reaching the Geomagnetic North Pole, but it had been a desperate race against time.

ON TOP OF THE WORLD

Mount Everest

I arrived at Heathrow after the Geomagnetic North Pole trip at seven a.m. on Monday, 27 April 1992, and was sitting behind my desk at Robnor two hours later, my holiday quota used up to just about the very last minute. The following month the whole team was invited to a reception at the House of Commons, where we mingled first with Archie Hamilton, the Forces Minister at the time, then Simon Coombs, my local MP for Swindon, and finally John Major, who stayed chatting about our experience for the best part of an hour. He asked me if I knew what my next trip might be. I was not even sure there would be a next trip, let alone where it might be, so I rather dismissed the idea. It was only later on in the year, in September 1992, that the next trip came looking for me.

I was reading an article in the *Daily Telegraph* about a Venezuelan called Ramon Blanco who had just returned home after climbing Broad Peak in the Karakorams, one of the world's few 8000-metre mountains. He had been part of an expedition organised by a company called Himalayan Kingdoms, which basically sets up climbing expeditions. I noticed, in the bottom right-hand corner of the page, a small advertisement mentioning that Himalayan Kingdoms would be taking a group of climbers to Everest in the autumn of 1993. I looked at this advertisement for quite some time. It had been ages since I had been on any serious climbing expeditions, but Everest had, after all, been my childhood dream. The longer I looked at the page, the more excited I became. I realised that this could be my chance, perhaps my only chance, to take on the world's highest mountain.

It made good business sense to go with Himalayan Kingdoms. If I organised my own trip, assuming I could and would be allowed to, it could cost up to £250,000; by going with Himalayan Kingdoms I would have to pay a tenth of this figure. In my excited calculations, I figured this meant I could go on ten Himalayan Kingdoms expeditions for the same price as an independent attempt.

There was a knock on my office door, reminding me that I had to go immediately to a Robnor board meeting. For the next hour I sat around the boardroom table in a complete daze. I am not quite sure what went on in that meeting; all I was thinking about was Everest. The dream was very much back on.

I rushed out of the meeting at a hundred miles an hour to get back to my own telephone to contact Steve Bell, the man who fronted Himalayan Kingdoms in Bristol. The news was not good: all places for the trip had been snapped up. What about reserve places? I asked in hope. No, they had gone too. In desperation I asked him if I could come down to Bristol and talk about it over lunch. Steve said that he was always available to anyone taking him out to lunch.

The following week we faced each other over some pasta. Steve told me that, even if I could get on the trip, I would first need to reintroduce myself to high altitude climbing, and he suggested I should take a trip to the Pamirs in Russia and climb the 23,000-foot Peak Lenin. I agreed to this, and begged him to consider me if anyone dropped out of his trip.

I never got to go to Peak Lenin. My personal life suddenly faced a rollercoaster of emotions, from joy to sadness in the space of a few days, which would ensure that for the next few months my mind was anywhere but focusing on mountaineering. My father's remission from leukaemia came to an abrupt end, and the illness returned with a vengeance. On 22 October 1992, meanwhile, my second daughter, Camilla, was born. Later that same day the doctor contacted me with news of my father. His condition had declined to the extent that the medical prognosis was now just four days to live. I found myself juggling emotions.

Claire returned home from hospital on the Sunday with Camilla. My father, although desperately ill, refused to be in hospital himself and came over the same day to see his new granddaughter. That night he took my brother, Mark, and myself to the local pub for what was clearly our last drink together. The fact that he refused to touch any beer merely confirmed his condition to me. I had never known him to pass up the chance to enjoy a pint with me before. The conversation concentrated on wills and pensions, company business and probates. Mark and I just did not know what to say. I decided to stay with my father for what turned out to be a very short amount of time. In the early hours of the Tuesday morning, at the age of just fifty-six, he died.

Even the thought of Everest vanished for the next few months, a time dominated by the funeral, seeing the probate through, and trying to pick the company up. I brought Mark into the company as a director, introduced a new set of structures so that all the managers were able to run their own departments, and by the summer of 1993 business was looking after itself.

That June Steve Bell telephoned me. Someone had been injured and there was a vacancy on the trip. My heart missed a beat. It was almost as if fate was thrusting my chance to climb Everest in my face. I told him I would think about it. I discussed the situation with Mark and a fellow director called Norman Smith. I told them I would be away for eighty days, and asked them if they would be able to handle the company and my absence. They said it would not be a big deal and, besides, it would be good to get rid of me for a while. I then decided to go for it, recognising that, with my lack of experience in recent years, I should forget about the summit and just use it as a training exercise. I got back to Steve to tell him I was on the trip. 'Right,' he answered, 'you've got two months.'

I knew exactly what he meant by this. I threw myself into a concerted fitness programme, running and rowing to build up my upper body strength, and working hard on my cardiovascular system to ensure that my heart and lungs would be able to face the Himalayas. By 8 August 1993, when I drove to Heathrow airport to meet some of the members of the team and fly to Nepal, I felt fighting fit, but whether this would be enough remained the big question.

I was turning, at least for the next couple of months or so, back from a polar explorer into a mountaineer. There are, I think, crucial differences between the two disciplines, and also similarities. Polar walking is consistently extreme. You can never escape from the cold, and you have to be aware that in polar conditions you can die, through something like frostbite, a very slow death. Men like Scott and, although he was never actually found, Franklin probably starved to death over a series of weeks. It is a different, more instant kind of danger in climbing. It certainly gets cold on a mountain like Everest, especially the higher you venture, but the cold lasts for only a short period. When the sun comes out you can almost cook in the heat. If something goes wrong, however, then it happens quickly. Few survive a fall or an avalanche or, for that matter, chronic altitude sickness. Men have died from heart attacks and strokes climbing Everest.

Walking in polar conditions does, at least, prepare you for climbing glaciers and coping with the severe cold during the night. Much of the equipment is very similar and the sixth sense needed for danger is prevalent in both areas. The need to explore and to push the boundaries of human endeavour further and further beyond your own, predetermined beliefs, remains the same. And, I suppose, you have to be a little crazy, certainly crazy enough to allow the challenge to far outweigh the real possibility of death. On Everest death is a major consideration. By the end of 1992 only 485 climbers had reached the summit since Edmund Hillary and Tenzing Norgay first beat the barrier in 1953, even though the number of those who have tried is probably ten times as much. The fact that 115 had died in attempting the climb speaks for itself. Everest has claimed the very best mountaineers in the world, including Britain's Pete Boardman and Joe Tasker. The causes of death vary from avalanche to falls, exhaustion to exposure, frostbite to drowning in rivers, illness to mysterious disappearances, but all are horrendous ways to go. Every climber who looks at Everest recognises that his fate depends partly on his skill and experience, but is mainly in the lap of the gods.

On arriving at Kathmandu in Nepal, the whole team was introduced to each other. At the helm was Steve Bell who proved to be quite a superb leader. A former marine officer, I would class him as one of the best climbers in the world; as a leader, he is even better. Lord John Hunt, the man who led Hillary and Tenzing, was a decent climber, but a far better leader of men. Chris Bonington, for that matter, although a fine mountaineer, was perhaps not quite in the same class as the likes of Doug Scott, Dougal Haston and Pete Boardman, but he has always possessed excellent leadership qualities and organisational abilities.

Roger Mear and Martin Barnicott, as the two most experienced climbers on the team, would act as guides on the climb. Ramon Blanco, the sixty-year-old Venezuelan, would try to become the oldest man in history to reach the summit. A guitar and violin maker back home in Caracas, he was a lovely, carefree man. Brian Blessed, the actor, was also on the trip. I always remember him for his marvellous performance as Augustus in BBC-tv's *I Claudius*, but he was a fine climber in his own right, and desperately wanted to tackle Everest. His immense determination, in particular, impressed us all.

The other climbers on the trip were: Alan Lees, a computer operator from London; Scott McIvor, a Scottish accountant working in Saudi Arabia; Lee Nobmann, a Californian timber tradesman; Mark Warham, a British banker; Gary Pfisterer, a lawyer from Massachusetts; Dave Callaway, a professor of physics from the Rockefeller Center in New York; Graham Hoyland, a BBC cameraman and sound recordist who would be climbing himself and helping Blessed; and Ginette Harrison, the only woman on the trip. She was a British doctor, who later became involved in a battle with Rebecca Stephens, the first British woman to climb Everest, to become the first British woman ever to climb the seven highest summits in the world's seven continents.

I soon discovered that nobody on the trip had ever reached the summit before, although many had tried on at least one occasion. Alan Lees had the most amazing kit on him, while Scott McIvor had been running thirty miles a day just to get fit for the trip. I suddenly felt like an intruder, coming in on the scene late and using this experience as nothing more than a training exercise while

A young boy in the Alps. My love affair with mountains deepens.

Steve Vincent and me, aged 18, in America.

Bartering for donkeys in Mexico.

In Zermatt, talking to an old mountain guide.

Ignorance is bliss. On top of Mount McKinley, 1980.

Ice rubble. North Pole expedition, 1983.

High Street, Resolute Bay. Hell on earth!

right It's all over! Cracked ribs
end my North Pole dreams, 1983.

below En route to the Magnetic
North Pole, 1984.

The polar bear that attacked me during the Magnetic North Pole expedition. It took for ever to load him on to the plane behind.

Pack ice slowing us up. North Geomagnetic Pole expedition, 1992.

above At the start of the Everest expedition, 1993

right Welcoming ceremony, Kathmandu Airport.

below First view of Everest, peaking over the Nuptse Ridge.

Everest base camp.

The Altar, where the Pujah takes place. Behind, the menacing ice fall.

Crossing a crevasse in the Everest ice fall.

The summit of Everest and the Hillary Step, taken from the south summit.

Natemba and me on the summit of Everest, 9 October 1993.

On the Western Cwm, with the Everest face behind. The sun was like a furnace.

above Pruitt Hut on Elbrus with the summit on the left, August 1994.

left Mount Vinson taken from base camp.

below Roger Mear on the summit of Mount Vinson, December 1994.

the rest saw this as their big, and quite possibly last, chance.

We spent the next couple of days getting to know each other, sightseeing and talking, incessantly, about Everest. A couple of nights after arriving in Kathmandu, we were all sitting in the lounge of the Summit Hotel drinking beer and listening to Tina Turner. Steve Bell suddenly entered, looking like a ghost. He announced that the permit he had originally obtained for fourteen people to reach the summit had suddenly been reduced to seven. Steve then explained that the only way around this problem was to say that seven of us would, in fact, be climbing Lhotse, the fourth highest mountain in the world, situated right next door to Everest. In climbing Lhotse you take exactly the same route as you would for Everest until, reaching the South Col at 26,200 feet, you turn right instead of left. Steve said that he had agreed with the Nepalese that any Lhotse members who climbed Everest could have their peak fee paid retrospectively. Everyone thought this was a reasonable solution to the problem of the reduced permit. We then had to decide who went on the Everest permit and who went on the Lhotse permit. Even with Steve's reassurances of the retrospective permit, I was anxious to be on the Everest permit from the outset.

Steve began to write the capital letter 'E' on pieces of paper, and threw them into a hat, together with a stack of blank pieces of paper. Steve, as team leader, Roger Mear and Martin Barnicott, as guides, and Brian Blessed, because of the BBC film interest, had to go officially for Everest, leaving just three places left for the rest to fight over. I happened to notice Steve screw one of the 'E' pieces up more than the others. By now, after just a couple of days in the company of people hell-bent on reaching the summit, I too had forgotten my limitations and was desperate to climb to the very top. A couple of people pulled out blank pieces of paper, which meant that they would have Lhotse permits. Then it was my turn. Looking into the hat, I saw the slightly smaller, more screwed-up piece and grabbed it, to reveal the letter 'E'. Now I was definitely up for it, and saw the whole episode as a good omen.

We flew from Kathmandu to a small village called Lukla, where we met up with our sherpas, cooks and porters. Now the team was complete, and from here to base camp, nearly a hundred miles away, we would be walking. The reasons for this are simple: firstly, there would be no other way of getting to the site of the base camp, especially with all the equipment we were taking with us; secondly, base camp itself is 18,000 feet above sea level, even if nearly all of the walk is through vegetation. This is more than 2000 feet higher than Mont Blanc in the Alps, but when you stand on the summit of the highest Alpine mountain, you are very much surrounded by ice and snow; in the Himalayas, in stark contrast, you would not fully realise the height you were walking to if it were not for the effects of altitude.

This, above all else, is the main reason for the walk. Altitude sickness, which is basically liquid on the brain or in the lungs, kills people, either in itself or by disorientating climbers enough to precipitate a fatal mistake. The only way to get around this problem is to spend enough time acclimatising to altitude, allowing our blood to thicken in the process enabling it to carry more oxygen, which is why we were all more than happy to spend our time walking to base camp. We had no alternative. If we had been flown straight into base camp by helicopter, we probably would have died within a few days. Of course, even a long walk does not guarantee that you will escape from the sickness. The difference between 18,000 and 29,000 feet is, in altitude sickness terms, enormous, and as I had never climbed higher than Mount McKinley's 20,320 feet before in my life, I had no idea whether I would be able to cope with what lay ahead.

The walk gave me the opportunity really to get to know the others. Ginette Harrison, for example, was a lovely girl. I would suggest that she is probably a better technical climber than Rebecca Stephens, but Rebecca is slightly stronger, both physically and mentally. Brian Blessed, despite being in his mid-fifties, was as strong as an ox. Technically he was not the best, but you could not find fault with his fitness, stamina and strength. He also happens to be a very fine raconteur, and he spent most evenings entertaining the rest of us with stories about his acting career and his fellow actors and actresses. I particularly started to enjoy the company of Dave Callaway, who had twice tried, and failed, to summit Everest before.

After walking through the Nepalese national park, we reached Nanche Bazaar, the capital of the Khumbu region. From near here you can first see Everest, in between the clouds. I noticed that Alan Lees was struggling to keep up with us on the walk, often coming in four hours behind the rest of us. At the time I thought he was just preserving his energy. In the local market I met a former sherpa climber who now ran a tea shop and stall. He was selling 'Z' stones at $200 each. I wanted to buy one to bring me luck for the climb ahead, but not at a price which matched half the Nepalese national average annual wage. In the end we made a deal: I told him that if I reached the summit wearing the stone around my neck, I would pay him the full $200, but if I did not, then the price would be reduced to fifty. We shook hands and, not surprisingly under the circumstances, he wished me luck.

It was at the Thyangboche monastery that I caught sight of Everest's summit. It was an exhilarating and frightening vision. I knew that I would be miraculously lucky to reach it, but grew ever more determined to do so. Here the local lama gave each of us a blessing and presented us with a piece of red string which we were to wear around our necks. I found it particularly useful because I could now tie my 'Z' stone to the necklace. On reaching Pheriche we came to a halt. We were now 14,000 feet up, and this is where we would stay for the next ten days in order to acclimatise more. The idea was to carry out some climbing, but always return and sleep low. I was surprised how fit and well I felt. I even began going out for runs until Steve Bell pulled me aside and told me to slow down and not to burn myself out as all the hard work still lay ahead of us.

From Pheriche we climbed to Lobuje, which is where Ginette Harrison and Gary Pfisterer suddenly became a couple for the rest of the trip and, for all I know, to this day. It became somewhat disconcerting to be sleeping five yards away from their tent and having to listen to the two of them enjoying themselves all night. Soon the rest of us were comparing notes on the subject. Finally, at 17,000 feet, we came to Gorak Shep, where a few locals still live. This was the last inhabited area before Everest began for real. Leaving a handful of small huts behind us, we struck across the Khumbu glacier en route to base camp, with the terrain dramatically changing from vegetation to ice, making sure to leave a path of rocks behind us in case we needed to climb back down again to Gorak Shep. It was a quite incredible sight. Apart from the fourteen of us, plus the sherpas who would be accompanying us up Everest, a fleet of large woolly yaks carried all our equipment up the mountain. Base camp, at 18,000 feet, was like a market town by the time we arrived. We discovered a small team of Spanish climbers from the Basque region nearby, and also a military team from France. From now on, however, we knew that we would be out on our own.

It was 1 September and the full extent of what I was about to do finally struck home. I was 11,000 feet from the summit of the world's highest mountain. The boy who had dreamed of this moment was finally on an Everest trip. Dave Callaway, the droll New Yorker, and I decided to share tents. We were of similar age and got on very well together, even if he had a nasty habit of shouting out: 'We're all gonna die!' Having twice been on Everest before, he only meant this as a dark joke, but in the end I had to tell him to shut up before someone on the trip killed him.

At base you could actually hear the mountain groaning at night. The sound of rocks and ice creaking and cracking in the wind did little for one's confidence, and at this height you were already aware of the thin air. We were to spend three days at base just familiarising ourselves with our equipment, and acclimatising. It was here that Alan Lees dropped out of the trip. Clearly suffering, he asked Ginette Harrison to look him over. The short-term diagnosis was that he had some kind of virus, but after being transported out of base by helicopter and taken down to hospital, Alan discovered that he had a heart complaint.

It was during my stay at base that I witnessed the full extent of the associated superstitions and the reverence in which the sherpas held the mountain. Another lama and a small entourage made the climb up to base camp in order to carry out a small but important ceremony, called a 'pujah'. They constructed a wooden altar, with scarves serving as prayer flags tied to the top of a pole sprouting from the altar. The idea is that the flags, flapping in the wind, release prayers towards Everest. Juniper burns throughout your stay on Everest, and gifts, such as Marmite and a bottle of Jack Daniels, were laid on the altar for the gods. We then threw rice in the air for good measure. I had always been a little superstitious in the past, but these events took me a step further from just wearing my lucky pair of socks. No sherpa would ever dream of climbing Everest without first going through this ceremony, and when I saw hardened, more experienced climbers than me throwing themselves into the service, I was quick to follow. I do not know whether there are gods living above Everest, or whether the mountain, as some of the locals believe, is a god itself, but I do know that climbing Everest is a humbling experience, and one that leaves you in no doubt that your destiny lies in the hands of the mountain.

We then started to climb. The plan was simple: we would climb a little to begin with before returning to base, then we would venture further, before returning once more. Eventually we would climb to the site of the first camp, at 20,000 feet, and stay. This process would continue until we felt confident enough to go for the summit from camp four. It meant that, in total, we would probably climb the distance of three Mount Everests, but we could not afford the risk of just assuming we could meet the challenges of height, weather and the route by climbing blind.

Every step from now on would be dangerous. Even tackling the Khumbu icefall, a massive river of ice constantly moving from camp one down to base, was riddled with pitfalls. The sherpas kept constructing ladders, bridges and thick ropes across a series of crevasses for the rest of us to follow. We made sure that we were clipped in at all times, except for the experienced sherpas, who found the sight of the rest of us slipping and sliding amusing.

Back at base the bonding process continued. We played Monopoly one night (probably the greatest height at which the game has ever been played) and Mark Warham, the banker, completely wiped the rest of us out. We also started to become friendlier with the Spanish team, mainly because our meals of rice, pasta and chips tasted slightly of kerosene, while our European friends still enjoyed mussels, prawns and wine. Whenever we found some excuse to go over and say hello, we were welcomed with open arms and invited in to join them for dinner.

I also began to suffer from a hacking cough, especially during the night. It was getting progressively worse, even though I was plying myself with Lemsips and Tunes. Roger Mear, who apart from being a respected mountaineer also happened to have walked to the South Pole in 1986 with Robert Swan and Gareth Wood, was good with suggestions on how to rid oneself of a cold at 18,000 feet. I spent much of my time with my head a few inches above a steaming bowl of hot water.

On 6 September we achieved our first carry to camp one. This meant a non-stop climb carrying around 50lb of weight on your back up to over 20,000 feet, and back again to base. Starting at seven a.m., it was imperative to get back to base by three p.m. before the heat of the sun caused avalanches. I paired off with Dave Callaway and, despite my cough, reached camp one with relative ease. Already, as I surveyed the inspirational scenery, I reckoned that just by reaching camp one it had been a bonus for a guy who had initially set out on a training exercise.

Three days later we moved up from base to camp one. We were now at the bottom of the famous Western Cwm, known as the 'Valley of Silence' by the Americans. In order to climb up to camp two, at over 21,000 feet, we needed to climb into the Western Cwm, but first we returned to base again in order to relax, and not rush ourselves into a dangerous position. It was tempting, of course, just to keep on climbing upwards, but it would also have been incredibly foolhardy.

On 12 September we carried up to camp two. Callaway

and I were now beginning to understand each other as climbers. The two biggest men on the trip, we gelled well. Roped together and climbing at a distance between us of fifty feet, once in the Western Cwm we were very much out there by ourselves. Other pairs were as much as a couple of hours behind or in front of us. During the climb the whole of the south-west face of Everest suddenly loomed, large and foreboding, to the side and above us.

My cough was proving to be painful. On descending once more, first to camp one and then back down to base again, I was checked over by Ginette and a Spanish doctor. My chest seemed to be in constant niggling pain, which turned to excruciating when I coughed. The feeling was that I had cracked a rib through coughing so much, a diagnosis which proved to be correct later. There is not much anyone can do to mend a cracked rib except rest, but having got this far there was no way I was going to give up. Steve told me the choice would be mine, but by now the Everest bug had bitten me so hard that only death would stop me.

On 17 September we all made the big climb from base to camp two, which proved to be a long and hard day's climbing. On the way down we were lucky a couple of avalanches decided to miss us out, but it was a close-run escape. Brian Blessed, Graham Hoyland and Steve Bell had to run like hell to avoid one avalanche, which Brian referred to as a 'white rhinoceros'. A couple of minutes later an even bigger one obliterated their tracks and enveloped camp one in a heap of snow crystals.

The next morning, during breakfast at base camp, a sherpa reported that a body had just emerged from the icefall. To our amazement and horror, it turned out to be the Australian Tony Tighe, who died at the top of the icefall due to falling boulders of ice, or 'seracs', on Chris Bonington's unsuccessful 1972 trip. It had taken his remains twenty years to move down from the top of the icefall to base camp. He was still semi-preserved, with his clothes and parts of his equipment clearly evident for all to see. It was a sobering thought that the man had died on the icefall which we were climbing every other day in order to reach camp one and beyond. It also reminded us, if we needed to be reminded, that Everest took no prisoners.

On 19 September we carried up to camp three. Now, at nearly 24,000 feet and much of the way up the Lhotse face, we really were climbing high altitude. We had to use a fixed rope during the climb in order to successfully negotiate a huge, almost vertical wall of ice. Even with the crampons and thick rope, you are only using your front points and you can feel your calves almost bursting out of the back of your legs. It was hard going, but everyone was out to prove that they were up for this, and capable of climbing all the way to the summit. I was still coughing away, but refused to let the pain prevent me from matching everyone else's efforts. On reaching camp three we dropped a stack of oxygen bottles and made a swift return to camp two and then, the next day, downwards to camp one.

The plan then was actually to descend all the way back to Pheriche for a few days of relaxation and holiday. Steve felt it was crucial to rest and to keep up our spirits. Most of us were ready for it in any case, and could almost taste the beers that awaited us. We were just about to leave when a couple of sherpas radioed the camp to say that a huge avalanche had totally wiped out camp three. Everything we had carried up had been swept away. The only good news was that we were no longer on the ice face, for it was patently clear that none of us would have survived.

For a moment it seemed that the whole trip was stuffed, unless we wanted to attempt the summit without oxygen.

None of us considered this to be an option. Steve Bell sent a couple of sherpas back up the mountain to recover any oxygen bottles, while Roger Mear agreed to trek all the way back to Nanche Bazaar to purchase as much oxygen as he could get his hands on.

The rest of us made our way back to Pheriche. It was good to be able to enjoy a hot shower, a decent meal, and to relax, but we were all despondent and concerned that our chance to climb Everest, having reached camp three, had been taken away from us. A couple of days later Roger returned with some oxygen, but not quite enough for the whole party. The original plan was to use oxygen from camp three to camp four at the South Col, at 26,200 feet. We would sleep using oxygen that night at camp four, before going for the summit and back again to camp three the following day. At a meeting in Pheriche we decided to split up into two teams. Whatever team we were in, we would not be able to use oxygen until we reached camp four, except for a small amount to sleep on only at camp three.

The big question was what team I should be included in. I decided, together with Dave Callaway, to seek out the advice of Natemba, the head sherpa, who had more experience of Everest than the rest of us put together. If you went up the mountain in the first team, it meant you had first use of the oxygen. The sherpas would be really going for it, because they were all on a bonus if they succeeded in just helping one person to the summit; after that, the number of complete ascents made no financial difference. The disadvantages, however, were that the first team had to put up the tents for themselves and the second team, and a fixed rope from the south summit at 28,750 feet to the Hillary step, 150 feet further up. There could also be deep snow, which would be hard for the first team, but easier for the second because a track would have been laid. If some of the members of the first team failed to reach the summit there would be some spare oxygen which would mean we would be able to go at a quicker and more comfortable rate. What finally swung it for me was that Natemba said he would be going in the second team. I figured it would be wise to stick closely to the sherpa who had already reached the summit once before.

Team one ended up comprising Bell, Hoyland, McIvor, Blanco, Warham, Harrison and Pfisterer, the second team myself, Barnicott, Mear, Callaway, Blessed and Nobmann. We made our way back up to base camp excited and fearful with the knowledge that we could soon be standing on the summit of Mount Everest. This would be it. We would be stopping en route, of course, to the top, but unlike before there would be no turning back. I had already lost 20lb in weight, and was slightly concerned about losing strength. Blessed, in contrast, having purposefully arrived in Nepal quite clearly overweight, was now down to his best size and maximum strength.

On 3 October the first group left base camp. The farewells were pretty emotional. None of us remaining at camp for the next three days knew whether our newfound friends would either make it to the summit or indeed ever be seen again. There was, needless to say, a great deal of bear hugs, back-slapping and best wishes. More rice was thrown, and off they went, watched by us until their tiny specks disappeared from view. For those of us left behind it was an eerie experience. Over dinner that night, all we could talk about was how we felt the first group was faring. We heard over the radio that they had made it to camp two without any mishaps, and that the weather forecast looked good. All we could do was keep our fingers crossed.

It was our turn to move on 6 October. The night before I had walked across to the Spaniards at base camp and said farewell. They strapped up my chest with bandaging, and wished me luck. I took a moment to kneel before the sherpa's altar alone. Although not exactly religious, I felt that I needed a great deal of help and guidance over the next few days, so I placed some rice on the altar and said a little prayer. I had also written a letter to Claire, which I asked Steve Bell to deliver to her if the worst happened. The letter basically said that if Claire were reading it then it would mean I had perished on Everest. It went on to say that I loved her, that she must continue to look after the children, and that she would have to realise that I had gone to a better world. I was not being negative when I wrote the letter and mentioned it to Steve before he left for his climb. I had every intention of returning, but as any mountaineer will tell you, you have to face up to the fact that any climb could be your last, especially on Mount Everest. I remember Steve just looked at me and said, 'Okay, Dave, I understand.' As I left my tent, filled with trepidation and excitement, I placed the letter on my sleeping bag. With the state of my rib, I did not seriously believe I stood much of a chance. I just planned to climb as high as I possibly could.

Our team split up into two groups of three: I was with Mear and Callaway, while Barnicott went with Nobmann and Blessed. It took us a long, hard day to climb from base, over the Khumbu icefall, past the site of camp one, up the Western Cwm and finally to camp two. The next morning we woke up brimming with excitement. We would be climbing to camp three, but we knew that this was summit day for group one. We set off early in the morning, our lights shining brightly from our helmets like miners down a coal shaft. After a couple of hours I noticed that Callaway was struggling. He kept stopping and was clearly suffering from terrible diarrhoea on the mountainside. I was beginning to get frustrated with the whole situation. Over the course of the previous sixty days or so, Dave Callaway had almost become a part of me. I was thinking to myself, 'Please don't fail again, Dave.' He stopped a couple more times before eventually untying himself from the rope; he turned round and began to walk back. I started screaming at him from higher up the mountain: 'Callaway, Callaway, just make it to camp three. Callaway. Come back!' Dave did not even turn his head. I said out loud to nobody in particular, 'You poor bastard.' Mear, watching the whole episode with me, pulled the rest of the team together. 'Come on, let's carry on,' he said, and suddenly I was back in climbing mode again.

As we drew closer to camp three Mark Warham suddenly descended from the heights. We all asked him if he had already reached the summit. Warham shook his head sadly. He had reached the South Col before suffering from oedema – a condition characterised by an excess of watery fluid collecting in bodily tissues – which forced him to give up. He could see the south summit from the South Col, and yet still had the guts to turn round. It must have been a desperate decision for the man, and a terribly brave one to have made under the circumstances, but it was undoubtedly the correct choice. A few feet higher could well have resulted in his death. As I watched him disappear downwards, I realised that two of the strongest guys on the whole trip were already out of the running, while I was hoping to reach the summit with a broken rib.

Twenty minutes later Roger Mear suddenly stopped climbing, moved to one side and sat down. At first I thought he was going to empty his bladder, but he unclipped himself and, because I was in the middle of the group, came over to me and handed me the rope. 'I don't feel at all right, I'm having problems, and I'm going down,' he said. Barnicott and Blessed were way behind us, further down the mountain, which meant just myself and Nobmann were left. We were both shocked by Mear's sudden and totally unexpected departure, but still felt relatively strong in ourselves. Finally, after an incident-packed day, we clambered into camp three late that evening.

The following morning, 8 October, we were to climb up from camp three to four at the South Col. The first group would have made it to the summit by now, or failed, but we had no way of finding out until we met them on the mountain. Blessed started out like an express train, brimming with confidence and strength. He shot across the Lhotse face, and then the Geneva Square towards the South Col like a man possessed. None of the rest of us could keep up with the man. Midway during the day the remaining members of group one started to appear. Ginette Harrison and Gary Pfisterer emerged first. They were jubilant, and we felt a mixture of elation and envy on their behalf. They told us how they reached the summit together, holding hands. Steve Bell, Graham Hoyland and Ramon Blanco arrived shortly afterwards. They, too, had made it to the summit, although all sported sunken eyes and looked rough. Ramon made history by becoming the oldest man to have climbed Everest, a record that still stands today, but he had paid the heaviest price for his efforts. The man was totally shot away. He had left us at base looking fighting fit, but now looked older than his age, dehydrated, and devoid of any strength.

Scott McIvor came down last. He, too, had reached the summit, but was now in a terrible mess. He, according to Steve who told me later, had come across a few problems on the mountainside with his oxygen. A Spanish climber was close by and came across to help Scott out. Later that evening, just before reaching his camp, the Spaniard had failed to clip himself in correctly, and fell 4000 feet to his death. For Scott, now in tears, all the exaltation of reaching the summit had been erased by this tragedy.

We chatted for a few minutes, but both groups were eager to get on their way. It was as if Everest was now posting danger signals at every turn. At six o'clock that evening we finally crawled into camp four at the South Col, a flat plateau littered with debris from previous trips. On the far side one could clearly see the final, inhospitable slopes of the mountain. It looked so near now, but we knew there was still so much to do.

As I made my way over to a tent I noticed a couple of dead frozen bodies. One was the corpse of an Indian climber, fully preserved and half hidden behind a boulder. The other, I was told later, was a German. These bodies, like quite a few others on the mountain, would remain for eternity on Everest. Nobody could bring them back down again because it was simply too high and too dangerous. I studied these bodies for some time, realising that they were probably better climbers than me. The South Col is a windy, desolate place to lie in rest, and it reminded me once again that I needed to remain lucky.

I was more than happy to be a sharing a tent with Natemba that night. The wind whipped up and I was finding breathing difficult. We were aiming to leave for the summit in the early hours of the morning, but as the wind whistled louder and louder around our tents I feared that, even at this late stage, the attempt could be over. It would take us a couple of hours to get ready for the climb. I asked Natemba what we should do. Barnicott's voice echoed across from his tent asking the same question. The sherpa decided that we should all prepare and then look at the situation after that.

At 1.30 a.m., impatient with the wait and almost bursting with adrenalin, I asked if we were going or not. Quite frankly, if foolishly, I would have gone by myself to try to reach the summit. Natemba agreed that we should all go for it. From now on we would not be roped up, and we would be out there on our own. There were four of the initial group left – myself, Barnicott, Blessed and Nobmann, plus Natemba and two other sherpas. Just as we were about to leave, Blessed suddenly piped up. 'I've got a problem,' he announced. 'I've got frostbite.' We looked and saw some on his fingers, but it is my opinion that it was his decision not to use oxygen, but to attempt a 'pure' climb, that had finished him off at this late stage. Blessed had suddenly tired and, at this high altitude, had burnt himself out. Barnicott offered to stay with him, but was told by Blessed and the rest of us to go for the summit. He wished us luck and saw us disappear into the night.

The climbing became tough. The going got steeper as the snow became deeper. I had read how Chris Bonington had struggled so much during this stage of the climb, through to the south summit. Three hours into the day, before dawn had begun to break, something made me raise my head and my torch shone directly into the face of yet another frozen body just a couple of yards away. It was, to say the least, quite a shock to be confronted by a man, fully preserved and sitting upright on the ridge. I never found out who he was, or whether he had reached the summit, but I only hope for his sake that he enjoyed a fleeting moment on top of the world.

As I rose, higher and higher, I was half expecting to experience something spiritual, as Bonington described when he finally made it to the summit in 1985. I suppose I was hoping to meet my father, or possibly even some angels. In the event, I saw nothing except the sun slowly appearing over Lhotse behind me. One hundred yards from a ridge where we knew we would be picking up more oxygen, I suddenly felt disorientated. I did not have a clue what was happening to me. I told Natemba, who

ON TOP OF THE WORLD

was close by, that I did not think I could make it to the ridge. The sherpa checked my valve and discovered that I had been climbing for half an hour without oxygen because I had been using only a half-full cylinder. Dragging my confused body up to the ridge, I was soon helping myself to some much needed oxygen, which rapidly restored my senses and strength.

It was here that Hillary and Tenzing made their final ascent to the summit. The sun was now beating down, and as I climbed up a gradual ridge to the south summit, I became so hot that I tore off my fleece and placed it on the ice for my return. I decided to stay close to Natemba. Barnicott had forged on ahead, while Nobmann was not too far behind. Each step had to be taken with care. Climbers had died at this late stage, and when peering through the holes in the cornice, or staring at the deep, deep drop down the south-west face, I could clearly see how fatal accidents happened.

Looking up I saw a jubilant Barnicott on top of Hillary's step beckoning me to join him. 'Come on, Dave,' he shouted, 'you're nearly there.' The step is only thirty feet high or so, but almost vertical. As I reached the top Barnicott helped to haul me up. I fell to my knees and hugged him, partly because he had just reached the summit, but mainly because I knew that if I could reach the top of Hillary's step I would make it to the top. Barnicott said that he would see me back at the South Col, and shot off downwards, leaving me to stare up at the final hundred feet to the summit.

The time will live with me for ever. At precisely 11.38 a.m. on 9 October 1993, I clambered on top of Mount Everest and stood there, on the summit of the world, in disbelief. When I had started out, I never imagined that this moment would happen. Now I was gazing out over the Himalayas and down to China on one side of the mountain and, way, way down to the south, the plains of India. I had three minutes to myself on the snowy mound that represented one of my major goals in life. I thought of my old schoolmasters at Writhlington, and then took a few deep breaths and tried to take everything in. I dug a small hole in the snow and stuck a bar of Twix in it for the gods, for surely they had helped me reach this point.

Natemba emerged, smiling as he climbed on to the summit for the second time in his life and, moments later, an ecstatic Lee Nobmann also appeared. In total I spent half an hour on top of the world. We took photographs, hugged each other, held back tears and then regained our concentration for a descent that could still claim our lives. The weather held out for us and we shot down to the South Col in no time to be greeted by Brian Blessed. The big man looked me in the eyes, and then proceeded to give me a huge bear hug, which prompted the tears to flow down my cheeks. After sharing a tent with Lee Nobmann that night, we were quick off the mark in the morning. Having reached the summit, we had no intention of hanging around on the mountain any longer than necessary. We dashed down from the South Col to camp two in a day, despite the fact that I discovered a touch of frostbite on my left big toe.

By now the first group had received news of our success, and all, bar a couple who went on to Pheriche to have their own frostbite treated, waited for us to arrive at base camp. Even as we clambered down through the icefall for the last time a sherpa tripped over on the ladder and was hanging in mid-air over a deep crevasse, clinging on to the side of the ladder with his hands. It was a reminder, as we hauled the sherpa to safety, that even at this stage the mountain still had time to claim another victim.

At five p.m. we finally crawled into base camp. Steve Bell, overjoyed to see that we had succeeded and returned safely, rushed out to greet us. 'Well done, that's brilliant,' he kept saying to us. In return I congratulated him for becoming, with sixteen people in total reaching the summit when you include the sherpas in the group, one of the most successful Everest leaders of all time. It was another emotional moment and I found myself crying again, as much as anything with the relief that I had not only reached the summit but lived to tell the tale.

Later, again grabbing a quiet moment for myself, I made my way over to the pujah to express my gratitude to whoever, or whatever, had been watching over me. Then I went over to the tent I had been using to discover my letter to Claire still lying there on top of my sleeping bag. I proceeded to rip the piece of paper up into tiny shreds. Claire, after all, would not now be needing to read it. I was coming home.

THE MAGNIFICENT SEVEN

The Completion of the Seven Summits

Even after Everest the thought of climbing the highest summits in the world's seven continents had not entered my mind. I suppose once you have made it to the very top of the world, there does not seem much else to do in mountaineering.

It was my adventurous friends who dragged me back into the world of climbing. Richard Mitchell and Neill Williams, who accompanied me on the way to the Geomagnetic North Pole, were delighted for me that I had reached Everest's summit, but my success only served to whet their appetite. I had missed out on my usual climbing sorties with the guys due to Everest, and then the commitments I had in the office, so when they suggested another trip in August 1994, my ears pricked up.

We decided on Mount Elbrus, for no other reason then that at 18,481 feet it stands as Europe's highest summit. Situated in the Caucasus Mountains between the Black Sea and the Caspian Sea in the far corner of Europe, Elbrus consists of two extinct volcanic peaks, with the one to the west the taller of the two. George Pollock, a friend of mine and the managing director of a company called Farepak Hampers, and Julian Champkin, a *Daily Mail* journalist who met me at base camp at Everest, also wanted to come along, so we all felt it wise to plump for a hard plod rather than a dangerous and challenging climb.

We met up at Heathrow on Friday, 5 August, to catch a flight to Moscow. We then flew on, the following morning, to a town called Mineralniye Vody where we were met by a Russian named Alex Koran who would be looking after us for the trip. He looked just like Sylvester Stallone, with huge rippling biceps and a tight-fitting T-shirt that barely covered his chest. He had arranged what turned out to be a ramshackle old bus to drive us to the mountains. After a while, in his pidgin English, he went round the group asking us how high we had climbed. Neill had been to 14,000 feet, Mitch had reached 16,000, George had only really walked up to 10,000 feet, and Julian, only on the basis that he had been to base camp at Everest, had made it up to 18,000 feet. When I answered 29,028 feet, Alex looked at me for a few seconds and then proceeded vigorously to shake my hand. His attitude towards us noticeably changed from this moment onwards.

We were taken to what turned out to be Leonid Brezhnev's former dacha, or country retreat. It was like an enormous private house and, I suppose, the equivalent of Camp David or Chequers. Boris Yeltsin was in power, and under him and his predecessor, Mikhail Gorbachev, Brezhnev's Russia had changed beyond belief. Now the old dacha served as nothing more than a private hotel.

Our first day comprised a hike around the area. Elbrus may, compared to Everest, only be 18,000 feet high, but you still need to be acclimatised to the altitude. The dacha was already 6000 feet above sea level, but by the time we had hiked across a glacier we had climbed to 10,000 feet. That would be enough for the first day, and on our return we were treated to some bortsch and vodka strong enough to burn a carpet.

The following morning Alex took his son, Peter, with us on a climb up a 12,000-foot mountain. Again, this was all part of the acclimatisation process, and the climb was nothing more than a steep hike. On reaching the top Alex hugged and kissed Peter and started to cry. It was his son's first summit and for both of them it was a special moment. We looked on and privately thought of our own children. Maybe I can do exactly the same with my daughters one day.

Six days after leaving Heathrow we were ready to tackle Elbrus. Catching a cable car from the bottom up to the first stage, our gear was then transferred to a big snow cat which piled its way through the snow until it reached Pruitt Refuge, where we were supposed to stay the night.

Pruitt Refuge was a large aluminium hut that stank of vomit and petrol fumes. We reckoned the vomit came from people who suffered from altitude sickness, but we had seen so much vodka imbibed over the last couple of days by the locals that this could have provided an alternative explanation. Somehow we managed to sleep overnight in such conditions, but were more than happy to get going the next morning for a further acclimatisation climb up to Pastuhov Rocks, before returning in the afternoon.

We were up again at four the following morning. This would be summit day. It was a beautiful night; the stars, lit up brightly in the sky, seemed close enough to touch. We did not need to be roped up to each other because we were not going to face any difficult challenges. Instead, we plodded along with just our crampons on. On reaching the 17,500-foot col where the mountain splits into two peaks, George had to turn back. He had twisted his ankle, which had ballooned up as a result, and we felt he could not venture any further. The rest of us continued to walk all the way up to the snowy summit. Everyone was delighted to be standing on the highest point in Europe. After the customary photographs, we made our way back down and reached our dacha by two in the afternoon.

I now had four of the continental highest summits under my belt, but still had no thoughts of completing all seven. As I go on to explain in detail in the next chapter of this book, Roger Mear had by this time persuaded me to join him on an attempt to walk across the Antarctic continent. In preparation, we decided to head down to the Antarctic in November 1994 to test our gear and take in Mount Vinson, the highest mountain on the continent, in the process. Finding ourselves with a bit of time on our hands in Chile, we decided first to travel to Aconcagua in the Argentinian Andes and attempt a climb. Our failure is recorded in the next chapter, but the trip was worth it for two reasons: first, because it proved to be an invaluable reconnaissance for my second attempt on Aconcagua a few months later; and secondly, because I bumped into Rebecca Stephens, the first British woman ever to climb Everest. She asked me if I was going for the seven summits. I told her that it had never crossed my mind; she replied, 'Well, you've done four of them, including the hardest one, Everest, so you may as well finish them off.' She was right, and her words started the old heart thumping again.

Rebecca, her climbing partner Dave Halton, Roger and I then flew down to Vinson, which can be found in the Ellesworth Mountains in the north of the continent. It rises to 16,860 feet, and definitely offers the coldest conditions. With the various crevasses we expected to confront, polar experience is extremely handy. Fewer than one hundred people have actually climbed Vinson due to the extreme cold and the cost of mounting such an expedition down in the Antarctic.

Roger and I would be climbing as an independent party. A Twin Otter plane landed us on a glacier at base camp. At 10,000 feet the temperature was already – 20°C. We made life a little harder for ourselves by pulling the sledge half-way up the mountain in practice for our forthcoming polar trip. Out in front, roped up to Roger with skis on, I kept finding myself sinking three inches into the ice as the whole area immediately around me imploded. This was a scary experience, and one I had not come across before. Each time this happened my heart was in my mouth because I kept thinking I was about to fall down a crevasse. It took some time to get used to.

A forty-eight-hour storm, with total white-out conditions, then meant that we were imprisoned within our tent. We were using one designed by Reinhold Messner, the first man to climb Everest without the use of oxygen. Basically, this tent had a black lining inside which in theory would make the temperature inside that much warmer. It also makes it easier to sleep in polar conditions when you face twenty-four hours of sunshine. The downside, however, is that if you are forced to sit out a storm in such a tent then you are in almost complete darkness. I hardly helped matters, either, by not drinking enough. In such temperatures, at altitude, you are losing liquid simply by breathing, and I became terribly dehydrated.

On the night of 21 December we noticed that the barometer was finally changing for the better. It was eight a.m. by the time we had gathered everything up and prepared ourselves, and as we burst out of our tent we walked straight into a still raging storm. The windchill factor must have lowered the temperature to −70°C, and the visibility was down to just twenty metres. Most climbers might well have decided to stay in their tent for the night in the hope that the storm would pass by morning, but these were the conditions we would undoubtedly face on our trans-Antarctic crossing, so it seemed appropriate that we should sample some of it now.

I found the going tough. My dehydrated condition had left me weaker than usual, and I was suffering from terrible stomach cramps. Roger kept asking me if I was okay, and expressing his concern that we were not climbing quickly enough. I had decided, however, that I would crawl up to the summit if really necessary because there was no way I was coming back down to Vinson again, at least not to climb it.

Climbing over a cornice, I suddenly saw a ski pole sticking out of the ice. This was the summit. As we both clambered on top of the highest point in Antarctica we shook hands and surveyed the scene. We both felt that the ski pole should not be allowed to desecrate what was otherwise a totally unspoilt and secluded part of the world. We therefore tried to pull it out of the ice, as if it was Excalibur, but neither of us possessed the strength to succeed. For all I know, it is probably still sticking out of the mountain.

After my previous failure, Aconcagua had to be next. Found in western Argentina, close to the Chilean border, the mountain rises to 22,835 feet, making it the highest in South America and the highest in the western hemisphere. I wasn't going to try it again with Roger Mear, so I turned to Neill Williams. I took him out for dinner on a Tuesday night in February 1995, and after I had poured four or five beers down him he agreed to join me on the trip. We were to leave that Friday.

The plan was to attempt the whole trip within a fortnight. The southern hemisphere summer comes to an end in February and it just begins to get a little cold, especially 22,000 feet up in the Andes. With the weather and our job commitments we wanted to get down there and up the mountain as quickly as possible, and be sitting behind our office desks again within twelve days.

Arriving in Santiago on the Saturday morning we stocked up with decent food and fuel for our stove and then caught the bus for the three-hour journey up to Punta de l'Inca, on the border with Argentina. Four months earlier the whole area had been covered with snow; now it was green and lush, and beautifully warm. I immediately felt a great deal more optimistic about my chances this time.

We spent the next two days walking the forty miles from Punta de l'Inca to base camp on Aconcagua. Local gauchos accompanied us, bringing their mules to carry all our equipment. The forty-eight-hour walk served as our acclimatisation process as we trekked higher and higher above sea level.

Base camp was at 10,000 feet. When we arrived we found ourselves mingling with other climbers from around the world. A couple of young Americans in their early twenties called Steve and Jack approached us and asked if they could accompany us up Aconcagua. Neill and I felt like old men as we explained that we would be plodding up the mountain and taking it easy. The boys were eager to get on with it, unaware of the dangers of haste, and they reminded me of Steve Vincent and myself when we succeeded, fortuitously, in climbing Mount McKinley.

We spent a day acclimatising at base camp before getting on with a load carry the following morning up to a point on the mountain at 16,000 feet called the Condor's Nest. It was a hard old slog again for me, carting everything we would need such as water, food, crampons, ice axes and other climbing equipment up the steep but relatively unchallenging slopes, but at least it was warmer and easier than in October.

The following morning we took the rest of our kit, plus our sleeping bags, back up to the Condor's Nest. The Americans also made the climb, and were noticeably slower in their progress. The next day the initial hares went at a snail's pace, and the two old tortoises, namely Neill and myself, completed a further carry to the 18,500-

foot Berlin Hut. We camped nearby in order to prepare for our summit bid in the small hours. The Americans joined us later. Although they were exhausted, they were desperate to join us for the climb to the summit. Mountaineers had given me their time when I was their age, so it was only right that Neill and I should now be helping them out.

We left for the top of South America at two a.m. We wanted to secure enough time to reach the summit and complete a descent by late afternoon, and we also wanted the ice to be nice and crisp. After Everest every mountain seemed easy in comparison, but Aconcagua is still dangerous enough to claim its fair quota of lives. Only the week before we climbed the mountain two Koreans had slipped, fallen and died of exposure. While we were attempting to reach the summit, the Argentinian military were out in force trying to locate the bodies.

By mid-morning we had left the American lads well behind us. They were clearly struggling, while Neill was going off like a rocket. I, too, felt much more comfortable than I had on Vinson, and the ascent was completed with no difficulty, except for the strain and sweat of any hard climb. Neill reached the summit fifteen minutes before I did, but waited for my breathless figure to join him. Instead of a ski pole, this time we found a wooden cross stuck in the centre of the summit. Looking around, as one always does on summits, the scenery was as beautiful as anywhere in the world. We felt that a cross was much more at home on top of a summit than a ski pole. After a few hugs and yet more photos, Neill and I set off on our way back down the mountain.

Within an hour we came across Steve, finding the going tough but clearly still strong enough to make it to the top. There seemed no sign of his mate, however. Two hours later, as we were well on our way back to the Berlin Hut, we finally found Jack. He did not look that good to me, and time was clearly running out. I advised him to give up and have another crack the next day. He insisted he had to finish the job right then, because he doubted he had the strength to try for a second time. I noticed that he had lost his sunglasses which, he explained, had slipped down the mountainside when he fell. I decided to lend him mine instead, to help him reach the summit. I wrongly believed that the baseball cap, which I pulled further over my face, would act as a decent substitute. We wished Jack luck, and went our separate ways.

An hour or so later my eyes started to close up. I knew it would be a risk lending Jack my sunglasses, but I felt I should, with my experience, still be able to get back down to the Berlin Hut without them, whereas the inexperienced Jack would need every help he could get. The snow blindness came on quite suddenly. It got to the point where Neill had quite literally to stick out his ski pole and lead me down the mountain. It was also beginning to get dark, and even Neill was beginning to grow tired. I was a little annoyed with my benevolence, knowing that if I had been that helpful on Everest I would have been dead by now. Jack should have taken my advice and tried for the summit again the following day, with a spare pair of sunglasses.

By the time we finally crawled into the tent beside the Berlin Hut, at around eight p.m. that evening, I could barely see anything. I was not too scared about my condition because I knew full well that snow blindness is always temporary, but I needed a good night's sleep. Normally I would have been out like a light within minutes after such a hard day's climbing, but both Neill and I were concerned about the lads. It was now pitch black outside, and as Jack in particular was evidently in a state, we knew they would struggle to find the hut again.

We decided they would need some assistance. Every ten minutes we banged some cooking pans and flashed our head torches up the mountainside. We assumed, rightly as it turned out, that they had been climbing for so long that the batteries in their own head torches would have run down by now.

It had got to midnight and Neill and I, desperate to go to sleep, were just starting to give up on the lads when we heard a joyful shout from above. We flashed our lights back up the mountain and saw the two of them waving their arms, about a quarter of a mile away. Despite our own tiredness, and my blindness, which was already beginning to ease, we were overjoyed to see them. If anything had happened to the lads, it would have marred the whole trip. On reaching the hut they both hugged us and thanked us incessantly for helping them out. Jack was in tears. Neill told them about my snow blindness, which only made them even more apologetic and grateful. Neill and I were delighted to have helped out, and we both agreed that it was probably more satisfying aiding the two Americans than it was reaching the summit of Aconcagua.

We completed the descent the following morning and walked the forty miles to Punta de l'Inca in not much longer than a day. As we left for Santiago we said goodbye to the Americans. To this day I have never heard of, or seen, them again. It is a strange feeling to think that we may have helped to save their lives, two people we did not know before, but that is the nature of mountaineering. Laws in the mountains are unwritten but strictly adhered to. We are all brothers in such an environment.

Now I was pumped up to complete the job. Six summits – McKinley, Kilimanjaro, Everest, Elbrus, Vinson and Aconcagua – had been conquered, and there only remained Carstensz Pyramid, a tough rock climb. At 16,023 feet, Carstensz Pyramid in Irian Jaya is the highest mountain in Australasia. Within six weeks of arriving at Heathrow I would be on my travels again.

The reasons for this urgency were twofold. For a start, I really needed to be concentrating on the South Pole trip at the end of the year; the other factor was that Claire was pregnant and expecting our third child on 20 May. Steve Bell at Himalayan Kingdoms arranged the trip for me. It proved to be a bureaucratic nightmare where various permits from the government, the police, even the tribal heads took some getting. Even so, Steve produced the goods and I was all set for departure on 21 April 1995.

My next problem was trying to find a climbing partner. Steve Vincent once again said no, Mitch was unavailable, and Neill, having used up all his holiday time on Aconcagua, said forget it. Graham Hoyland was working, and Steve Bell was busy elsewhere. In the end I turned to an electrician friend of mine called Paul Harman, a competent climber but with limited experience at high altitude. The fact that I had not been rock climbing for many years was of some concern to me; the fact that Paul had never been to a third world country in his life, and was about to face a demanding rock climb, worried me immensely.

There is a difference in technique and skill between rock and ice climbing. With rock climbing your partner inserts protection into the rock while you feed out the rope behind. Should you slip at any time you will only fall as far as your last piece of equipment. When you reach your partner's position you remove the nuts and friends from the rock and venture on to place in more protection further up the rock face. In other words, you keep leap-frogging each other. As a result accidents in rock climbing are less common than in ice climbing, where you rely on your ice axes and the crampons sticking out of your feet to hold on to the ice.

Paul and I arrived in Jakarta on 22 April. We were met at the airport by our guide, Djojo Sumardo, an experienced climber who had reached the summit of Carstensz Pyramid on three separate occasions. This made me feel a lot happier – at least one of us knew what the hell he was doing. The following day we flew to a beautiful island called Biak, near Bali. As Paul observed the increasingly tribal food and accommodation and felt the mosquito bites on his arms, his jaw began to drop. He was not exactly enamoured with Jakarta, but by Biak he started to say something which, over the next week, would become his stock phrase: 'Hempie, what the hell have you got me into?'

Our next destination would be the Balium Valley, an area only revealed, apparently, to the rest of the world some forty years ago. The people who lived here were almost Stone Age in their manner. A small Cessna plane, normally used by missionaries, took us right into the midst of the valley. As we landed on the grassy airstrip we could see little mud huts dotted around. As soon as the plane stopped local tribespeople converged from all directions. The women were naked except for grass skirts, designed in a way to show whether they were married or not. The men were also naked except for long penis gourds. I had never been to such a place before in my life and marvelled at the fact that here must be one of the few totally unspoiled, non-commercialised areas in the world.

We faced a hundred-mile, seven-day trek through a jungle full of the most amazing wildlife, ranging from bats and snakes to monkeys and sloths. The locals would be acting as our porters. The jungle became quite dense in places with vegetation, but they made short work of it, thrashing their machetes and clearing a way for us to follow. They also happened to be extremely friendly, if a little curious at first. They only got to see a handful of white people each year, and we were the first to arrive in their part of the world in 1995.

At four o'clock each afternoon they would suddenly stop, seemingly without anyone saying a word. They would all then spread out into the jungle before returning with their arms full of wood. Within a quarter of an hour, using some tarpaulin that we had supplied, they had built a shelter big enough to house all fifteen of them. We remained in our tents nearby to sleep, but joined them for food. Dinner always consisted of a local vegetable called 'uebe', which tasted like a yam. Occasionally, if they were lucky, they lobbed in a bat or rat which they trapped during the day's trek. Paul and I were conscious of not upsetting them but we drew the line when it came to either bat or rat stew.

Inside the shelter the atmosphere was superb. The tribesmen would all be singing and laughing, especially if something amusing had happened during the day. On one of the days I slipped right over on to my backside. They all thought it was a real hoot. The going, however, was slow, and for all the fun and enjoyment I was concerned about the lack of urgency. My mind kept going back to a heavily pregnant Claire at home. Over lunch I showed the porters a photograph of my family. This really seemed to break any remaining ice. They started telling me, through Djojo's interpretation, how many children they all had. Then I explained that Claire was pregnant, and how it was imperative to get me to the mountain and back again as quickly as possible. It seemed to do the trick. From this point on they upped the tempo and reached Carstensz Pyramid within the allotted time.

When we arrived at base camp at 12,000 feet the temperature, which had been a pleasant sixty degrees in the jungle, had dipped to near freezing. This did not seem to bother the semi-naked porters, and neither did the slippery and watery conditions as they clambered over rock. Most climbers would be roped up at this point, but these guys thought nothing of it. They literally skipped across potentially dangerous areas with huge loads on their backs as if it was a walk in a park. From base camp, however, Paul, Djojo and myself would be on our own. The rest found a cave which they made their home while we peered up towards a massive and almost vertical rock face above.

It was now 2 May. At four a.m. we roped ourselves up and started the climb. Paul had continued to swear at me for getting him into this situation, but he performed well above my expectations and insisted, when I was beginning to raise doubts, that we could succeed in reaching the summit and returning to base within the day. Over the next few hours we spent a great deal of time abseiling up and down a series of ridges like yo-yos. Some of these abseils were pretty exposed and, with drops sometimes as steep as 2000 feet, very demanding. The altitude was beginning to drain my energy, but Djojo was hopping up and down the mountainside like a kangaroo.

At the final ridge before the summit I was so exhausted I took my pack off my back and left it behind. It took every last ounce of strength to haul my body over this last obstacle, made a great deal harder by altitude. It took me ten minutes to recover and pull my pack up after me before Paul, roped up to me, could then follow up the mountain. From this point onwards, however, the going was easy. Within another half an hour we had reached the summit and surveyed the mixed scenery of alpine conditions at the top to jungle down below. A small wooden plaque confirmed that Carstensz Pyramid was the continent's highest mountain.

I arrived home on 15 May. Claire ended up giving birth to Amelia on 1 June, which was the perfect end to a highly eventful month. I had become the third British climber to complete the seven summits and, in doing so, I had come across some of the most wonderful people and environments in the world.

It was now time to turn my back on mountaineering and return to polar adventuring, where there was so much still to achieve. The next twelve months would prove to be the coldest and the most dangerous of my life.

PART TWO

ATTENTION TO DETAIL

The South Pole Trip, 1995–6

In November 1993 I attended the Everest reunion dinner laid on by Steve Bell and Himalayan Kingdoms. Most of the team were present that night, including Roger Mear. I had got to know Roger reasonably well, although I would not have said we were best friends. Still, he had vast polar experience, as well as being one of the country's leading climbers, and had worked for the British Antarctic Survey.

During the dinner Roger asked me if I had any further plans. I had not really given it much thought, but I told him that I quite fancied looking at the South Pole. Whether this would be solo, with a partner or a group, supported, unsupported, with snow mobiles or whatever, I did not know. A chord had clearly been struck. Roger said that it all sounded interesting, and then added that he would phone me the following day. Two days later Roger was sitting in my office.

Ranulph Fiennes and Dr Mike Stroud had failed earlier in the year in their attempt to become the first people to cross the whole of the Antarctic continent. This was the idea Roger put to me. I really was not sure about it. I had been away for three months climbing Everest and now had a mountain of business to sort out. More importantly, a corporation was interested in buying Robnor, my Swindon-based company, and we were talking about a great deal of money. The overriding impression I received from reading Fiennes's book recounting their attempt to cross Antarctica was that he and Stroud did not put enough time into preparing for the trip. This, I felt, was the major reason for their extremely brave, but ultimate failed, expedition.

Roger came down for a second visit the following week. By now he had worked out the budget for his suggested trip. I never actually thought obtaining the money would be a problem, but I was concerned about the time needed to organise insurance, transport, equipment, food, and everything else necessary for such an expedition. With my business commitments, I just did not have the time to do all this. Roger said that he would look after it. I then agreed to his idea, and we set a date of early October 1994 to begin the crossing.

From then on we talked on the telephone virtually every day. Right from the start Roger was scathing of Fiennes and Stroud. I was actually quite supportive of them, recognising that what they had achieved had been magnificent. They were only 300 miles short of their intended finish, at the end of the ice shelf, having successfully crossed the continental land mass, and their average daily mileage had been colossal. Roger just felt the two had messed things up.

Once Roger had produced various computer lists it became clear that it was possible we could succeed in our aims. I was beginning to get quite excited about the prospect of the South Pole and beyond. I suppose, deep down, having reached the Magnetic North and Geomagnetic North Poles I was a little scared of failing again at the North Pole. I figured that the South Pole would be a fresh challenge, with no polar bears nor open water. I also wanted to follow in some of Ernest Shackleton's footsteps.

Shackleton is my hero, rather than Robert Falcon Scott. I felt Scott was too pompous, an old establishment figure who had to carry out things a certain way. What I liked about Shackleton is that he flew in the face of authority and was more in line with my own character. Like me, he was given a hard time by the Royal Geographical Society who never seemed quite to approve of his antics. I remember being told by an RGS fellow, when in my early twenties, that I would never be asked to lecture at the RGS because I had been educated at a comprehensive school. With twenty-nine expeditions to date behind me, I still have not received RGS approval or support, nor been asked to present or lecture to them.

Throughout 1994 Roger worked on the trip while I stayed in the background concentrating on other matters, but the longer the year went on the more I grew concerned. Although Roger continued to criticise Fiennes and Stroud, I felt that we, too, were being inordinately slow in getting our act together (in hindsight, I should have found some time from somewhere to help out more). At the start of September I called him in for a meeting. I told him we had a month to go before we started our attempt to cross Antarctica and, by my reckoning, we were deluding ourselves. We would find ourselves in the same boots as Fiennes and Stroud. I told him I wanted to postpone the trip for a year, but still fly down to Patriot Hills, the starting point for Antarctic trips, in order to test out the equipment. I also felt it would help us psychologically to get familiar with the environment. I then suggested we could climb Mount Vinson, at 16,000 feet the continent's highest mountain, to ensure that all our kit could withstand the cold weather. Roger agreed, which was just as well because the night before we were due to leave for Santiago in Chile our ski bindings were still being fitted to the skis. My ski boots did not fit, the sledges were not ready, and our clothes had turned up just three days earlier. In some cases they were so small I could not even pull up my zip. Looking back there was no way we could have covered ten miles in Antarctica like this, let alone try to cross the whole continent.

Having arrived in Santiago we discovered there would be a short delay before we could fly on to Patriot Hills. I suggested that we nip on a bus trip to the Argentinian Andes and try to climb Aconcagua. Roger had tried once before but failed to reach the summit. It would also provide an extra test of our cold-weather equipment. Once we had reached Punta de l'Inca, on the border between Chile and Argentina, we bumped into an astonished Rebecca Stephens and a group of British mountaineers assembled to help Rebecca tackle Aconcagua. They could not believe that Roger and I should just turn up in the middle of the Andes and catch them on the verge of beginning what was supposed to be a top-secret climb. Rebecca had, of course, just become the first British woman to climb Everest and was now in a seven-summit race with fellow climber Ginette Harrison. With her was her boyfriend at the time, John Barry, a brilliant climber and the best raconteur in the mountaineering business; the accomplished climber and guide Martin Barnicott, whom I had last seen at the Himalayan Kingdoms reunion dinner; and Dave Halton, who had been with Rebecca on Everest.

It was the first time I had met Rebecca, and we got along fine. I had known John Barry for years, and obviously knew the other guys as well, so it turned out to be something of a party atmosphere. Roger, however, wanted us to keep to ourselves, saying that we would climb Aconcagua at our own pace. He spent a fair bit of time knocking the others. Rebecca, he opined, was no Alison Hargreaves when it came to climbing. John Barry also received a fair bashing about a previous trip, even Steve Bell and Bob Swann, the polar explorer, got it in the neck. I was beginning to see what others had warned me about: being with Roger was like living with somebody with permanent PMT.

A few days later we found ourselves at 18,000 feet on the mountain. We were 4000 feet away from the summit, and as we woke up that morning we knew it would be summit day. John and Rebecca were nearby and, having taken a look at the ghastly weather, decided to stay put for the day. We, on the other hand, had to go for it because our food supplies had all but gone. It was bitterly cold and our equipment was not completely up for it. After half an hour Roger suddenly announced, 'Well, I don't know about you, but I'm going down.' That was that. There was no discussion, he just decided to bale out.

I was faced with no choice. I had to go with Roger, as my climbing partner, but felt immensely disappointed, not only for failing to reach the summit but also because I did not think we had given Aconcagua our best shot. It also made me think long and hard about Roger in Antarctica. When the chips were down, and I was half-way down a crevasse, would he be the best man in a crisis?

Rebecca, who succeeded in reaching Aconcagua's summit, joined us as we flew first to Punta Arenas in southern Chile and then to Patriot Hills, and finally to Mount Vinson. The mountain requires all-round polar climbing ability, mainly because it gets incredibly cold. During the climb Roger turned his criticisms towards me. Having been sitting behind a desk for most of the year, I was now being a little slow in tying some of the knots required during the climb. He clearly began to feel I was not up to the planned Antarctic crossing. Having reached the summit, Rebecca spent some time talking to the BBC about her achievements. Once again, Roger was demeaning the whole feat behind her back. As we flew back to

England in time for Christmas, I decided to re-evaluate the whole situation.

In January 1995 I went up to Roger's cottage in Derbyshire. At his request I had written out a list of all the sponsors we had, and where I felt we could obtain the rest of the money required for the trip. Once I had provided him with a copy I was quite prepared to sit down and talk again about the crossing; Roger had other ideas. He told me that, having discussed it with his wife, he had decided to have a crack at a solo crossing of Antarctica, but if I wanted to do anything myself down there then he would be more than happy to lend his advice.

It was here, in his study, that I decided to attempt the solo and unsupported walk to the South Pole. Roger, in attempting to cross the whole continent solo, would by definition become the first Briton to reach the South Pole unsupported and solo. That is when I looked at him and thought, 'Right, you bastard, I'm going to beat you at it, but I'm not going to tell anyone until the last minute.' Looking back, Roger did me a favour that day back in January 1995. Not only did it mean that I avoided a probably divisive partnership in the inhospitable wastes of the Antarctic, but it also gave me all the motivation I needed to reach the Pole first.

The strange thing is that I do not feel particularly bitter about Roger's actions. I actually felt a sense of relief that my proposed affiliation with the man was now over. I do not think we or the trip would have worked out and, as I said, it made me incredibly motivated, both before and during my own solo walk to the South Pole. I discussed the matter with both Mitch Mitchell and Neill Williams, who had accompanied me on the 1992 Geomagnetic North Pole trip, and they agreed that it was the best thing that could have happened. They, too, expressed their concerns about whether Roger would have been the best partner if something happened to me during the trip.

While we were all down at Mount Vinson a Norwegian girl called Liv Arnesson was in the process of becoming the first woman ever to walk to the South Pole, solo and unsupported. She spent four years planning the trip and proved to be wonderfully able in Antarctic conditions. This only served to whet my appetite further to attempt the same trip myself. I met up with Annie Kershaw, who runs Adventure Network, a company based in Beaconsfield and Punta Arenas in Chile which helps to organise all Antarctic expeditions. She had taken over the running of Adventure Network after her husband, Giles, was killed in a plane crash in the Antarctic. At first sight this petite, attractive, blonde Scotswoman is disarmingly feminine, but deep down there lurks a core of steel. In all my business dealings she is one of the shrewdest, most professional people I have ever come across. Despite the death of her husband, and the male-dominated character of her business, she has proved to be extremely successful. She has grown into a real authority on Antarctic expeditions, and she provides a wealth of information for research. Trying to get a discount off her, however, is about as easy as walking naked to the Pole.

I told Annie my plans and swore her to secrecy. She also provided me with Liv Arnesson's number in Oslo. When I bothered to think about it I realised that while the British had recorded a string of polar failures in recent years, the Norwegians, in contrast, had been spectacularly successful. It was to them that I decided to turn. Ignoring the advice and equipment provided by Roger, I contacted Liv – who sent me a list of magnetic variations, her routes and her equipment – a compatriot called Steiner Sveen – who helped to get my boots – and a man who would become one of my closest friends, Borge Ousland.

Borge is one of the world's most accomplished polar

explorers. He also happened to be attempting a solo and unsupported crossing of Antarctica himself that winter and, as a result, found himself in direct competition with Roger Mear. Yet he still found time to advise me. Apart from faxing me a complete breakdown of weights and manufacturers, perhaps the best piece of advice he gave me was to start training by pulling tyres along a beach, to simulate a sledge. It was a simple idea, but brilliant. Thanks to the Norwegians, I had everything I needed within four weeks. And this was still only June 1995.

I also went to see Sir Vivian Fuchs and Dr Charles Swithinbank, both of whom lived in Cambridge. Sir Vivian made his name back in the 1950s when he crossed the Antarctic on the Commonwealth expedition using a tractor train. As one of the leading lights, and as someone I have always turned to before my polar expeditions, he was my natural first port of call and, as always, his views were highly valuable.

Charles is an experienced glaciologist. He's in his late sixties now, but his advice concerning routes was spot on. We spread out a series of maps across his living-room floor and pored over them for many hours. At the end of the conversation Charles wanted to make it clear that he was more than happy to help me, but the route would have to be my choice. He did not want to be blamed if anything were to happen to me. Having been blamed by Reinhold Messner after he went down prescribed glaciated routes on previous Antarctic expeditions, Swithinbank was playing it safe this time. I felt a little sorry for him. If Messner did not want his advice, then he should not have sought it in the first place. I could not see the point of blaming someone else for falling down a crevasse.

Meanwhile, plans for the 'Ultimate Challenge' were in an embryonic stage. The idea first came up during a meeting between myself, Mitch and Jock Wishart. Why don't we take a bunch of novices up to the Magnetic North Pole the following March? I think that Mitch, Jock and, after consultation, Neill were all keen to carry out another expedition after our successful trip to the Geo-magnetic North Pole in 1992, but I also liked the idea of leading a large group comprising friends and complete newcomers, just to show how it is done and how ordinary punters can, if they possess enough character, succeed as polar adventurers.

Suddenly I had two trips to think about. At least with the Ultimate Challenge I had partners carrying out most of the preparation. I suggested to Neill that he should contact Roger Mear to get some names and addresses to help him organise the trip. When Neill finally got hold of him, Roger told him to get all the names out of the telephone directory, as he had to. As you can imagine, Roger was not the most popular person in our camp.

Things were really hotting up now. During my climb of Carstensz Pyramid that May Paul Harman, my fellow mountaineer, first put the idea of sailing to the Magnetic South Pole into my mind. I could just about do it, in between the South Pole and Ultimate Challenge trips, so now there were three trips. Looking back, it was all a little crazy, but I was consumed with excitement and adventure, and despite trying to juggle the sale of my company, the birth of my third daughter Amelia, and the planning and preparation of three trips, I seemed to thrive in the situation I found myself in.

The budget for the South Pole trip was £150,000. That was my target and I reached it thanks largely to generous and trusted businessmen, most of whom had supported me on previous expeditions, people like Rikki Hunt at Burmah Fuels, who would later join me on the Ultimate Challenge; Malcolm Wallace at EMR (European Metal Recycling); Clive Mann from Whitehead Mann (a recruitment services company); and John Nelligan at Britannia Music. I flew to America to see Jim May, our main sponsor on the 1992 Geomagnetic North Pole trip, who ended up endorsing me again.

My biggest sponsor was Burmah, with £30,000, followed by Buxted Foods with £10,000, but in general I obtained most of the £150,000 through networking. George Pollock, for example, the managing director of Farepak Hampers, supported me to a small degree with funding, but he mentioned me to other companies who in turn added contributions. When you end up with nearly fifty sponsors, £150,000 is suddenly not so much to raise. Most of them got photos and brief mentions which were of use within the company. At no time was I placed under pressure from any of my sponsors. In fact, it was quite the reverse. I feel that, in some cases, the individuals behind the decisions to endorse me were reliving their own adventures through me, but nearly all of them told me that I was stark raving mad to be walking to the South Pole.

Most of these discussions were completed over the mobile telephone. In March 1995 I had set up a second company, Global Resins, which provides traffic and construction industry resins, and was concentrating on overseas work and the finalising of terms for the sale of Robnor. After what seemed like an eternity of meetings and bartering I finally sold Robnor to the Mason Corporation in September. The final completion meeting took a solid sixty hours, and when it was over I was both exhilarated and exhausted.

September was also the month when the selection process began for the Ultimate Challenge. We had already advertised the idea through a brochure and launched the concept to the national broadcast and print media in July from the deep freeze in London's Smithfield Market. We received over 500 applications, a figure whittled down to 150 as soon as they discovered they would have to find £15,000 to get on board, either from their own pocket or through sponsorship. But the rest all trooped down to Sandhurst where Mitch, a major in the British army, happened to be serving at the time. We laid on three tests for the hopeful adventurers. A psychologist called Chris Jones conducted a series of psychometric tests on an individual and team basis just to see the interaction within groups and also the leadership qualities required for trekking in polar conditions. Then Mitch, Neill, Jock and myself split the group into four and interviewed each individual. I ended the session by conducting a lecture about the Magnetic North Pole. After Sandhurst we managed to reduce the number to twenty, which is where I had to leave it in order to concentrate on the South Pole. But the others took the novices on thirty-mile route marches, and a paratroopers training course which we called 'Tough Guy'. The twenty were reduced to ten in my absence, although I kept tabs on the situation from Antarctica on the radio.

I just about had time to find a boat and a crew to sail down to the Magnetic South Pole, assuming I would return from Antarctica, before setting all my sights on the walk to the South Pole. In the couple of weeks prior to leaving on 20 October for South America I was training in France and Germany, either pulling my tyres along the beach or just generally getting into good shape. The BBC agreed to film me starting out, and to broadcast progress reports.

I sent Annie Kershaw at Adventure Network my deposit, and then set off for what would be the biggest test yet of my adventuring years.

Saying goodbye to the family was obviously difficult. For a start Amelia was just four months old. I would be missing Christmas, the New Year, our wedding anniversary, and both Alicia's and Camilla's birthdays. The children did not appreciate the enormity of the trip ahead, but Claire certainly did. She was pretty tearful, and I had a large lump in my throat. I told her that my will was in the top drawer of my desk, but she would not be needing it because I promised I would be back in January. It was the first time I had been away on a solo trip since the Magnetic North Pole in 1984, and it would be my first polar trip since 1992. It was undeniably one of the toughest and most dangerous trips of my life.

There was a particular aspect, however, that still concerned me as I left the British Isles. I had just completed the most amazingly busy last few months, and a combination of getting my three polar projects together, setting up Global and selling Robnor had left me exhausted and unfocused. I had a farewell drink with Neill Williams in my local pub. He told me, in no uncertain terms, that I should pull out of the South Pole trip. He said that I had been working too hard on other matters, my mind was not in the best shape, and I was risking my life. Mitch agreed with Neill when I spoke to him the next day. Even Tony Rolls, a neighbour and fitness fanatic who helps to get me in shape before my trips, was telling me I just was not fit enough. Maybe they would all be proved right.

Roger Mear should have started out three weeks before me on his attempt to cross Antarctica but fortunately, from my point of view, the weather was so appalling that Adventure Network could not fly him out until a week before I was due to start. I was far from happy that Adventure Network had given him this advantage, especially as Roger and I were both in Punta Arenas, and I begged Annie Kershaw to let me fly out with him on the same plane. But Adventure Network was already fully booked, and I just had to wait my turn. In the end Roger left fourteen days behind his schedule, setting off from Bearkner Island, which would be a slightly longer route than mine to the South Pole.

Punta Arenas is the last major town in Chile before Cape Horn. It is best known by seafarers making their way around the Cape, but it has now become a tourist stopover for the Antarctic. It is always cold and windy in this dusty, old, corrugated tin-clad town, with only a statue of Ferdinand Magellan in the square to boast of in terms of points of historical interest. Although I am not a religious man, I went to church in Punta to pray before leaving for Antarctica. I also went to the Magellan statue. There is a long-standing tradition that if you touch Magellan's toes before leaving for the Antarctic, it will ensure a safe return to Chile. I almost bit off Magellan's toes in my efforts to obtain security.

There was quite a collection of adventurers in Punta Arenas at that time. Apart from Roger and myself, Feodore Konikov had turned up. He was intending to follow the same route I had chosen in an attempt to become the first Russian to walk, unsupported and solo, to the South Pole. I had no problem with this at all. We came from different countries, and therefore had different goals. Besides, Feodore was a giant of an adventurer: he had sailed around the world solo twice without stopping, climbed Everest, and had been to the North Pole, solo and supported. He was immensely experienced, and seemed never to fail in what he set out to do.

There was also a couple of French Canadians, Thierry Patrese and Bernard Voyear, both of whom were very good sportsmen, hoping to become the first Canadians to walk unsupported to the South Pole. They were very helpful and friendly, exchanging ideas and equipment with me. Finally, Borge Ousland arrived. I was particularly pleased to see him after all the help and friendship he had offered me. Roger was also in Punta. If he was surprised to see me, he did not show it. My anger with Roger had long gone, to be replaced by motivation to beat him, although I still had a grudging respect for his ability. When I saw him leave a week before me I was disappointed and dejected, but I also knew that it was a long, long way to the South Pole.

This left the two Canadians, Borge, Feodore and myself. Bernard's girlfriend, Natalie, gave me a small present which I was under strict instructions not to open until Christmas Day. Feodore looked like Jesus Christ, with long dark hair and a beard. One night there was a knock on the door. It was Feodore, and he presented me with a dead fish as a token of friendship and respect for a fellow polar adventurer. I gave him some Mars bars in return, and from that moment onwards we became firm friends.

Annie Kershaw brought me in to her office the following morning. She told me that if she failed to receive an Argos reading or a radio message within twenty-four hours of my starting out Adventure Network would fly in and pick me up. An Argos system is basically a tracking system which sends back your position each night to base, via satellite, in Washington DC, from where the unit is supplied, then they fax the details down to Annie. I tried to argue with her, pointing out that my batteries could go flat or sun spots could muck up the communications, but she would hear none of it. I persevered because I felt my reservations were justified. I might not contact them for legitimate reasons, such as falling down a crevasse. If this was the case, Annie replied, then Adventure Network would come in and possibly save me. On the other hand, I countered, a failure to contact may be down to a trivial reason, in which case Adventure Network would be hauling me out for no reason. Annie was adamant: at a cost of £65,000 just to fly over to the Antarctic with all the equipment, they would only be making the one rescue journey.

The Argos itself had caused me quite a scare. For six months I had been talking to a Scottish company until, with a week to go before leaving, they told me there was a problem and they would have to try to get hold of another one for me. In the end I picked one up from Swindon on my way to Heathrow airport to catch my flight to Santiago. On opening up the package I discovered it was an Argos designed for a fishing boat, which was therefore much heavier than the Argos I required. The whole trip was in jeopardy. Without an Argos system I knew I would be unable to venture a foot on Antarctic ice. Eventually, thanks to an American rival firm called NACLS, a new Argos was delivered to me in Punta Arenas just in the nick of time, and only after frantic last-minute telephone calls and a great deal of help from my cousin, Nick Hempleman, who ended up being my gopher in Punta Arenas, checking stoves, weighing everything, breaking down food and testing the Argos system and radio frequencies.

At last, after ten days in Punta Arenas, Adventure Network flew myself and Feodore into Patriot Hills, the only blue ice runway on the whole continent strong and flat enough to withstand a Hercules plane. It was now 6 November. Patriot Hills is where tourists are flown for day trips to see the penguins and to have their passports stamped, and it is also here that all adventurers first arrive before flying off in Adventure Network Twin Otters or Cessnas to their designated starting points.

With just two days to go before I was due to begin myself, it was time to check every single item I intended to take with me. I went through all my medical kit with the doctor based in Patriot Hills. He ended up advising me as to how I could reduce the weight of the load on my sledge. So out went a pair of scissors and tweezers because I already had a Swiss army knife, crêpe bandages were slung out because I could always use a silk balaclava, and I decided that if I became sunburned I could simply apply snow instead of some of the cream I had brought. I inspected everything down to the tiniest item, from polishing the runners to double-checking the screws on the bottom of the sledges. Then there was a final check on all my navigation and magnetic readings.

On 7 November we set off from Patriot Hills to Hercules Inlet on two snowmobiles. Geoff Somers came with me. He had vast experience himself as a polar explorer, and had agreed to be my radio man at base. He was a man for whom I had a great deal of respect, and he would be my only point of contact throughout the whole trip. By going together Feodore and I would be halving the costs. We had already reached an agreement where I would set off half a day before him, so that nobody could accuse either of us of not attempting the walk solo. I was concerned, however, that Feodore would shoot past me within a day or two. The man was awesome. He used to eat raw onions, and I remember once commenting on how cold it was outside. He just looked at me and said, 'It's the Antarctic. It gets cold here.'

Then I compared our equipment. I had all the up-to-date stuff; Feodore, in direct comparison, had rusty old skis, pieces of string which held his ski pole together, and a tent which just did not look strong enough to withstand the strong catabatic winds we both expected en route to the South Pole. I then had a go at lifting all his gear, and it felt like double the weight of mine. All in all it made me feel pretty bad, and pretty psyched out by my new-found friend. Feodore was as strong as an ox, and I, in comparison, suddenly felt rather weak.

We all ate together that night at Hercules Inlet in our

tents. It was a strange atmosphere, a mixture of excitement and anxiety. That night I barely slept a wink. Instead, I got to thinking about the next sixty days or so. I thought about the crevasses, the strong headwinds picking up speed as they zip across the continent, and then I pictured myself struggling against layer upon layer of sastrugi, the Russian word for snow dunes created by winds which blow the snow and ice into mounds of up to twenty feet in height. The surface is like a deeply furrowed field, and such conditions can be found all the way to the Pole. As I lay there I felt a pit in my stomach and a mounting fear I had never quite experienced before.

I was up by five that morning, in the brilliant daylight that Antarctica in its summer months produces all day and night. I cooked some breakfast, stoked myself up for the day ahead, and then went across to the other tents to say my farewells. Both Geoff and Feodore hugged me and told me they would see me at the Pole. I nodded back and grinned. As I trudged off to my sledge, wrapped the harness around my shoulder and prepared myself for my first pull of the longest, most arduous trip of my life, I had just one thought in my head: I hoped to God that Geoff and Feodore were right.

THANK YOU, MRS T

The realisation hit me as suddenly as an Antarctic storm. Now I was on my own, and despite all my previous experience I was feeling extremely frightened. There I was, at 79°58' south, standing on an ice pack at Hercules Inlet, fifty yards off shore. This was where my journey would officially begin, just so that no one could ever say I started from inland. Ahead of me lay 600 nautical miles of the most barren and uncompromising terrain on earth. In some ways it was great finally to be on my way. It was a beautiful day, with a deep-blue sky and absolutely no wind, and after all the waiting, drip-dripping like a Chinese torture, I found myself with my back to my companions facing the one direction that led me to the South Pole. But I had no idea what fate lay ahead of me, and whether I should even have been attempting the expedition in the first place. These were my overriding thoughts.

As I made my first pull and felt the sledge move behind me with its 285lb of contents nestled on top, I immediately started to plan ahead. I told myself that if I could get over the first ten days I would make it to the Pole. I would have to be patient and under no circumstances should I start like an express train. The trick would be to go easy to begin with, warming myself up but not burning out halfway to my hoped-for destination. Something in the region of eight hours' walking a day, resulting in a distance of twelve miles, would do the trick.

I hoped I could remain positive on what was only my first day, but within an hour's hard walking my mood had been consumed by negative thoughts. For a start, it was tough going. From Hercules Inlet the direction was upwards, at times approaching twenty-five degrees in slope. The sastrugi hardly helped either. Instead of a steady ski it turned into a plod, up and down over the lips of ice and snow caused by the wind, in a steady upwards direction. After three hours I looked back over my traces and saw all the tents at Hercules Inlet with steam coming out of the top of them, exuding warmth, friendliness and security. I thought to myself, 'This just doesn't stack up. I've been going for nearly half the day, and I can still see those bloody tents.' They seemed as close as ever.

Then I remembered the significance of the day. The eighth of November was not only my brother Mark's birthday, but also my eldest daughter Alicia's sixth birthday. I had no time to think about such matters prior to leaving because my time was fully taken up in last-minute preparations, but now, alone with only my thoughts, I turned to my family. I did not feel too bad about Mark, wishing him the best for the day and hoping he would sink a pint for me, but when my attention turned to Alicia I felt lousy. Singing happy birthday to her as I trudged along the ice hardly made up for the fact that for the third successive year I was away on my adventures when I should have been at home with my girl. The year before I was half-way through my first, aborted attempt on Aconcagua in the Andes, and now I found myself in Antarctica. There I was, in the middle of nowhere, being totally selfish and anything but a good father.

These thoughts then evolved into trying to figure out why I was out in the Antarctic at all. What was the point of it all? And did it really matter? For while I was out there, alone and already suffering, the rest of the world carried on as normal, and I was nothing more than an irrelevant speck moving slowly along in the last wilderness on the planet.

The one consolation at times like this is the beauty of the place. When the sun is shining and the sky is deep blue, there is nowhere more beautiful in the world. The sheer whiteness, the purest white you can ever imagine, glistens in the sunshine, and because you are out there completely by yourself you tend to believe that this is your kingdom. It was good to be back in the kind of environment that most people would only want to sample for an hour or two, but for me it was becoming almost a natural habitat.

After eight hours of plodding slowly through the ice, however, it was with some relief that I started to unpack the sledge that night and put up my tent. The first day was over, and it was good to start getting into some kind of routine. I figured that I needed at least one day behind me just to get used again to the polar conditions, not just climatically but also from a mental viewpoint. Just about the first thing I did was relieve myself in the snow. I mention this daily function only because, despite my complete solitude, I still found myself turning my back in order to pee privately, as if a queue of people were watching from the other side of the tent.

I emptied virtually all the contents of the sledge into the tent – my food, my three sleeping bags, my clothes, my first aid kit, my radio equipment, and so on – making sure to tie a loop attached to the tent round my foot just in case a sudden gust blew it away, which would immediately end the trip.

The big shock came when my global positioning system (GPS) revealed that in eight hours' walking I had managed to travel just six miles. Six miles! I couldn't believe it. I had been walking my balls off all day, and managed to cover just half of the distance I was supposed to if I were to reach the South Pole in fifty days. I immediately started to do sums in my head. The plan was simple: twelve miles for each of the fifty days would cover the 600 nautical miles. My emergency supplies meant that I could last a further ten days if necessary, but already after just one day I was six miles down on schedule. Then I discovered that, instead of climbing what I thought had been 2000 feet in altitude, it was only 230 feet.

It was a depressing first evening meal of dehydrated pasta that day, but as I prepared myself for bed, with the sun still shining brightly outside during a time of year when there is never any night, I tried to be positive. I wanted to take it slowly at first, after all, so I was bound to go further as the trip went on. The load of the sledge would lighten as I piled through my supplies, and it would not be uphill all the way. I had to counter high sastrugi, I had to get used to the conditions, all the equipment was fine, and I had no frostbite. In any case, I figured as I fell exhausted into a deep sleep, what's six miles out of 600?

The alarm on the cheap plastic watch I obtained from some petrol station failed to wake me up the following morning. I was so fatigued from the previous day's exertions that I overslept by an hour. Breakfast proved to be a slow process. I had no organised system in place, and instead of doing a number of things at the same time I plodded my way through the process, act after act. Getting the stove going before melting snow into boiling water took time, and when I finally got round to eating the warm muesli I could not help but think of a decent fry up back at home. By the time all this was finished and I had packed up the sledge and was ready to go, it was midday, and a vital chunk of the day had already gone. This, I thought to myself as I started out again, was the worst start to a day in which I had hoped to make up some of the lost ground from the first day.

My mood was hardly improved by the thought that during the day ahead I would face a whole series of crevasses, some of them huge and all of them potential death traps. It was a scary thought, for despite the certain cold and blizzards that awaited me, the crevasses presented the one element that could kill me straight away. I recalled other polar explorers, brave people like Belgrave Ninnis whose body was never found after he fell down a crevasse. His companions that day back in 1912, Mawson and Mertz, looked back to discover that where Ninnis, a team of dogs and sledges had been, there was nothing. Looking down into a large, dark gap in the ice that appeared to have no bottom, all they could hear, faintly and in the distance, were the wounded cries of a dying dog.

Some of the crevasses can be as deep as 300 feet, big black holes which normally mean certain death to a person who, because he or she is tied in a harness to the sledge, falls down like a torpedo. Within an hour I came to my first, stretching some 200 feet in length and about eight feet in width. You can usually recognise them ahead of you because the winds have created a small lip of snow hanging over the edge. I looked at the snowy ridge in front of me, and immediately began to ponder whether I should risk crossing the ridge, or take the long way round the length of the crevasse. The ridge was full of snow, but the problem was that I had no idea what, if anything, was underneath it. I started to prod first, and then whack the ridge with my ski stick. It stayed firm, and I was sorely tempted to cross, but then I lost my nerve and took the detour.

It was when I discovered that the whole process had

lost me an hour that I decided to get brave. The trick when walking in polar conditions is to establish a rhythm, however slow and plodding it may be. By stopping at each crevasse, checking the strength of the ridge, and then deciding to walk all the way round, I realised that the trip would take me years, not weeks. There would be fields of crevasses stretching all the way to the Pole, and my time meter was ticking.

By the time I reached the second crevasse I thought, 'Bugger it, I'll ski across.' I gave the ridge a good prod, just to make sure I wasn't committing suicide, untied my harness and connected a rope to the sledge, and then took a long run up. By the time I hit the ridge I was at full speed, with my heart firmly in my mouth. Thankfully, the ridge held firm and, once safely on the other side, I hauled the sledge across and got on my way. The adrenalin was pumping inside for quite some time after that, but my confidence was also building. I came to a third crevasse and repeated my actions without any problem. The fourth one came and went, and even the fact that I nearly lost my ski stick prodding through the next crevasse, a two-foot tiddler, failed to dent my growing confidence. I looked down the deceptive hole where my stick nearly fell and could only see black, but I was able to step neatly across the gap, and then haul the sledge behind me.

For the second time in two days the bad news came when, having pitched my tent for the night, my GPS revealed that I had once again covered only six miles. That put me twelve miles behind schedule after just forty-eight hours which meant, at this rate of walking, I was already two days into my emergency quota of ten days. The fact that I had climbed 500 feet in this time raised my hopes a little, because I was well on my way to reaching the 10,000 feet height of the South Pole, but I was still despondent over the small distance I had covered.

That night, over a less than appetising dish of dehy-drated chilli con carne, I started to think of ways of reducing the load on the sledge which would, in turn, help me to speed up. I decided that if I was going to fall down a crevasse I would die, so there was not much point in carrying an ice axe or a rope designed to get me out. You have to remember that in the cold, physically exhausted after a hard day's walk, your mind may not be in the most sound state, and the all-consuming thought that you must get to the Pole no matter what clouds over everything else. So I buried the equipment which could save me if I were to survive a fall down a crevasse in the ice.

I woke up on day three looking forward to seeing Patriot Hills. My route passed close by and I was hoping that when I made my radio call that night to Geoff Somers we would be able to blast each other off the airwaves. It was just my luck that there was a really strong wind which meant that all I could see was white ice and no sky. There was absolutely no chance of seeing Patriot Hills, even though I would never be as close again. It was important under such conditions to make sure that no part of my flesh was exposed to a chill factor of – 50°C which would freeze skin within seconds.

It was slow going. Every fifteen minutes I had to produce my compass and make sure I was still walking in the right direction. Every seventy minutes I unpacked my flask and made sure to take a good swig of warm soup, and eat a chunk of chocolate or a few peanuts from my special munchy bag. On a good day you could see for miles, so that something you focused on in the distance would seemingly never appear to be getting nearer as you walked, but on this day I had to make do with a different clump of sastrugi a few metres ahead of me, so poor was the visibility. It turned the day into one solid block, rather than a series, of small achievable goals.

I had mixed emotions when I discovered that night that, despite strong winds, I had travelled seven miles during the day, one mile further than on each of the first two days. I initially felt quite pleased with my performance until it struck me that it still meant a further five miles down on my schedule. My mood darkened when, trying to contact Geoff at Patriot Hills, we could barely hear each other even though this would be the nearest I would ever be to him on the whole trip. The reception turned out to be so poor that I was just about able to provide my position, and left it at that. A good chat and a laugh would have to wait for another two days, the next time I was due to call in.

That night I faced the fact that I might not be able to complete the walk. At my current speed I would need a hundred, not fifty, days to reach the Pole. Then I looked at more ways of cutting down the weight on the sledge. It sounds stupid now, but I was reading Margaret Thatcher's autobiography *The Downing Street Years* each night before I turned in, and I decided that I would bury whatever pages I had read each day to lessen the load. It was important to stimulate my brain in the conditions, so I made a point of reading at least ten pages before ripping them out. The difference it made to the weight was negligible, but every little effort made a psychological difference. As a result, there are little buried caches of the thoughts of Baroness Thatcher, a day's journey apart, all the way to the South Pole. Whoever finds them will wonder why and how they ever got there.

It was blowing another hooley on the morning of day four, but I was beginning to get used to my own routine and, as a result, was able to get going thirty minutes earlier. This morning routine began with the alarm clock waking me from a deep sleep. It would always be this way. If I left it until I woke up naturally it would probably be afternoon before I even had breakfast. I would then boil water on the stove for my first meal of the day, a less than desirable mixture of muesli, sugar and milk. I would drink a litre of this plus another litre of tea, and have soup boiled up in my flask to drink through the day. Then I could turn my attentions to the day's walk.

I was hardly feeling confident about my chances, but reckoned it would be just as windy at Patriot Hills, where the Twin Otter waiting to pick me up was stationed, so I may as well keep on going. If anyone had seen me each day out there in such conditions they would first have wondered why, and then realised how stupid I looked. The main reason for this was because I used old clothing bags as gaiters, which made me look completely daft. But, although we may well now be living in a technological world, I have always been a great believer in sticking to what is proven, especially in a place where getting it wrong can result in extremely uncomfortable consequences. As a result, I stuck to old-fashioned equipment. My boots were the same design as those Roald Amundsen wore back in 1912 when he pipped Robert Scott to become the first man to reach the South Pole. You need a very thin wool inner sock, then a vapour barrier to stop the sweat moving outwards from your feet and freezing, which is why I used a Sainsbury's shopping bag, would you believe, on each foot. I then wore a thick woollen sock on top of these, and an ordinary canvas outer boot, which resulted in nice warm feet with no frostbite, the whole thing weighing only half the weight of leather.

Nevertheless, a combination of headwinds blowing straight into my face that day and high sastrugi made it another hard toil on the ice. This is the time when you feel at your loneliest, and the enjoyment factor one can quite often derive from the beauty, peace and tranquillity of the environment is down to a bare minimum. The end result, I discovered that night, was just another six miles.

The facts were beginning to look bleak now, and at a very early stage of the walk. I was still barely covering half the distance I should have been, and I was falling further and further away from ever making the Pole on time. Yet still I remained upbeat about the situation. I had now climbed 1000 feet, a tenth of the total altitude, in just four days, which meant that the land would get flatter and therefore easier for me to walk on, a fact confirmed by the contours on my map. Then I resorted to what was becoming a nightly routine – the reduction of weight on the sledge. I brought the medical and maintenance kits into the tent and started to chuck out items such as half a tube of suntan cream, a large handful of grease, and some restraining straps. Then I started on the kitchen items. Out went a spare cooking pot, an extra fork, four out of my six lighters, a screwdriver and some masking tape. By my reckoning, another four pounds in weight was buried in the ice that evening.

During the night the wind really started to whip up, and I could hear and feel the tent beginning to flap about. A long, groaning whistle grew louder and louder as the night went on, and I grew more frightened by the hour. My first concern was whether the tent was secure enough to withstand what was clearly turning into a full-blown blizzard. Then I thought about the consequences of a long-drawn-out storm. Back in 1983, when I failed to make it solo to the North Pole, the worst blizzard I have ever had the misfortune to encounter kept me rooted inside my tent for ten days, virtually ensuring my failure. As I tried to sleep I could not help but wonder whether that experience was about to be repeated.

Within a split second of waking a few hours later in the morning my first action was to stick my head out of the tent to gauge the conditions. All I could see was snow, blowing furiously and swirling round and round in the air. Past experience has taught me that sometimes such conditions can seem worse than they actually are once you are standing up outside, but having left the tent to sample the blizzard I came to the rapid conclusion that attempting to walk in this would constitute suicide. Perhaps, just perhaps, I might have been able to walk with a companion, because at least we might have been able to see and therefore help each other out, but to be by myself out there would probably have resulted in my death. I reckoned that I would lose the tent either taking it down or constructing it again that evening, and that I would definitely have suffered from frostbite. I had no alternative but to sit the storm out, hoping that it would last hours rather than days.

During this time I was thinking furiously about the lost time, and how I could reduce the weight even further. Obviously, the thought occurred to me that the storm could last for weeks, but I did not need to make any rash decisions just then and, besides, I had a duty to my sponsors who had forked out £150,000 to make this trip possible. I am sure that none of them would have accused me of not trying, but I still felt I owed them a little patience.

The hours turned into a day, a whole day lost to a storm. After five days I should have covered sixty miles and been crossing from eighty to eighty-one degrees, a moment which would have a huge psychological impact. The reality was that I had walked just twenty-five miles and not even reached half-way to the first degree change. Incredibly, in just five days I had fallen the equivalent of seven days behind on my schedule. As I began to radio Geoff Somers I really started to panic. The literally cold fact was that I just was not getting there.

There were many crucial moments during this trip, and

the radio call that night proved to be one of them, even if the motivation I found would only last twenty-four hours. I must have sounded downhearted when my voice crackled over the airwaves at Patriot Hills. Geoff, in contrast, was upbeat. 'Look, Dave,' he began. 'Twenty-five miles is twenty-five miles nearer to the Pole. Keep sticking your nose out into the blizzard and see if there is a chance soon to get going. You are going to get to the Pole, and you had better get there because you have promised me a dinner at the end of all this.'

Now, if someone without polar experience had been on the other end of the line saying this I would have told him where to go, that he did not know what he was talking about, and that I was coming home. But I was almost in awe of Geoff because he had been out in similar conditions on many occasions. He had been there and done it, so the last thing I was going to do was to give up over the radio to Geoff. That night I went to sleep still determined to keep on going, and hoping that the blizzard would be gone by the morning.

When I woke up on day six it was clear that the blizzard was still with me but, on further inspection, I decided that the winds had died down to a still dangerous but manageable level. The weather meant another slow day's trek, not helped by constant sastrugi formed by the whipping winds. After six hours the sledge suddenly hit the lip of a sastrugi. For nearly six days I had been dragging the sledge smoothly over them, but this time it stuck and stopped dead in its tracks. For a split second I kept going before suddenly being jerked backwards, almost off my feet, straight on to my arse. I lay there, with my skis in the air, crying out in agony. The whole of the area around my coccyx had been jarred. I felt a piercing pain and immediately knew I was in trouble.

The day's walk ended abruptly at this moment. Having

slowly erected my tent, and discovered through my GPS that I had covered yet another six miles, I started to take painkillers. The tablets seemed to make no initial impact. The pain was excruciating, which only served to worsen my morale and make me wonder how badly I had damaged my back. My attempt at the North Pole back in 1983 failed partly due to a fall on the ice which resulted in two cracked ribs. Was history about to repeat itself in the Antarctic? Ignoring the advice on the bottle, I chucked a load of extra painkillers down my throat. This may not have been the cleverest action to take, but these were desperate moments on the expedition, and they required desperate actions. Then, leaning back and trying to find the least uncomfortable position, I began to take stock of my worsening situation.

The facts were not encouraging. I was well behind schedule, and it was clear that I was never going to be able to catch up on lost ground in such pain. I was feeling extremely sorry for myself and, after virtually a year without seeing my family due to horrendous business commitments abroad, very homesick. It would make complete sense to pull out right there. I was close to Patriot Hills and it would have been a cheaper exercise to quit there because Adventure Network would not charge to pick me up. Few would ever get to hear of the failure, because I had made a point of keeping the publicity down until I had succeeded, and I would simply return the following year, re-evaluate and, no doubt, have another crack at the South Pole.

All it would have taken was one push of the 'emergency evacuation' button on my Argos position transmitter and a plane would have flown me out within hours. My God, it was an incredible temptation. It could all be over with just a simple prod of my finger. I called up Geoff Somers at base back at Patriot, and discovered that despite my slow going I was faring better than both Roger Mear and Feodore. Both had covered less mileage than me, and were suffering in the uncompromising conditions the Antarctic had decided to throw at us all. I had become so caught up in my personal obsession to reach the Pole, and my resultant hardship, that I had forgotten I was involved in a race with Roger Mear to become the first Briton ever to reach the South Pole solo and unsupported. Despite everything that had happened to me, I was clearly winning the race.

Geoff proved once again to be priceless. If I had ever been a heavyweight boxer, I would have had him in my corner for every fight. He told me he respected me, and that I was doing all right. He went on to refer to the others out there on the ice as 'poor bastards', whereas he referred to me as 'wonderful'. He probably meant none of it, but it was so good to hear. Even so, my gut feeling was to hell with it all. So what if I was winning the race? The fact remained that I was in terrible pain, and I could not see how I could even get close to the Pole in my condition, and at the pace I had been plodding at. I could not see Mear succeeding either, so there did not seem an awful lot of point in walking a little further than my rival to record an ultimate failure. My old reasoning – better to be a living failure than a dead hero – seemed once again to be making sense.

I experienced quite a few moments during the trip when I felt like packing it all in, but the night of day six undoubtedly proved to be the major turning point. It was a complete accident that I had brought Mrs Thatcher's autobiography along in the first place. It was the thickest and best value-for-money book on sale at Heathrow airport, and as I admired the woman enormously and required a large book to provide reading material for as long as possible during my trip, I bought it. Idly flicking through the pages that night, prolonging the moment when I was going to push the button on the Argos, I came to a phrase her father often said to her, something which stuck in Mrs Thatcher's mind ever since: 'It is easy to be a starter,' she wrote, 'but are you a finisher?' I looked at this sentence, and then read it over and over again, before putting the book down beside me.

My thoughts then turned to my eldest daughter, Alicia, and all her friends at school. They were plotting my course on a map in the classroom, and I thought of that map and how pathetic it would look if the little girls' line was to come to an abrupt end after just six days. Then I remembered Jock's pleas not to come on this trip. He could be guaranteed to turn round later and say, 'I told you so.' Then I thought of all the others, the friends and the doubters, all of whom were expecting the moment when I pushed the emergency button. I would be following in a long line of failed British expeditions. While explorers and adventurers from countries like Norway and Russia continued to break down barriers, the British seemed to have this knack of cocking up.

I picked up the book again, found my place and ripped out the page with the quotation on it. Instead of burying it in the snow together with the rest of the pages I had read, I placed it in my top pocket. From then on, I would look at those words each day to remind myself that I had started, so I was bloody well going to finish. I accepted that I was well behind schedule, and that I was making a total pig's ear of the attempt to reach the Pole, but I had made the decision right then that I was not going to give up until my food had run out.

I am not sure whether it was the huge dose of painkillers or the distraction of this new-found motivation derived from Mrs Thatcher but, whatever the case, the pain seemed to ease and I started to plan ahead. Let's just get over that first degree, I told myself. I had another nine to cross, of course, but suddenly that moment when eighty degrees south turned to eight-one degrees south became a vital goal for me to attain. After that, I worked out, I would walk an extra half hour, whatever the hardship, until eighty-two degrees. Once past that mark, I would add a further thirty minutes to the day and so on until, by the time I reached the Pole, I would be walking an extra four hours each day. How I envisaged I could do this given the facts of the trip up to that point I will never know, but it is surprising what a mixture of cold, pain and motivation can do for you. If it could be bottled, it would gain incredible results in the sporting arena. I went to sleep safe in the knowledge that the trip was still on.

It was just as well I was in such a positive frame of mind, because I woke up on the morning of day seven to discover my first true white-out in the Antarctic. Surrounding my tent was a very thick, totally white fog, walking through which messes up your balance so much that you experience a sensation of being upside down.

I had taken my three painkillers and was beginning to notice some weight loss. I knew there would be more crevasses out there, somewhere in the swirling cotton wool that lay ahead of me, but my mind had been made up the night before, and a furtive glance at the ripped-out page in my top pocket only served to confirm my conviction. It was desperately frustrating that on a day when I hoped to walk twelve miles I was stuck again, this time in a white-out, but I started walking nonetheless, confused in the fog and a little scared.

As I trudged through the thick soup, I even convinced myself that I deserved everything that was happening to me. I looked back on my other adventures and came to the conclusion that on trips such as Everest I had been incredibly lucky. I had reached the summit when many far more accomplished climbers had perished. I had come through everything in my life with nothing more than a few cracked ribs. This, I reasoned, was pay-back time.

I was therefore upbeat when I pitched my tent that night and discovered that, despite the pain and the white-out, I had managed to cover another seven miles. By now I think I had released the pressure placed upon myself by the desire to reach the Pole. That goal had been changed to just lasting out the sixty days before my food supplies ran out. Looking back, this clearly helped my mental state. Each day I was falling further and further behind schedule, but it somehow stopped bothering me. The point was I was still there, alive and hanging in.

On any trip I believe what really makes you able to survive is the ability to address any problem that suddenly confronts you. After all, you are there on your own, and nobody else can help you. I realised that simply chucking painkillers down my throat would not be enough to enable me to speed up my pace. I therefore made a corset for my back, which I wrapped around my body, by ripping up a sleeping mattress and tying it together using sticky tape. This kept my back straight in one position for the rest of the time, even if it meant that I waddled across the continent like one of the hundreds of thousands of penguins who live on its shores.

For day nine, read day five. Another blizzard made it impossible to trek anywhere, and although I was obviously concerned about how long the severe weather conditions would last, I was also thankful that it would give my back, and the rest of my body, a day of much-needed rest. It also gave me time to think. Although my sights had been reset, I found myself up to my old trick of working out how I could still make it to the Pole. If the load of the sledge was reduced to half its original weight by, say, 85lb, I should in theory be able to pull it twice the distance. I had achieved this on my Magnetic North Pole trip and, at a push, past experience had taught me that I might be able to cover as much as eighteen miles in a day.

Every hour my thoughts would be broken and I would stick my head out of the tent to see if the blizzard was calming down. Then I would return to my nest, either to read more of Mrs Thatcher or to make further plans. The reduction of the sledge's weight was never far from my mind. During the day I decided to get rid of my Sony Walkman and all my tapes. Then I decided to sling out my crampons which, for a climber, was a big move to make. I was now stripping down to the most trivial possessions. Out went a spare pair of shoelaces, the ties on the sleeping bags, and so on until I was convinced I was not carrying a single ounce of excess weight.

Midway through the day the winds eased sufficiently for me to get going. Under normal circumstances I might have remained in the tent, but I wanted to record some distance by the end of the day, and was therefore amazed when, a few hours later, I discovered that I had covered six and a half miles.

That night I made what turned out to be one of my longest radio calls to Patriot. It was incredible how I was stuck in the middle of the loneliest place on Earth, and yet the most mundane messages were being sent or received. Claire, apart from sending her love, wanted to know whether she should pay for three cases of Rothschild wine which had not yet been delivered. Jock was saying that some of the sponsors had not paid up yet for the trip, and asked what he should do about it. And I was developing a raunchy rapport with a girl called Sue, who was a cook back at Patriot Hills.

It began with me asking her to make me an apple and blackberry pie for when I finally returned. Food, understandably, became an obsession as the trek towards the Pole went on. She agreed, but wanted to know what

I was going to give her in exchange. And so the theme of the conversation, relayed backwards and forwards by Geoff, went on, with the whole of British Antarctica listening in, ready for the next instalment as if it was the Gold Blend advert. It was all innocent fun, of course, but even little details like these help to keep up your morale.

The wind blew from the west on day ten, and with the altitude dropping from 2700 feet to 2600 feet, the walking was relatively easy, at least compared to my previous excursions. The back was holding up thanks to the pain-killers and the corset, and my mood was amazingly good. By that evening I calculated that I had only nine and a half miles to go until I crossed over from eighty to eighty-one degrees, and that would signal my first celebration on the trip, and a good excuse for a brandy. which, conveniently, I had refused to discard while lessening the sledge's load. Another seven miles the following day meant that I was just two and a half miles away from a point which was fast becoming as significant as reaching the South Pole itself.

I had no difficulty starting out bang on eight o'clock on the morning of the twelfth day. This time I needed no radio calls from Geoff Somers, or any motivation from Mrs Thatcher. This was the day when I knew I was going to pass through one vital degree. This was going to be the equivalent of my birthday. The weather conditions were kind to me, and the day and the miles seemed to fly past. By six o'clock it was time to stop and face the moment of truth.

By that time I had settled nicely into a routine. I would get the cooker going, and then start taking my clothes off. This would take up to half an hour, by which time the pot would be boiling. I would place my gloves on top of the cooking pan in order to melt off the snow, and then the flask of piping hot soup would be made up. It all boiled down to time management, but on this night it went out the proverbial window. As soon as I had erected the tent I took the GPS out of my pocket and, still fully clothed, peered excitedly at the reading. Not only had I crossed over into eighty-one degrees, but by recording eight miles for the day I had produced my best walk of the trip.

It was time to celebrate. I found the bottle of brandy, packed purposefully at the very bottom of the sledge, and took a swig. The bottle had lines drawn on it, denoting each degree point I would pass on my way to the Pole. It was tempting to down the lot, but I drank the amount up to the next line, and returned the bottle to the depths of the sledge. Then I opened my 'special treat' bag, which consisted of a packet of pork scratchings and an Earl Grey tea bag, and sucked on each scratching as if it were nectar. Boy, did I know how to throw a party!

Looking at the situation in a logical light, I had no cause to celebrate. For a start, eighty-one degrees was merely an imaginary line, but I was treating it as if it were a glass entrance through which I had just come. It was just one degree, and I had another nine to go. I should have been there within five days, not twelve, so in theory I had three emergency days left of supplies, assuming I could maintain a pace of twelve miles a day from that point on, right the way up to the Pole. When one considered that I had just recorded my best mileage, and this was four miles down on what I would now have to produce, it was a tall order. Yet logic, thankfully, did not come into my thinking that night. I had this funny feeling that someone, maybe my late grandfather or late father, was watching over me. It almost became a spiritual moment for me.

There were hundreds of dangers ahead of me: more fields of crevasses, a higher altitude to reach, and plummeting temperatures. I could easily get frostbite and, of course, there was the big question mark over my back.

But this was the moment, huddled up alone in my tent with my brandy and pork scratchings, that I knew, deep down inside, that I would make it to the South Pole.

CLOSE TO THE ABYSS

I woke up on day thirteen looking forward to what I saw as a fresh start. I had crossed over the degree barrier, the pain in my back was bearing up, and I possessed a new-found confidence in my chances of reaching the Pole.

Then I remembered the fact that it was the thirteenth day since I set out from Hercules Inlet. This could have been a negative factor; I am, after all, a fairly superstitious person by nature, made more so by the fact that I have on so many occasions thrown myself at the mercy of the elements and fate. I wear round my neck, for example, a chain of beads with the 'Z' stone in the middle on a piece of red string given to me by a lama from Nepal. He blessed me and the stone before I began my climb to the summit of Everest. They are supposed to give you good luck, and on the basis that I managed to survive the Everest trip, I have worn them ever since.

I initially decided I did not like the sound of 'day thirteen', confirmed when I stuck my head out of the tent and discovered that I faced another total white-out. When this happens the Antarctic is just like a desert. The powdered snow is very dry, so that if you bend down and blow it scatters all over the place. Still, undeterred I set off, trudging through the pea soup, knowing that even though I could not see anything ahead, each step was taking me that much closer to the Pole. At times like this it really is all in the mind. The psychology of polar walking determines, ultimately – together with the luck that we all need – whether a trip is successful or not.

On reaching the end of what I considered to be a real bum day, I discovered that I had managed to walk eight and a half miles which was, by that extra half a mile, my best walking day of the trip to date. Things got even better the following day when I discovered that not only had the white-out changed to a beautiful clear day, I could now see the peaks of the Pirrit Mountains ahead, forty miles away, but seeming so close that I felt I could almost touch them. That day I clocked up a further record of nine and a half miles, even though a strong headwind blew straight into my face.

Looking at my map that evening I continued with a little game I devised using the British Isles. The distance I faced between Hercules Inlet and the South Pole was, more or less, the same as between John O'Groats and Land's End, roughly 680 miles, or 600 nautical miles. By tipping my map upside-down and pretending to walk down the motorway, I reckoned I was well past Aviemore and heading for Glasgow and the Scottish borders. Each day I added on another eight miles, or whatever the distance I had covered, and marked off the small Scottish town I had just passed through. It may sound peculiar, but it was important to add a little familiarity to the trek.

I found other ways to lighten the load. This time I resorted to removing the contents of a plastic container, putting them inside a stuff sack, which is lighter, and then ditching the container. The sledge was by then losing a good three pounds a day as I went through my provisions and devoured each daily munchy bag I had prepared back in Punta Arenas. On the other hand, I was also starting noticeably to lose weight, and although I still felt comfortable, except for the back pain, I knew there would be times ahead when the hunger would become unbearable.

It may have taken me twelve days to reach eighty-one degrees, but I managed to halve this time to cross over into eighty-two degrees, breaking three daily distance records in the process. By day eighteen, the day I crossed over the degree barrier and treated myself to another swig of brandy and a bag of pork scratchings, I was up to ten miles. This was all very encouraging. I may still have been behind the daily mileage rate I had set myself on day one, but I was slowly moving up the scale, and gaining altitude at the same time. I had become acclimatised to the conditions, I had grown used to both my equipment and routine, and the sledge was getting lighter. I reckoned that by the half-way stage I would be up to, and maybe even beyond, twelve miles' walking a day, especially as I would continue to add on an extra half an hour each time I crossed over into a new degree.

The other important factor is that at the start of eighty-one degrees I had made a conscious decision to become much more disciplined. Perhaps I was a little hard on myself, but I attributed some of the blame for taking twelve days to reach my first degree to the fact that I had not been fearless enough, and that I had been slack. I would take longer than I should during tea breaks, or decide on the spur of the moment to stop and have an unscheduled tea break, on the basis that it did not really matter. Then I would sit down on the sledge, look around at the beautiful contrast of colours, and spend half an hour deciding that it was not a bad old life.

As soon as I started to look towards eighty-two degrees I became far more disciplined. For example, instead of lying in bed for a few minutes after my trusty old Casio watch alarm went off at 6.30 a.m. (I also had a £3000 Breitling watch, but it did not have an alarm – there was no way I was going to chuck that in the snow to lessen the load!), coming round and thinking about the day ahead, I would jump straight up into a kneeling position. It was a small point, but an important one. As soon as I was kneeling on my bed, the day and the routine had begun. The whole course of action then became a matter of time and motion. By 6.50 my breakfast and hot drink would be ready, and by 7.00 I would be packing away my final things. I would remove my inner tent and then make a square hole with my spade where I had been sleeping and make sure I had a crap, before adding my ten pages of Margaret Thatcher and anything else I could offload from the sledge. I would then place the snow back in the hole and whack it into a smooth and firm cover with my spade. If anyone ever discovers these holes, they may get the wrong impression of what I thought about Baroness Thatcher's book.

I was ready to start packing my sledge by 7.30 at the very latest. This was the best part, especially if I had completed everything inside the tent by, say, 7.28. If this was the case, I would reward myself with a two-minute lie down on the thermarest. That two minutes would be the only two minutes of rest, save for a couple of tea breaks, until I pitched up my tent that night. I spent those two minutes wondering just what the day ahead would bring, whether it would be a good or bad day, or even if I would be able to see it out. Then I would smother some sun cream over the few parts of my exposed face, in particular my nose, and get going.

I had specific places on the sledge for various items. If it was packed poorly there was always the danger of it tipping over, so I always had to create the right balance of weight, both in length and width. I would always place the day's munchy bag at the front end of the sledge, where it would be easier to get to, as well as my compass, the map and my two flasks of hot drink. It was vital to feel comfortable before you finally got going because, unlike in England where you can quite easily shift your trousers or shirt, you cannot dress yourself again without having to pitch up the tent and take everything off, a process which would dramatically delay your day's walking. If my balaclava was just a fraction out of place, rubbing my neck as I walked, then I would put up with it for the whole day.

I also decided to conduct a small ceremony at each degree. After eighty-one degrees I held up my thumb, and by eighty-two degrees I was able to add my forefinger to the collection. I had ten degrees in total between Hercules Inlet and the Pole, and would therefore 'remove' each digit on my hands along the way. It was symbolic more than anything else, but it helped in the psychological battle. It meant that as each degree was passed I would not only eat pork scratchings and enjoy a swig of brandy, I would also go through my fingers ceremony.

By now the first small signs of frostbite were beginning to reveal themselves. It began at the end of my nose. Ridiculous as it sounds, the first thing to be affected was my vanity. I reckon I've got a big enough nose as it is, but the effects of frostbite turned it into a horrible, big and bulbous sight.

By the start of eighty-two degrees I was also counting my fingers and checking out my feet. The problem about frostbite is that you just cannot tell if it's coming on. You just suddenly discover you have it, so it is vitally important to keep checking that you have feeling in your fingers and toes. Each morning, one of the first things I did once I had left my tent was to wrap each individual finger around my ski pole, counting them and gripping tightly. Each hour during the day I would then devote to one finger, and by the time I reached my second thumb on the other hand I would reward myself with a slice of salami. I would also punch my feet hard on the ice, creating extra circulation and warmth.

The bigger potential problem was in the area surrounding my inner thighs. I discovered a series of red patches with a tinge of blue on their outer rim. They grew increasingly sore and began to sting. I first put it down to chafing. Other adventurers say that when this happens they wash and clean out all the sweat, but I believe it is better to build up an oily base in such circumstances.

I spoke to Geoff Somers about it on the eighteenth night over the radio. What transpired was that because I was wearing just one pair of thermals and wind pants, my legs were getting too cold. It is a fine balance to reach, because you must not let your legs get too sweaty, but I was beginning to get frostbite and needed to take immediate action. By wearing a second pair of thermals the problem cleared up, but it took a further twenty days to disappear completely. I reckon I was a day or two away from full-blown frostbite, which would have been very serious.

By day twenty I had broken my walking record again, this time notching up ten and a half miles. I was slowly edging closer and closer to that mark of twelve miles a day and, better still, a huge field of crevasses I expected to confront never materialised. Each year they can get filled in either by blowing snow or just movement, but the downside is, of course, that this same movement can create new uncharted crevasses.

My mood swung the following day, 28 November, not because I had a particularly bad walking day, but because I got to thinking about what I could have achieved if I had bothered to pack a para-wing. This was the first time in the whole three weeks that I had experienced winds from the east. When the wind is in the right direction you can use the kite to take some of the pressure off the sledge and your body. Even Scott used a sail, just like a yacht, to help him reach the Pole.

I had thought long and hard about taking one with me. There is no doubt about it, if you get a good day you can travel thirty, maybe even fifty, miles by taking advantage of the winds. But the downside is the fact that you lack control over them, and they add extra weight to your sledge. Previous deployments of the kite, such as during the attempted crossing of the continent by Sir Ranulph Fiennes and Dr Michael Stroud in 1993, resulted in accidents. Stroud went into a crevasse and was lucky to live, while Fiennes was pulled over and injured himself. Reinhold Messner also tore a muscle when he tried with Arved Fuchs. The common denominator here was that none of these trips was solo, so that when one hurt himself, the other was on hand to help out.

Before I left for Antarctica, I had a bit of a play with a para-wing on the beach at Punta Arenas and discovered, as soon as I hit wind, that I had next to no control. With nobody else to help me on my way to the Pole, all it would take was for me to twist something as I was dragged along through sastrugi, or down a crevasse, and that would be the end of the trip. I therefore decided to leave the para-wing behind, and at the time I considered it to be the right decision.

But on the twenty-first day the wind suddenly came from the east at a speed of around 20mph, and I faced what appeared to be relatively flat land ahead of me. I got to thinking about what might have been. It was just possible that I could have covered fifty, sixty, maybe even eighty miles that day simply by clipping myself in, sitting back and enjoying the ride. My mood deteriorated the more I thought about what might have been. I could have enjoyed two brandy and pork scratchings days in just one.

The following day was yet another white-out, which

was the last thing I needed with my new-found depression. The wind moaned like a distraught ghost all around me. All day, apart from frantically checking my compass to make sure I was staying on course, I still thought about the fact that the ice I was trudging on could have been skimmed across if only I had packed my para-wing. I forgot about the burden of the extra four pounds of weight and the dangers of injuring myself.

Day twenty-four should have been one to celebrate: it was the day I passed across eighty-three degrees, which meant my usual treat in the tent that night, and the finger ceremony. But the date was 1 December, and I could not help but think about my family. Up until then, apart from my first-day feeling of guilt, I had managed successfully to shut out such negative emotions, but on this day, the first day my daughters would open up their advent calendars, it really got to me. Suddenly I was back home in Lacock. The children know that they are not supposed to open up the door on the calendar until after breakfast, but they are usually up very early through sheer excitement. In our family, at least, 1 December denotes the official beginning of the run-down to Christmas. We always get an advent calendar with chocolates behind the doors, and I started to envisage the two elder girls eagerly discovering their goodies. I wondered what the picture was behind their doors that day, and what colour wrapping the chocolates were covered in.

I then got to thinking about Christmas in general. We have a sort of ritual where we all traipse down to a local farm and spend ages selecting the right Christmas tree to bring home. Then I chop it down and bring it back home. I started to worry about whether Claire would be able to do this, and how she was going to put up the tree herself.

I also found the constantly changing terrain a little daunting. On the twenty-fifth day I was, according to the map, supposed to come to what looked like a big icy hill, some five miles across. I kept looking at it as I neared it on the map, but like the so-called crevasse field a couple of days before, the hill never materialised. This continent truly is amazing. In the space of just a couple of years a whole hill can disappear as the land re-forms.

I cheered up considerably that evening when my GPS reported that I had covered eleven miles, which was a new record on the trip. I had also climbed a further 600 feet, which meant that I was close to 4000 feet above sea level. By the end of the next day I had made it to 4244 feet in altitude, but there were two more important factors which gave me a much-needed lift.

By reaching this stage I was able to change from my large-scale map to a much smaller and more detailed one. That seemed like a significant moment to me, even if I had not yet reached half-way. The other point was that, during the day's walk, I caught my first sight of the Thiel Mountains, which not only meant that my navigation was spot on, but also gave me the kind of thrill that any mountaineer would experience. From a distance they look like the Swiss Alps, spread out over 120 miles, and reaching up to 10,000 feet in height. As I still see myself as first and foremost a mountaineer, such a sight is like a magnet to me. Most of the Thiels have never been climbed before: some of them have not even been seen by mankind. I would be walking past them, about thirty miles to the east, but I could not help constantly glancing over towards them and at the orange glow the low sun in the sky provided over the peaks, making a sunset that lasted all day and night.

I was still taking the Thatcher quotation out of my top pocket each day to inject myself with motivation, and as I passed by the Thiel Mountains I checked on my map of Britain and realised that I was now crossing the Scottish border and making my way into Cumbria. The days seemed to alternate between good and bad, either mentally or practically. Day twenty-seven, for example, saw me walk eleven and a half miles, despite facing a howling blizzard for most of the day. But the next day I hit a problem. While making contact on my HF radio, Geoff Somers told me they had not received my Argos position. It had been agreed that if my Argos malfunctioned I would have to contact base each night. If, for whatever reason, I failed to do so, this would spark off an immediate rescue operation which would end the trip. By default the whole expedition would be screwed up.

I played around with the aerial and twiddled the on–off button, but the next night base still did not have a position for me. This concern became all-consuming for me. On 7 December I crossed over into eighty-four degrees and finally managed to reach the magical twelve miles in a day mark. I was down to just one finger on my left hand, was well down the motorway back in Britain, and drank another notch of brandy, but I had this vision of being hauled off the ice protesting because my Argos had failed me.

A change of battery did the trick. Luckily I had brought a spare one with me, but the whole communication format had to be changed through fear of my remaining battery running out of gas. There had been days when I had needed to leave the Argos on for up to six hours in order for camp to get my position. As a result, I made base work out exactly the best times to turn the thing on so that I wouldn't need to run my battery for more than around half an hour each day.

By now I was down, if that is the right word, to three painkillers a day to counteract my back. My arse was a bit sore and I resorted to rolling up pieces of toilet paper and putting them between my thermals and my buttocks.

But the bigger problem was my nose, which was virtually shot away. I started to stick some taping over it to give it a bit of protection but, in hindsight, that only made matters worse because the plaster would grow cold and wet, and this only exacerbated the problem. It was not just big, it was throbbing constantly. White blisters appeared on the end of it which have left scars ever since, and I have lost the feeling at the end of my nose.

I am not a great fan of frostbite, it has to be said. There are some polar explorers who take the attitude that you are not a real man unless you have experienced frostbite, rather like a rugby prop forward with cauliflower ears. But the effects of my nose have remained with me to this day. Apart from the scars, my nose goes very red at the first hint of cold weather, and much of the feeling I once possessed in it has never returned. The lining inside was also damaged, for which I shall have an operation once I can find some time.

On the plus side, I was doing better than Roger Mear. He was still recording three miles a day, and even when he used his para-wing to make twenty-five miles in a day, it left him a long way behind me. This provided great motivation for me, and also enhanced a feeling of dogged belligerence. The last thing I wanted him to do was to rub my frostbitten nose into the ice by getting to the Pole before me.

The thirtieth day was the biggest landmark of the trip to date. Not only did it represent the exact half-way stage of my allotted sixty days, plus ten emergency extra days, but it was also the day when I passed across eighty-five degrees, exactly half-way to the South Pole. This was another brandy day, of course, but I was also able to change over to my right hand with my fingers ceremony.

At this point I came to a large area of disturbed ice. I had never come across such a sight before in my life. What stood before me was, basically, a huge area of blue ice with lots and lots of blocks of solid blue ice balancing on top. It was like a scene straight out of a science fiction film, as if a UFO had landed and melted everything around it. This was pure ice, which meant having to walk twelve miles on an ice rink. I slipped over twice during the day, each time fearing that my dodgy back would give way. The funny thing was that each time I slipped I looked around embarrassedly, rather like the person in the street does when he lands on his backside on a crowded pavement. I must have looked a complete prat sliding over, but I had to remind myself that nobody, or nothing for that matter, was watching.

During the course of the next degrees I began clearly to notice a change in my body. The obvious one was in the way I looked: I had grown a fairly bushy beard, and what particularly bothered me was that the end of it was as white as the snow and ice that surrounded me. There I was, in the middle of nowhere, worrying about what I saw as confirmation that I was growing old. The sledge by now was 120lb lighter then when I first set off from Hercules Inlet, but I was climbing higher and higher, which meant that it was starting to get really cold. I also began to notice how, the more weight I lost, the less strength I seemed to possess. After the trip was over I worked out that I had lost over half a pound a day, having started out at a healthy fifteen stone. It was already beginning to tell.

The disgusting food I consumed every day was becoming more and more enjoyable as my need for energy grew. Of the three main evening meals of the day – chicken and mushroom mix, pasta, and chilli con carne, which was really dried powder mixed with boiling water – the pasta was my favourite, and I began to think earlier and earlier during the day of the main meal. It was only on day thirty-eight that my thoughts changed to looking forward to an evening of pork scratchings and brandy, and a time to celebrate passing through into eighty-six degrees. That night I eagerly made up the tent, got the cooker out, removed the scratchings and the brandy from the sledge, and switched on my GPS. To my horror it read half a minute off the eighty-six degrees; I was behind the mark by half a mile. At this point I faced a moral dilemma. I had everything out ready to celebrate the passing of another crucial degree. Should I now cheat, on the basis that I would reach the mark within thirty minutes of walking the following morning? I was sorely tempted, but in my new, disciplined manner I simply put everything back and decided to carry out the routine properly the next day.

By now any independent observer might have concluded that the first signs of madness were beginning to become evident. I had decided, for example, to name my skis. My right ski was christened Gandalf, and my left ski became Merlin. I quite liked the idea of naming them after the only two fictional wizards I could think of, mainly because I felt that the skis were looking after me. I had also begun to start calling my sledge 'Boy'. My days would not even start until I had shouted out, 'Come on Boy, another good day today!' I was treating my sledge like a faithful dog. When the sledge slid into the back of my legs, I would shout, 'Slow down there, Boy.' Then I would go a bit further and add, 'That's right, Boy, this is the way to go.' All this may sound completely mad, but I actually believe it helped to maintain my sanity, and my discipline. Without someone, or something, to talk to, I may well have gone nuts.

The biggest problem was when the sastrugi would cause Boy to flip over. On day thirty-nine this must have happened at least ten times. Looking back the following admission might sound disturbing, but at the end of that day I grabbed hold of my ski stick and proceeded to hit the sledge over and over again in a frenzied attack, until collapsing in a crying heap, my cheeks wet with tears. It may sound quite funny now – and it must have resembled that well-known *Fawlty Towers* episode 'Gourmet Night' when John Cleese hits his car with a branch from a tree as a punishment for letting him down – but at the time it was clear that all the frustration that had been pent up inside suddenly reared its head. I was not actually doing too badly, but I think it was the pressure of standing on the precipice of time that caused this sudden outburst. I knew I could not afford to lose a minute more if I was to be successful in reaching the Pole. It all just seemed to pour out, all thirty-nine days of my emotions, and I remember afterwards, as I wiped away the tears, feeling a great deal more relaxed as a result.

I suppose such a breakdown underlines the fragile mental state you find yourself in in such conditions. I was still on course for the Pole, just, but it had been a hard day and it was pretty obvious that, at least inwardly, I was in turmoil. This state of mental frenzy has only ever happened to me once before, when I was trying to walk to the North Pole, but although I gave my sledge a bit of a beating then as well, it was nothing compared to what took place that day in Antarctica. Funnily enough, once I had calmed down and recovered, my only thought was not that I had just acted in an extremely worrying fashion, but that I was a stupid bugger because I could have snapped my ski stick.

It seemed to do the trick for me because the next day I completed thirteen miles, again a new best for me during the trek. I immediately put it down to my new, relaxed state of mind. Whatever anyone might think of my actions the previous day, the demons I possessed inside me had to get out of my system. Looking at the map of the British Isles that night, I reckoned I had long gone past Manchester and was heading into the Potteries. Suddenly Birmingham did not seem too far off.

The forty-first day turned out to be yet another whiteout, but by now I had even grown used to this. The problem came on day forty-two. During this day, and indeed the next day, I had to give a passing impersonation of Indiana Jones, because from morning to night I faced a non-stop series of crevasses; like Harrison Ford, I had to get round these obstacles to get through to the next stage. Coupled with this I encountered the highest sastrugi of the trip, with some reaching as high as fifteen feet. In theory the sastrugi should have been smaller as I climbed higher and nearer my intended destination because less wind was coming off the Pole, but this was not the case. So much for the reference books, I cursed, as I hauled the sledge over each lip of ice.

The following day was just as bad. I started to punch the ice with my ski stick in front of me to try to identify a crevasse before it identified me. During the twelve miles I managed to complete that day there must have been a crevasse every fifty feet or so. They were all big bastards, and I just tried to ski over them as quickly as I could. On a couple of occasions, while actually in the process of crossing over a crevasse, my ski stick went through the ice to reveal a large, yawning black hole below. While the pressure of the stick being thrust into the icy bridge crossing the crevasse caused the area to give way, the ice around the hole stayed solid, enabling me to cross. The point is by the time it has dawned on you that your stick has gone straight through the ice, you are just about over to the other side of the bridge.

By night time I was more thankful to have completed the day without any mishaps. This had been one of the most dangerous days of the whole trip, and I had survived unscathed. As I put up my tent for the night and prepared my meal I was pretty chuffed, because I knew the next day I would be passing through eighty-seven degrees, and I was beginning to imagine what it would be like to reach the Pole.

At about nine o'clock that night I went through my final ritual action. I took a pee in a plastic bottle and tipped the contents out on a specially designated area of ice. If the ground is solid ice the liquid usually spreads around a bit, but if it is snow you normally hear the fizzling sound of the urine disappearing into the melting powder. This time, however, I heard absolutely nothing.

It was almost as an afterthought that the lack of sound struck me. I was safely tucked up in my sleeping bag, nice and warm and ready for a much-needed sleep after what had been an exhausting day. But I felt I had better check to see what had happened to my pee. As I reached over and looked where I had tipped the bottle upside down beside me, all I could see was a deep blue hole. It took a couple of seconds for the scene completely to register in my mind. I had pitched my tent on a snow bridge over an ice-walled abyss, and the full weight of myself and the tent was balancing precariously on a thin layer of snow.

Naturally I gave my predicament some thought. If I got up and tried to move the tent I might well go through the ice and plunge to my death. I then reckoned that the very fact that I had not fallen down the crevasse as I pitched up for the night was a good sign. But in reality I was very tired, pretty cold, voraciously hungry and frightened. When you are in such a state, your mind does not function normally. Whatever the reason, I figured that if my time was up, then it was up, and there was nothing I could do about it.

There was something else as well, something which is hard to explain to someone reading this away from the harsh realities of Antarctica. No matter how much research and preparation I had put into this trip, when you are faced with such conditions, both physically and mentally the practicalities of polar exploration dissipate. For, as I lay down for the night, I genuinely felt that someone was really watching over me. I am not a religious man, so I knew it was not God, but I reckoned it might well have been my hero, Ernest Shackleton. The point about Shackleton was that he always returned from his adventures. It is very difficult to explain in the cold light of day, but I just sensed him inside the tent that night. If he was acting as a guardian angel, then he was the right one. Despite the obvious danger I was in, I felt completely at peace with myself. The snowy bridge could have given way at any time during that night. Whether I would wake up the next morning would be completely in the lap of fate. But with Shackleton watching over me, I fell asleep within a few seconds. Below me, a deep blue hole was waiting.

'CAN ANYONE HEAR ME?'

It took a few seconds for me to remind myself where I was when I woke up the following morning. My next reaction was relief that I had woken up at all. Then I had the precarious job of assembling all my gear and getting off the ridge without it all caving in. The whole morning routine went to pieces on this occasion because, rather like the final scene in *The Italian Job* when the coach is hanging over the edge of a precipice, everything depended on keeping the right balance inside my tent. I did not even bother standing up, but crawled around on all fours, or rolled over from side to side. As soon as I was out of the tent I immediately snapped my skis into place and slowly hauled my sledge across the remainder of the ridge and to relative safety on the other side of the crevasse.

At this point I sat back for a few moments and let out a huge sigh of relief. You go through so many lives when you are a polar explorer. I had notched up quite a few from my previous polar trips in the north but this, I reckoned, must have accounted for at least two extra lives.

The fact that I faced yet another miserable white-out soon snapped me out of this retrospective mood. These were becoming more and more frequent, by that time perhaps as many as one every five days. White-outs only serve to remind you of your solitude and your vulnerability, but by now I was feeling mentally and physically strong. The back, although still painful, was holding up, and I felt buoyant about the prospect of reaching the Pole. Onwards I trudged as the pea soup wrapped itself around me.

That night my GPS reported the good news that I had crossed over eighty-seven degrees. This, of course, sparked off the usual ritual of brandy, pork scratchings and my fingers act. Just three more fingers to go, and 180 miles. On my British map this meant that I was down to Worcester now. I decided to change my route at this point. Instead of walking down to Land's End, I decided to go from Cardiff to London along the M4 motorway. This was because I live close to the M4 just outside Chippenham, and knew virtually every single mile to London. Now it would be a case of not just passing towns, but service stations and signposts.

I was up to 8000 feet in altitude now, and it was getting bloody cold. My thermometer read – 37°C, although the windchill factor more than doubled this temperature. This would mean frostbite within a matter of seconds if bare flesh were exposed. It also made attempts to have a pee quite comical. Trying to find your zip through your Parka coat with two pairs of gloves on, and then wading through two sets of thermal underwear, and then finally your pants, did lead to the odd accident. Of course you then had to try to be as quick as possible because that is one place on which you definitely do not want frostbite.

The following day I received news that Roger Mear had pulled out of his walk across the continent, having decided he was quite clearly not going to achieve his goal. By doing so he left me in the clear to become, if successful, the first Briton to reach the South Pole unsupported and solo. I gathered he had given up a couple of days before at roughly 84°20', a good 180 miles behind me.

After everything I have written about him, you might assume I would welcome this news, but the truth was I felt terribly sad for him. I genuinely muttered to myself, 'You poor bastard.' I recalled my failed attempt to reach the North Pole back in 1983. I made the same mistake Mear made this time round by going out and securing pre-publicity. When I returned to England I was hammered by the media; I knew Mear would also have to return to England, with his tail between his legs, and face the music. What the public does not understand is that there are only a handful of people who can muster the sponsorship and technical support necessary even to start walking to the South Pole. More people have walked on the moon than walked to the South Pole from the edge of Antarctica. So I knew what Mear would be going through. We did not always see eye to eye, but he was an experienced polar explorer, and with his removal from the equation it left just me, inexperienced in comparison, flying the flag for Britain.

The forty-seventh day happened to be a particularly bad day for me. It was 24 December, and my thoughts immediately turned to home. Like most families in Britain, Christmas Eve is a day of routine for us. My children get to see their cousins for the only time of the year, which results in excitable mayhem, and then in the evening we all prepare a tray for Father Christmas with a mince pie, a glass of sherry, and a carrot for Rudolph. Once the kids have gone to bed we fill up their socks and stockings and hang them on their beds, and then I down the glass of sherry, eat the mince pie, and place teeth marks in the carrot. That has always been my job. I remember trudging through the snow and ice that day singing 'Jingle Bells' over and over again, and worrying whether Claire would remember to take a bite out of the carrot. I was actually trying to work out how I could get a message to Claire to remind her about the carrot routine, at eighty-seven degrees in the Antarctic!

The next day, of course, was no better. I had contemplated having a complete day off on Christmas Day. My calculations told me I could afford to do this and still reach the South Pole on the sixtieth day. I was now averaging over thirteen miles a day, and with an extra half hour's walking after each degree I knew, barring an accident, that I would make it. But I was still some distance away from my goal, and I could not start to get complacent. So Christmas Day turned out to be the same as every other day – a long, hard, cold trek.

It was impossible not to think of the family that day. I imagined the kids opening up their presents, and Claire, smiling bravely through it all. I knew that they would talk about me, and I knew that they would be worried, especially Claire, who was being put through all this anguish again. We were going to celebrate Christmas again when I returned, and that was when I was going to give her a present. It meant that for the first time in fifteen years she had no present from me to open on Christmas Day. As I hauled the sledge over a succession of sastrugi, I kept asking myself how I could be so damn selfish. It was all very well messing up my own life, but it was completely out of order to mess up my family's as well. All in all, it made me feel pretty lousy about myself, and in this type of mood I decided to quit for the day half an hour earlier than planned.

I had been wondering for a couple of days how I was going to celebrate Christmas, alone with just the wind and ice. At least, I mused while unpacking the sledge, I had a white Christmas! I decided to make it a brandy day, even though I had not yet crossed over into eighty-eight degrees. I had also been saving a packet of dehydrated fruit cocktail which I devoured that night. It was hardly turkey and plum pudding, but it had to do.

Then I turned my attention to the one present I had to

open. As the twenty-fifth drew nearer I began to wonder more and more what Natalie's present could be. That night I finally opened it up to discover a small branch from a Christmas tree. It had lost most of its needles by now, and looked more like a bare twig, but it was wrapped up in a page from a magazine highlighting a nude girl advertising perfume. I am not sure now which was supposed to be the Christmas present, the tree or the girl, but either way I laughed. Back at base Geoff sang 'We Wish You a Merry Christmas' to me over the radio.

Two days and a further twenty-five miles later, I heard the news that I would be joined by five Russian women. They had left it very late to try to walk the whole way to the Pole, after not having enough money to pay Annie Kershaw at Adventure Network. In the end they decided to be dropped off at eighty-eight degrees and walk just the final 120 miles. Geoff asked me to provide weather conditions for the women from where I was in order to give them the green light to be dropped in.

I was furious. The last thing I needed was five women up my arse so close to the Pole. I suppose I was paranoid, after all the effort I had put in, because I feared that if I made contact with them I would be accused of being supported on my walk. I didn't want anything to do with them, but I was assured that nothing would be dropped in for me and nobody would suggest anything other than that I had completed the walk solo and unsupported. Reluctantly, on 29 December, I radioed in a good weather report, and that night their plane landed within a hundred yards of my tent.

I hope you can forgive me for thinking, momentarily, of the prospect of being joined by five women, alone in the middle of nowhere. I observed them as they emerged from the plane. I had been away from home for a long time now, but the sight of five middle-aged Russian women with metal teeth failed to arouse me. To be fair, I had a white bushy beard, a terrible nose, and I had not washed for over seven weeks. There is no question about it, I stunk to high heaven. The lack of sexual appreciation must have been mutual.

I went up to the pilot and co-pilot, produced my diary and asked them to confirm, in writing, that I had not received any fuel, gas, food, or anything else. The ladies offered me a banana. My God, I wanted that banana. I could have killed for it. Food had become the number one fantasy for me as the trip and my discomfort had developed. But I refused on two counts: accepting it would immediately mean that I had been supported and, even if I had been allowed to eat it, past experience from my North Pole trip told me that after fifty-one days of eating dehydrated food, a banana would pass through me like a dose of salts. I was afraid to appear too rude, but I think they understood my reasons. Even so, I spent half the night wondering if they were talking about how off-hand the Englishman was. The plane flew off, and the ladies ski'd away and pitched up their tents a quarter of a mile away. I was pleased to see them go. After all this time in solitude, I had come to treat the Antarctic as my domain, and it felt as though these women were trespassing.

The next morning I set off and never met them again. I saw their tents, of course, but I did not want to say goodbye. There was still much work to be done. They stayed there three days to acclimatise, and then made a mile and a half on their first day. I was still going well and was looking forward to crossing over the outer rim on the map, where the longitude lines end and the final push for the Pole begins. But my mood changed the following day, the fifty-fourth of my walk, when I heard some morale-damaging news, and then injured myself again.

Geoff told me over the radio that Borge Ousland had

just pulled out of his attempt to cross the continent. The Norwegian had made it to the Pole, but after a further two days' walking the other side he suddenly pushed the emergency button. This was a huge shock to me, mainly because apart from the fact that Borge was a good friend of mine, he was also my hero. I used to ask Borge in my mind what he would do when faced with any problem on the ice. I saw him as 'Mr Invincible', so to hear the news that even he could not meet what was undoubtedly a stiffer challenge than the one I had set myself, was not good on the morale front.

Neither, for that matter, was another close shave at a crevasse that set off my back again. As usual I was skiing along, poking ridges with my ski stick to test their strength. My stick went clean through a thin crust of snow into a black emptiness. I immediately lost my balance and, for a split second, thought I was about to plunge down the gaping hole. Luckily I regained my balance, but in jerking myself straight I managed not only to damage my back again, but also to pull a couple of muscles in my leg.

I was in a lot of pain, and immediately upped my dosage of painkillers. If this had happened a couple of weeks before I may well have pushed the panic button myself, but I reckoned I was less than a week away from the Pole and counted myself lucky that I should hurt my back again with such a short time to go. Even so, sixty-odd miles now seemed a long way. People have attempted to climb Everest and failed to reach the summit by one hundred feet. I've actually walked past a frozen body on the south summit, just a half hour's climb from the actual summit. Look at Robert Scott. Having reached the Pole he failed to make his food depot, one of a series he had laid down on his outward journey for his return, by just eleven miles. It made me realise it was not over yet, not by a long way. I decided to halve my food rations in case my injuries slowed me down.

As if all this was not enough, the date happened to be New Year's Eve. Back at home the whole family gets together and always goes off to a hotel to see the new year in over dinner. I checked my watch at six p.m., exactly midnight back in England, and thought of everyone linking arms and singing 'Auld Lang Syne'. As I continued walking I made a resolution to myself: after the summer I would see much more of my children.

On New Year's Day I crossed over into eighty-nine degrees. The lines of longitude were so squeezed together as I homed in on the Pole that my GPS could not actually register them any more. It was an incredible feeling to get down to my last finger, and to know that I was on the final part of the walk. A combination of the excitement and fear caused by my injuries meant that on this day, day fifty-five, despite the extra pain in my back and leg, I managed to walk fourteen miles. It was also the first day on the whole trip that I started to get emotional about actually reaching the Pole. For the first time since I set out from Hercules Inlet eight weeks before, I could feel the Pole almost in my grasp.

The following day was bitterly cold; in fact the whole of that last leg was so desperately cold that I kept my Parka on throughout. That night I worked out I had just twenty-two miles to go to the Pole, and on my British map I was virtually at Maidenhead in Berkshire on my way down the M4 to London. As I cooked my dinner I heard the sound of an aeroplane. At first I couldn't figure it out. Then I recognised a familiar sound. My house in Lacock is close to RAF Lyneham, where Hercules planes are often heard flying in and out. This was the sound of a Hercules, and I suddenly realised it was landing at the American research base at the Pole. It gave me a tremendous lift, and although I kept reminding myself that I still had twenty-two miles to go, I felt like an excited child.

Day fifty-eight was a beautiful day to walk in the Antarctic. It was cold but fresh, and the blue sky and no wind made it almost a pleasure. In the middle of the afternoon, about fifteen miles from the Pole, I could just make out the tips of two antennae. I had stopped for a quick tea break when I saw these two black dots. It was obvious what it was: I had caught the first sight of the research station at the Pole. I no longer needed any maps or compass readings, although I took a final bearing on the Pole in case of a final white-out. All I had to do was walk directly towards the dots.

It was here that my thoughts turned again to Robert Scott. I knew that I would eventually reach a research station, but back in 1912 Scott did not know whether he would find mountains, canyons or crevasses at the Pole. He possessed no photographs, no maps, and no idea what would await him. Can you imagine what thoughts went through his mind when he, like me on this day, first caught sight of something in the distance? Maybe at first he might have thought the black dot ahead of him was an outcrop; then, at some point, he must have started to think about the possibility of the black dot being a tent. Scott must have tried to put such a thought to the back of his mind, but the nearer he walked to the Pole the clearer the sight ahead of him would have become. He must have been totally shot away when it finally dawned on him that what he could see was Roald Amundsen's tent, confirming that the Norwegian had won the race to the Pole. I know there are lots of views arguing that because his men had scurvy and gangrene they would not have survived in any case, but it is my belief, having walked to the Pole myself and having suffered many of the same emotions, that he resigned himself to his and his men's fate the moment he saw Amundsen's tent. The man's nature was to succeed. If he had become the first man to reach the Pole, his tail would have been so up that he would have covered with ease that last eleven miles to safety at the food depot he had erected en route.

It was a subject I dwelt on a lot as I walked. The elements have remained the same, of course, but at least the modern-day adventurer has maps, photographs and an education in the psychological effects of such a walk, plus knowledge of the correct diet and nutrition. I also knew exactly how to navigate, and my Argos would assure that I could be hauled to safety within a few hours of signalling. Scott's men, in contrast, were on a journey to the complete unknown, with open wounds and life-threatening illnesses. What brave, brave men they were.

For much of the next day the tips of the antennae seemed to get no nearer. The air was crystal clear. With nothing to indicate scale the judgement of distance is almost impossible. But then, with under ten miles to go, I could make out the silver dome of the research station at the Pole. Then I started to see some colours, the red of the buildings, and steam pouring out of a roof. I came to a ski-way where the planes land, and as I crossed over it I started to worry about being knocked over by a plane. It would be extraordinarily unfortunate, but I was so near to achieving my goal that any unlikely event concerned me.

It was when I caught sight of the flags fluttering in the breeze, and in particular the Union Jack, that my emotions finally broke free. Kneeling down on the ice, about half a mile from the Pole, I broke down and cried. The tears caused my goggles first to steam up, and then to freeze over. I had to spend ages clearing the ice off my lenses. Throughout the final half-mile walk to the Pole I continued to cry, constantly wiping my goggles to prevent the same process from reoccurring.

I had been warned to expect a frosty reception from the Americans on my arrival. They viewed people like me as tourists who got in the way of their research. Sure enough, as I walked into the area surrounding the research station I observed how they all seemed to have their backs to me, talking among themselves. It seemed bloody rude of them not even to acknowledge my arrival after what I had been through. Still, I had not done it for them, but for myself, and on approaching the pole and the orb that denotes the exact geographical position of the South Pole, I thought about kissing the pole. In the end, through fear of my lips freezing against it, I hugged it tightly, still crying with a mixture of relief that the trip was over, and ecstasy that I had overcome everything to become the first Briton in the record books to reach the Pole solo and unsupported. It was my greatest achievement.

It was fifty-nine days since I began my walk, back on 8 November. The date now was 5 January, because by reaching the Pole I had crossed over the international time zone and entered New Zealand time, an extra day ahead. It meant that the time had become seven in the morning, and I had technically missed out a whole night's sleep. I looked back over the first ten days of my trip, when I would have laughed at the ridiculous thought of actually reaching the Pole.

After a few minutes the Americans turned round and came over to me, clapping and cheering and shaking my hand. They explained that as my goal was to get to the Pole, they did not want to come and spoil what was a very personal moment for me. They reckoned, quite rightly, that I wanted my own space for a while. A British scientist called Bill made a big point of shaking my hand before skating off and then reappearing with a cup of hot tea. Then the head of the research station congratulated me and welcomed me to the South Pole. Having initially decided that these guys were unappreciative bastards, I completely changed my opinion of them when I realised how they had all come out, in incredibly cold conditions, to see me home.

I took a few photos and then started to wonder where Feodore was. I had been invited in by the scientists for breakfast but, although I politely informed them I could eat the arse off a dead rhinoceros, I wanted to wait for my friend and colleague and see him home first. I had been told over the radio for days that he had been burning up the miles and was drawing nearer and nearer to me, but even I was surprised when he suddenly appeared at the Pole just three hours after me. I had set out half a day ahead of him back at Hercules Inlet, and we had more or less stuck to the same pace throughout the walk, although if his equipment had been as modern as mine he would probably have shot by me. By reaching the Pole Feodore became the first Russian to walk, unsupported and solo, to the bottom of the world.

I gave him some space before skiing over to hug him. We both cried and took more photos before the Americans finally persuaded us to have breakfast. Inside the aluminium dome of the research centre were warm portakabins where the food was served. I had lost 36lb in weight since beginning my walk, and I could have killed for a decent meal. But as soon as I began to drink some orange juice my whole body fell apart. My nose was really painful, and my back was in agony, but my first priority continued to be food. While they served Feodore and me with a huge fry-up I kept apologising to the Americans about how I smelled. They told me to forget about it, but they also suggested that we should both have a shower and, if we wanted, a sauna.

We were amazed. After fifty-nine days trekking in the frozen wastes, there we were being offered a sauna at the South Pole. Bill went and got me some clean clothes and then Feodore and I toddled off down to the showers like two over-excited kids. As we shared the soap and shampoo, neither of us could stop laughing. It was just brilliant to rub shampoo into my hair and soap on to my body. The dirt was piling off, and my fingers and cheeks were tingling with the first taste of cleanliness in two months.

The lavish breakfast resulted in much of the rest of the morning sitting on the toilet, but I also found time to see the base doctor. She checked all over my body for blisters and frostbite, and when she came to my nose she just shook her head and exclaimed, 'Not very nice!' She told me it would heal naturally, if slowly, and then gave me more painkillers for my back.

I spent the afternoon enjoying a guided tour of the research station before I found myself in a rather ridiculous race. The scientists, from time to time, like to stage a race on a half-mile course around the actual pole jutting out of the ice. On completion they award themselves with T-shirts saying that they had just completed a round-the-world race. Feodore and I asked if we could each have a T-shirt, but the base commander refused on the grounds that we had not completed the half-mile course. Never mind the fact that we had just walked 680 miles across frozen wastes of Antarctica, rules were rules! Feodore and I then clipped our skis back on, tied ourselves up to our sledges, and trudged round the course, swearing with virtually every step we took. Only then were we presented with our T-shirts.

That evening I settled down to phone home with the good news. I was told, because of the satellite transmitter, that I was allowed one call, and it had to be collect. Claire should have had an inkling by now that I had reached the Pole, but I wanted to be the first person to confirm this.

The first problem I came across was the operator at McMurdo Sound, on the New Zealand side of Antarctica. Although I argued that the Amundsen–Scott base commander had given me permission to make this call, the operator insisted on confirmation. I then had to go and find the commander, who thankfully made his way down to the telephone room on my behalf. Finally I heard a clicking sound down the line as my home numbers were punched into the system, followed by three rings. I couldn't wait to hear Claire's voice and to tell her that I was safe, and at the South Pole. Instead I heard a recorded male voice say, 'This is David Hempleman-Adams. We're not here at the moment, but please leave a message.'

I couldn't believe it. This was supposed to be the big phone call home, and Claire wasn't in. The operator's voice piped back, 'There's nobody answering.' I begged her for one more call and, without my address book on me, tried furiously to think of another family member's number. The only one I could think of was Aunt Audrey. The operator tried again, but this time the telephone just rang and rang. Terrific! Does anybody know, or care for that matter, that I'm down here, with my nose frozen off, having just created a small slice of history?

I could tell that the operator was now growing extremely impatient. I pleaded with her for one more chance, and started to remember my grandmother's number. I wrote it out on a piece of paper. Was it 523102, or 523103? The operator ordered me to hurry up, so I plumped for the first number. This time the call was answered, and I heard a woman say hello down the line. The operator explained that it was David Hempleman-Adams at the South Pole, and then asked if the lady would accept the collect call. I was already beginning to get worried. The lady asked the operator what she meant by the term 'collect call'. The operator patiently explained that it meant that she was expected to pay for it. Then the lady asked, 'And who did you say is calling?' The operator repeated my name. Finally the lady back in England said, 'So let me get this straight. You want me to pay for a phone call made by some strange man at the South Pole?' The operator replied, 'Yes, that's right.' There was a small pause, and then the English lady announced her decision: 'NO!', and she slammed down the phone.

Once I got over the initial disappointment of failing to tell anyone my good news, I saw the funny side of it, and decided to go and have a few beers with Feodore and my new-found friends from the research station. We knew that the Cessna from Patriot Hills would be arriving in the morning to take us away from the South Pole, so after a fitful sleep we packed away our equipment and waited for the plane to arrive.

Geoff Somers was the first person out of the plane once it had come to a halt on the ice. He is a typically reserved Englishman, so when I went to give him a big hug he backed off and shook my hand instead. But he was genuinely thrilled for me, even if the first words he said were, 'So, Dave, what took you so long? And what's all this nonsense about your back?'

A few minutes later two Twin Otters landed next to us and a bunch of elderly tourists from New York piled out, snapping away with their cameras. It was not what I needed at the time, because it made me feel as if what I had just done had been diluted. Why walk to the Pole when you can catch a chartered plane, like the American tourists? As I had spent fifty-nine days walking there, I held the South Pole in some reverence, so I found the experience of watching these tourists particularly galling.

All they seemed to want to do was touch the pole and get a stamp in their passport. Feodore and I did not need to say anything to each other. We understood precisely what each of us was thinking.

I waited until the masses had left to look around the research station, and then made my personal farewell to the Pole. Looking back, it was as if I was kissing my wife goodbye at the airport. I touched the pole, and thanked it for tolerating me, and for delivering me. Then I made my way to the waiting Cessna.

Geoff, the pilot, Feodore and myself all clambered into the plane. The Cessna is only small, and as we were all big men we felt like sardines packed into a can. A moment of farce happened just as we were about to take off and leave the South Pole. The hitherto friendly base commander had a complaint to make. I had the headphones on and heard traffic control deliver a message saying that the base commander wanted his trousers back after lending them to me when I had first arrived. I had already returned them to the base doctor, but the base commander insisted on checking with the doctor first. So the four of us sat in the Cessna for ten minutes until, finally, a voice crackled over the radio, 'Okay, we've got the trousers, you can go now.'

It is a six-hour flight to Patriot Hills from the South Pole in a Cessna. As we took off and circled the Pole, I looked down and wondered if I would ever return. I still do, for that matter. Midway through the flight the BBC World Service suddenly came on the airwaves, and I heard the presenter announce that David Hempleman-Adams had just become the first Briton to make it to the South Pole, solo and unsupported. I then heard the dulcet tones of Jock Wishart providing the details. That was me they were all talking about! This is when I first realised that the rest of the world knew of my exploits. I was not looking for fame, but I had a warm glow inside me as I dozed off.

On arriving at Patriot we were met with party streamers, champagne and cake. There were about ten people at the camp, and all came out personally to congratulate us. Sue, the cook, who had been keeping British Antarctica hooked to the airwaves with her suggestive talk, presented me with her promise made during the first part of my walk, when times were at their toughest. The apple and black-berry pie with custard went down a treat, and afterwards I made a small speech thanking everyone for their support.

The following morning the tourists from the South Pole turned up at Patriot. I came into the mess tent for my lunch to find the place heaving with them. Having grown used to solitude, I could not stand this and walked out again. Geoff Somers knew what I was going through and he left a meal for me to eat later. It was good to be back in civilisation again, but it would take a little time to readjust.

Later that day I caught the Hercules back to Punta Arenas in Chile. As I boarded the plane I said goodbye to Feodore. He, believe it or not, was staying down in Antarctica for a little longer in order to climb Mount Vinson. That man really is incredible. I have failed to get in touch with him since, but intend to do so soon. Although I was wearing clean clothes, I still had to wear my old outer clothes. The crew on the Hercules were polite, but eventually they asked me if I could move down to the back of the plane, away from the same American tourists who returned with me. When the girl from Adventure Network collected me at Punta Arenas, the first thing she said was, 'Cor, the Hercules crew were right. You are a bit smelly!'

The shower and shave in the hotel room where it all began two months earlier were bliss. There were twenty-two phone calls waiting for me from the media around the world, who had somehow tracked me down to this small Chilean town on the tip of the world, but my first call was to Claire. It was three in the morning back in England, but this time she answered. She said well done, and added that she had missed me. We then made arrangements for my return. We decided to meet in Calais and have a short holiday at a friends' house nearby with my three daughters, Alicia, Camilla and Amelia. Besides, a load of TV and radio satellite vans had arrived outside my house in Lacock, so it seemed as good a reason as any to escape.

Just before I left Punta Arenas for Santiago, Adventure Network's Annie Kershaw asked me if I could give a lecture about my recent antics to – wait for it – the same American tourists who had so annoyed me. As a favour to Annie I agreed, and when the tourists discovered who I was, and what I had just achieved, they were really nice to me and extremely interested. Of course, it made me feel terribly guilty. Perhaps my mental state was not as good as it might have been back at the Pole, because in Punta Arenas my view took a 180-degree turn, and I suddenly started to appreciate the fact that these sixty- and seventy-year-olds had, in their own way, been courageous by getting off their arses and travelling down to the South Pole.

More press calls waited for me in Santiago, where I stopped overnight before flying to Paris. They explained to me that the world was particularly interested in me because I had not only reached the South Pole unsupported, but also climbed Everest, which made me one of only two people ever to have done so. It had also made me the first person ever to have climbed the seven summits and reached the Pole. The connection, I suppose, is the top and bottom of the world.

My brother Mark picked me up in Paris and drove me over to Calais where I waited for Claire and the children to arrive. A bottle of champagne greeted me in my room, which I thought was a nice touch. It was 10 January, it had been nearly three months since I had left my home, and I was aching to see my family again.

Not long afterwards there was a knock on the door. I opened it and was almost bowled over by the rush of three small children running and then leaping into my arms. Claire walked in behind them, hugged me, said well done again, and then took a step back. I asked her what she was doing. She replied, 'I'm looking at your nose. See you got a bit of frostbite!' Then we both laughed.

PART THREE

A NEW DANGER

The Magnetic South Pole Trip, February–March 1996

The idea of sailing to the Magnetic South Pole first came about during my climb of Carstensz Pyramid. I was with my climbing partner, Paul Harman, talking of my plans to start walking to the South Pole later that year, and also to the Magnetic North Pole with a team of novices. Suddenly Paul turned round and suggested, if I could find the time, an attempt on the Magnetic South Pole as well, on the basis that by reaching all three poles I would undoubtedly become the first man to do so in one year. The seed was sown in the jungles of Indonesia. Later research revealed that, indeed, no adventurer had ever achieved what I set out to do.

I knew that Jock Wishart, for a start, would go ballistic when I told him I was planning another trip in between the South Pole and the Ultimate Challenge trip to the Magnetic North Pole, mainly because he would fear that I would be placing the latter operation in jeopardy should anything happen to me, or even if I were delayed. But my decision was made, and I decided only to tell Jock when I was about to leave Tasmania for the Magnetic South Pole. Then it was too late for him to do anything about it.

The plan was to return from the South Pole in early January, take a couple of weeks' holiday in France with Claire and the children, and then head straight off back to Antarctica. The timing of the trip was predetermined.

I knew I could sail to the Magnetic South Pole on open water in February and March, but any later than that would mean the start of the southern hemisphere winter, and the sea surrounding the Pole would freeze over into pack ice. I also had to be sure of exactly where I would be travelling to. The Magnetic South Pole is located at around sixty-five degrees south, 140 degrees east, but it does tend to move. I therefore obtained the most up-to-date co-ordinates for its location by contacting the British and Australian Magnetism groups. At the time of our sailing the Pole was located at 64°7' south, 138°6' east.

The next problem was how I was going to reach the Pole. I was offered the chance to lecture on a Russian ice-breaker full of tourists who fancied a trip down to Antarctica, but I did not see any sense of achievement in that. You might wonder what the point was of reaching the Magnetic South Pole at all in a yacht when I could have done it, in much more comfort, on the ice-breaker, but by doing so it would have removed any semblance of achievement. After all, nobody knocked Sir Francis Chichester after he circumnavigated the world in a yacht, against all the elements, when he could have sailed on the *QE2*.

I first approached my friend, Skip Novak, the famous American Whitbread sailor. We met while climbing on the Haute Route in the Alps. He has a boat called *Pelagic* specially adapted for icy conditions, so he had to be the first call. Skip said that it would be brilliant to be involved, but he had other commitments, and could not have sailed his boat, based in Punta Arenas, round to Hobart in time before the southern hemisphere winter set in. The contact was useful, however, because Skip put me in touch with a number of people, including an Australian called Don McIntyre.

A former BOC sailor, McIntyre telephoned me one

morning at my Robnor offices in Swindon. He and his wife, Marge, had just returned from spending a whole year living in a ten-by-ten-foot prefabricated hut on the Australian-owned part of the Antarctic continent. Their reason, believe it or not, was to see what the experience would be like. The place where they lived, near to Mawson's Hut, is supposed to be the windiest place on the planet, and, of course, during the winter months the couple would have experienced twenty-four-hour darkness. Before Don left he even had his appendix removed in case, with no medical facilities available, he developed appendicitis. It seemed to me that the risks were enormous, not only to their health but also to their marriage, but they survived the ordeal and now had a boat available to charter. In fact *The Spirit of Sydney* had sailed down to Antarctica to pick the McIntyres up and return them to Hobart, so it had already proved its seaworthiness in such uncompromising conditions. Don had spent £250,000 on upgrading the boat for Antarctic sailing, and told me that it would be ready within six weeks. I chartered the boat for £36,000.

The boat was a sixty-two-foot sailing yacht specifically designed for solo sailing, but it had been re-rigged with bunks inside which could accommodate up to twelve people. Twelve would be too much of a squeeze, so I decided on ten, comprising three crew and seven punters, including myself, each of whom would help to pay for the trip. The whole trip cost me £40,000, so by obtaining some sponsorship and charging each of the punters for the trip I was just about able to cover the costs.

I advertised in the sailing and yachting world press and received a reply from a Swiss doctor called Oliver Houseman who also happened to be an accomplished sailor, and a diesel engineer called Roy Lewington from Lancing in Sussex. I decided to ask Ron Brooks, my father-in-law, if he would like to come along. He had been a sailor for a long time and was very experienced. He was coming up to sixty-five years of age and had always been very proud of my achievements, so I thought I would give him the trip of his lifetime. The other three spaces went to Graham Hoyland, the BBC sound man from the Everest trip, Julian Champkin, the newspaper reporter from base camp at Everest and Elbrus, and Rebecca Stephens who, like me, fancied a change.

Everything was now set. Arriving back in England after our French holiday on the morning of Saturday, 27 January, I rejoined the family, who had returned a couple of days before because the girls had to go back to school. This, at last, was going to be my Christmas Day. The next day I was due to fly off to Tasmania with Ron. I had put on over a stone in weight, and my nose felt a lot better for the respite from the cold. I have always recovered pretty quickly from my polar ordeals, and this was to be no exception.

I was dressed up in my dinner jacket and looking forward to a fantastic day when I suddenly thought I should pre-book our seats for the long flight. Phoning up Garuda Airlines I asked if I could pre-book, only to be told that my secretary had somehow got my dates wrong, and that my flight was leaving on the Saturday, my Christmas Day. It was ten in the morning and I had less than two hours to pack and get up to Heathrow from Wiltshire in time. I thought about the rest of the team who, having made their own way to Hobart from all corners of the world, would be waiting for me to arrive. As team leader, I could hardly turn up late.

Then my thoughts turned to Claire and the kids. I assumed Claire would go berserk. The children had all been a bit clingy when I had first returned from the South Pole, and now I was about to walk out on them again.

They were standing in their party dresses and I had to tell them that I had to leave right then. There were a few tears, of course, but Claire was marvellous. I suppose she had long resigned herself to putting up with me and my ridiculous adventures. It took me a rushed fifteen minutes to pack everything before my brother, Mark, picked me up and drove me to the airport.

I phoned the airport every half an hour to let them know I was on my way, and that the plane must not leave without me. I made it by a matter of minutes, and as I sat back in my seat next to Ron, I realised it was not the best way to start off a new trip. I hoped it was not a bad omen. Meanwhile, Ron was as happy as a sand boy. He was going back to sea again and, unlike me who had packed three tons of ginger biscuits, scopolamine patches to place behind my ears, and a crate of sea-sickness tablets, he travelled empty-handed.

We arrived in Hobart late in the afternoon the following day and were met by Don and Marge McIntyre. They had been back three weeks since their Antarctic holiday, and seemed to have coped well with what I would have thought was a brutal ordeal. The first thing Don did, before even taking us to the boat, was sit us down and tell us the uncensored truth about our proposed trip.

For a start, he told us, you will get two or three weather fronts a day down there, and massive lows where the barometer will fall through the floor. Then he underlined the most frightening part: we were on our own when it came to any possibility of a rescue. Helicopters based at Casey and McMurdo in the Antarctic would be too far away to get to us in time. Worse still, we would not be in any shipping channel because we would have sailed too far south. There would be no army or naval base to aid us, so our only hope would be a distress signal, and even then it would probably take too long to save us from the icy and hazardous waters. He ended this encouraging chat in typical Aussie style: 'Frankly mate, if you or the boat goes over, you've had it.' Thanks Don.

He changed his tone once we arrived at the marina and stared up at the *Spirit of Sydney*. 'Isn't she a beaut?' he said. I agreed, not really knowing what I was talking about, but by doing so I prompted a long eulogy from Don about her sleekness, mast, engine, and just about everything else. He took me inside and showed me where the bunks were. The distance between them could not have been more than eighteen inches. I grabbed a particular bunk which was both good and bad news for me. I wanted one with enough head room, and also one which was low under the wrong assumption that, wary of sea sickness, I might not be moved around so much. The flip side of this decision, however, was that I was going to sleep below the waterline, with only a matter of a few millimetres of aluminium between me and a cold bath.

Roy and Oliver had already slept the night before in the yacht. Oliver was an accomplished helmsman, but what would make him particularly useful was, of course, his medical experience. Suitably, he had arrived with a box of tricks which would come in useful during the voyage. Roy was another experienced sailor, having crossed the Atlantic on a number of occasions, but his particular forte was to keep an eye on the engine.

That night the rest of the crew met up in a flat Don had organised for us. The yacht's skipper was Steve Corrigan who, for some unknown reason, was known as 'Nig'. He was a veteran of twenty Sydney to Hobart races, had sailed down to Antarctica on *The Spirit of Sydney* to collect Don, and was vastly experienced. In his weather-beaten way Nig had seen life. His girlfriend, called Ez, was coming too. She was short and stocky and had more balls than most men I know. Although she had a great deal of sailing experience, she was the type of tomboy who liked to be seen farting and belching with the best of them. I wasn't too keen on that aspect of her personality.

The final member of the crew was Pete Bland, a former Melbourne Grammar boy who only made the team the night before we set off because the original member, Jay, had somehow managed to pull his back. Pete flew down from Melbourne at a moment's notice and leapt at the chance to join up, unpaid, just for the adventure. As it later transpired, he was to play a crucial role on the trip.

As I observed everybody greeting each other it occurred to me that, although I was the team leader and had put the whole damn trip together, I was probably the novice and would need as much guidance as possible from my fellow crew members. At this point I thought it might be a good idea to contact Jock Wishart. I'm not sure, but I think I could hear him hitting the table when I phoned him. Back home he was steaming ahead with planning the Ultimate Challenge and was rightly livid that my cover story of going skiing had changed to a trip to the Magnetic South Pole.

As an experienced sailor himself, Jock wanted to know whether I had any idea what I was proposing to do. He tried to tell me to forget about it for a couple of years. Then he reminded me that if I went off and killed myself, or even slipped in the ice and the wet and broke my arm, then the Ultimate Challenge would be stuffed. He was right, but if I did not attempt the trip now I would not become the first person ever to reach three poles in a year. If you mention the magic word 'first' to any adventurer it provides a compelling argument.

Don explained to us that he had a problem with the electrics on the boat. Someone was flying down from Sydney which meant that we had an extra day to kill in Hobart. That night we all went out for a meal. Some of the talk was about my recent trip to the South Pole. I did not dwell on it too much, however, because I was among adventurers who had done their bits in their time and, secondly, I always find it difficult to talk about a trip in the past when I am focusing on a new adventure. We all had hundreds of questions to ask the skipper who, in turn, tried to prepare us for what the roughest seas on the planet would throw at us. He tried to find the right balance between excited optimism and warning us that we were not going on a nice cruise. When he talked of the hundred-foot waves, I laughed along, until I saw the serious look on his face.

Then we discussed watches. Nig would take one, with myself, Rebecca – or 'Becks' as we all came to call her – and Graham Hoyland who, at the time, were a couple. Pete Bland took the second watch, together with Ron and Julian. Ez was in charge of the third watch. She was the least experienced of the crew, but she had Ron and Ollie to accompany her. The shifts were either three or four hours long. The six a.m. to ten a.m. was a nice one, but the midnight to three a.m. was by far the worst, closely followed by the three a.m. to six a.m. shift.

At last we were ready to set sail. It was the morning of 1 February, and the whole crew were glad to be off and running. After thirty minutes, with Hobart slowly disappearing behind us, we suddenly remembered that we had left all the milk behind. It was annoying to have to turn back, but we decided we could not go a whole month without milk at breakfast or in our teas and coffees.

After that little hiccup we set sail again and, at least for three hours, it was a very enjoyable experience. Dolphins swam alongside, and sailing down Hobart Sound was as pleasant a time as we could wish for. Then, unbelievably, our communications went down. Faced with the thought of sailing to the Antarctic without a phone, radio or fax, we came to the reluctant decision to turn back again. We limped back into Hobart marina in the early hours of the following morning.

Already there were murmurs of discontent. We all privately began to wonder if the boat was up to the voyage ahead. I was concerned that, having paid all this money, we had lumbered ourselves with a Jonah. The skipper calmed things down, assuring us that these things happen all the time, and that it would only mean a day's delay. I began to look at my calendar and think of the Ultimate Challenge, while Graham Hoyland thought about his climbing trip to the Himalayas that directly followed this adventure.

We all slept in the yacht that night and, once an electrician had sorted out the communications, we set sail again down through the Hobart Sound until, after five hours, we met the infamous Southern Ocean Swell. It happened almost without warning. The swell is like a rollercoaster of waves which do not break; it is, if you like, the hors d'oeuvres before the main course, the ocean itself, which, because it has no land to break itself up, provides the most ferocious conditions. We all had to clip ourselves on to the safety line, holding on for dear life while the yacht veered at forty-five-degree angles. This was still in the channel, and already the yacht's rails on the other side were under water. I was thinking to myself, 'Christ, I know we're running late, but we don't have to kill ourselves on day one.' This, as I was later to discover, was nothing.

Just before reaching open water we passed a tiny village called Dover on the coast. The skipper felt we should stop and make last-minute checks, now that we had achieved some hard sailing. It was just as well he did. While the rest of us inspected the insides of a local bar, Nig stayed behind to carry out some tests. As soon as he walked into the bar we could tell by the look on his face that something was wrong.

'We've got to go back to Hobart again,' he announced. He had discovered an earth leakage in the aluminium hull of the yacht. Rather like a battery, the yacht was dissolving in the sea water. The trip was close to being over again. Graham mentioned the Himalayas again, and I became seriously concerned about the Ultimate Challenge. The close-knit camaraderie we had rapidly developed was sinking fast. We sailed back to Hobart, five hours' away, and returned to the flat disillusioned and disheartened.

Finally, the next morning, 5 February, we heard the news that this time the yacht really was in good shape and was ready to set sail. I think we had all independently decided that if there was one more hitch we would pack up and go home. We had lost five days and, as we sailed out of the marina, I was fully expecting to be back again within the day.

This time there would be no stopping. We all agreed to steam out into the ocean. After five hours, having sailed by Dover, we passed the last piece of land until Antarctica. This was the Southern Ocean. I had read about it many times in accounts of Ernest Shackleton's journey from Elephant Island to South Georgia in an open boat which, for me, is the greatest adventure ever. For nine months Shackleton and his crew were locked in ice and drifting. When the ice finally crushed his ship, *Endurance*, they took to the ship's boats and, after a remarkable struggle for survival, made Elephant Island in the South Falklands. From here he sailed on Easter Monday, 1916 in one of the boats, *James Caird*, covering the 300 miles to South Georgia to seek help. It was one of the greatest ever feats of seamanship and navigation in an open boat, taking them across the stormiest seas on earth. It is because of feats such as this that I felt comfortable with the thought of Shackleton, the great survivor, watching over me.

As we entered the Southern Ocean the crew enacted an emotional and important ceremony. Ez produced a large bunch of rhododendrons, handed them over to us all, and then asked us to throw them over the sea to give thanks to the gods for a safe passage. This, apparently, is a common procedure for anyone entering the Southern Ocean, for it is felt that this particular sea is so powerful that your fate rests with something more than just your own ability. Far from scaring me, I felt rather relieved that we had been asked to do such a seemingly strange thing. I looked across at Steve Corrigan, a hardened sailor, and saw him throwing the flowers into the waves with gusto. I thought to myself, I'm with you on this mate. Like Everest, the Southern Ocean must be feared, respected and never taken for granted. These guys, whether Nepalese sherpas in the Himalayas or weather-beaten sailors facing the Southern Ocean, know the environment and the elements better than me, I mused, so I fully respect their views and traditions. Oh, and by the way, I had made sure to put on my 'Z' bead again.

This time there were no hitches with the yacht. We powered into the Southern Ocean and, although the swell remained frightening for a novice such as me, the likes of Nig seemed to be totally at home steering the bouncing, lurching yacht. The sailors' vocabulary was a little off-putting at first. I had to get used to the fact that the kitchen became the 'galley', and the toilet, for some reason, was known as the 'head'. But I felt at ease on watch, especially as Nig took the controls most of the time, enabling me either to navigate or to make the teas. As the hours passed into days I was allowed to steer the yacht more and more, always under the watchful eye of the skipper. Even the clipping on was something that came naturally to me from climbing up fixed ropes at high altitude.

I found the amount of sea covered, after my experiences walking twelve miles a day at the South Pole, remarkable. On day one the *Spirit of Sydney* sailed 160 nautical miles. The next day we covered 202 nautical miles. By day three we were up to 230. Within a short amount of time the crew became very competitive. Who could helm the yacht the furthest each day? Who could cook the nicest evening meal? Who could surf down the biggest wave?

It all meant that, at least for the first week, the voyage was hard but pleasant. We all slept and snored in a room no bigger than a small living-room, and we all went about our daily business almost permanently at an angle of forty-five degrees. After what I had to endure at the South Pole, the standard of food was almost gourmet in comparison. It was not unusual, for example, to enjoy a leg of lamb with mint sauce and roast potatoes, or a good steak. I may have lost 36lb in weight on my way to the South Pole, but I actually gained weight on my way to the Magnetic South Pole.

The further we sailed the rougher the sea became. The sea began to crash over the sides of the yacht and, on occasion, into the cockpit. One night I was helming when I was suddenly surrounded by luminous jellyfish floating around the cockpit. I became paranoid about falling overboard. We were all wearing harnesses over our waterproof jackets and at no time were any of us not clipped up.

As we passed through the roaring forties and into the screaming fifties the conditions deteriorated noticeably. On the fifth night, during a storm, Ron was on his way down into the cabin from the deck when he lost his footing and smacked his head on the side. It was handy that Ollie was there to insert five stitches, but it left Ron feeling embarrassed and reminded him that down here in the Southern Ocean this was stuff for big boys. As for me, I looked at Ron's head and felt guilty that I had persuaded him to come along in the first place.

It was becoming colder, both in the air and in the sea where the temperature had dropped from sixteen degrees in Hobart to just seven degrees. There were no other sailing yachts by now, and we did not even need to have our steaming lights switched on – we were well out of the last shipping lanes. The wind also started to pick up, but this only seemed to work in our favour. We were covering 230 nautical miles a day on a voyage which, if you look on a map, may seem deceptively short but in reality is far greater than sailing across the pond from Europe to the United States. The howling gusts helped to blow two or three severe weather fronts past us on most days, which resulted in the biggest waves I have ever seen in my life. To me they looked like tidal waves. They were certainly reaching one hundred feet in height. In fact they were so tall that when we surfed down them into the trough, the sails could not pick up any wind at all, but when the yacht reached the top of the next wave, we were blown full blast down the other side and into the next trough. We were permanently wet by now and experiencing an emotional mix of exhilaration and fear.

Ollie became the second casualty after cracking his head on the cabin wall, having been thrown against it by an unfriendly wave. He inserted the three stitches himself. I wondered when it would be my turn to injure myself, and thought of Jock's warning that it could only take one slip on the whole voyage to scupper the Ultimate Challenge. Julian, meanwhile, had been puking his guts up for most of the trip and had turned a permanent shade of green. I watched him throwing up into a bucket and felt genuinely sorry for him. For a while I thought about giving him one of my scopolamine patches, but I knew I only had enough for myself and did not want to go through what he was suffering.

Besides, I was having fun and games with my bunk. I discovered, only once we were well and truly on our way, that if I was lying on my bunk when someone turned the radio on, I would be treated to a small electric shock. I was the only one affected by this strange phenomenon, which we all put down to the fact that I was next to the aluminium hull. I spent half my time on the bunk sticking my head out over the side like a bird in a cuckoo clock to avoid being zapped.

By 11 February we had crossed over the South-East Indian Ridge, the conversion in the Southern Ocean which signals the start of the roughest and coldest part of this great expanse of water. Nig told everyone to look out for icebergs. We were not to worry too much about the big obvious ones, but to concentrate on the little peaks of ice jutting out of the sea. They were the ones to be wary of because, travelling at speeds reaching thirty knots, a collision would result in a tear in the hull which would mean the end of the trip, and quite possible the end of us all. I sat in my bunk listening to the icy water a matter of millimetres away on the other side of the hull and thought, 'And if we do hit an iceberg, it will be me who cops it first!' Still, I was cheered that evening after helping to make a roast lamb dinner which was voted best meal of the trip.

By now we had sailed into what I termed the 'freezing' sixties. The mercury on the barometer was falling through the floor. As we sailed further and further south the spray was beginning to freeze on the deck and on our clothing. We were all now in our thermals, with no part of our flesh exposed to the biting cold, made far worse by the windchill factor of the Southern Ocean. It highlighted an important difference between this and mountaineering: on a mountain you could dig yourself into a tunnel to avoid the worst of the weather; out here, exposed on a yacht tossed around like a rubber duck in a bath, we were just in the middle of it all, with nowhere to run and hide. In one of the sixty-knot winds a life-raft was ripped clean away from its moorings.

In another storm I watched poor old Ron cross the cabin horizontally like an Exocet missile, which took some doing for a 6ft 3in man. It was down to Ollie to sew his head back together again. I could only stand by and feel wretchedly guilty. Ron was as strong as an ox, but this, together with the concussion he suffered as a result of the accident, knocked his confidence.

In fact by now the whole experience on the yacht was surreal. While the waves, and sometimes fellow crew members, were crashing around me, I would sit on my bunk, watch water constantly run past the window, eat chocolate and listen to Van Morrison blaring out on the ghetto blaster.

The threat of icebergs had us all out on deck squinting through the fog. On the previous trip to pick up Don and Marge McIntyre, they had come across icebergs much further north. We were all wondering what had happened to them. By all accounts some of them had been the size of Wales, so none of us could work out where they had disappeared to.

My nose, unfortunately, had begun to deteriorate again after making a half recovery from the South Pole trip. Blisters began to reappear from the cold, which made me stand out from the rest who had not suffered from frostbite before. The instruments were beginning to get covered in ice, the spray was freezing within minutes of splashing on the decks, and we could not stand out for any more than twenty minutes each turn. When we were out there, those not steering spent most of the time chipping away on the ice that had formed on the decks. We used anything we could get our hands on, from chisels to hammers, axes to knives. As more and more ice developed so the anxiety grew that the weight of the ice could result in the yacht tipping over. As I looked down into the icy sea, this was not a pleasant sight. As usual, food cheered us all up that night. It is amazing what sausage, cheese and onion, potatoes followed by Christmas pudding, brandy and cream can do for the morale.

By Valentine's Day the magnetic compass could no longer be used because of the proximity of our destination. We reverted to using the good old GPS system. We woke up to a huge storm, and I remember looking across the bunk at Becks who sat there looking as white as a ghost. She asked me if I was frightened, because she certainly was. I was as scared as Becks, probably more so than during my walk to the South Pole, but I told her that the yacht had seen and done it before, we were in good hands, and that there was nothing to be frightened of. As I was saying this I was far from comforted by the fact that the first British woman ever to climb Everest was scared. That said, Becks then stood up, put her goggles on and went straight up on deck to carry out her helming duties.

It was then that we heard the worst news of the trip so far. I was lying in my bunk, trying not to get zapped, when I suddenly heard Nig shout out, 'For God's sake, you're going to fucking kill us all, you daft bitch.' I ran upstairs to see what all the commotion was about, and saw Nig staring accusingly at his girlfriend. Ez had somehow managed to get a warp, or rope, from one of the sails over the side and caught up on the propeller. The engine drives the small propeller, and by wrapping the warp around it it meant the engine could not function. This was a serious problem. It meant that we did not have any battery power, which in turn meant that we could not use any of the

above Carstensz Pyramid, the highest mountain in Australasia.

right On the top of the Carstensz Pyramid, the last of the seven summits, May 1995.

below Thierry, Bernard, Feodor, Borge and me at the Magellan Statue, Punta Arenas, before setting off individually for the South Pole, November 1995.

The South Pole, a small village of cold scientists.

I've made it! At the South Pole and happy, despite the obvious frostbite on my nose.

Graham Hoyland, Rebecca Stephens and me, the three members of the South Magnetic Pole crew to have climbed Everest.

Leaving Hobart for the South Magnetic Pole, February 1996.

En route to the South Magnetic Pole.

On board *The Spirit of Sydney*. The less than salubrious sleeping accommodation.

The moment when Graham Hoyland nearly lost his life. Note the ice on deck.

The crew at the site of the South Magnetic Pole.

The Ultimate Challenge team at the North Magnetic Pole.
Different people, but just one expectation, May 1996.

-50°. First day at Ward Hunt Island. North Pole expedition, March 1997.

Crossing frozen lead. This could sometimes be more than one mile across.

Our rescued man, Alan Bywater.

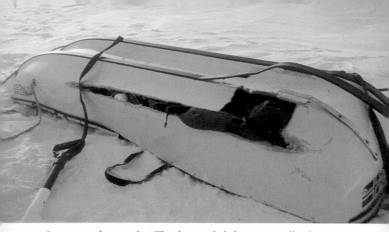

So near and yet so far! The damaged sledge; eventually, the runner came off and the bottom fell out.

My girls: (clockwise) Claire, Amelia, Camilla and Alicia
© Les Wilson

instruments. The GPS was made redundant, and we were therefore unable to navigate.

The experienced sailors on board knew that Ez had made a basic error but nobody actually said anything, except for the caring Nig. As for me, I probably would have made the same mistake on day one, given the chance. The professionals likened it to climbing without tying on properly.

Of course, by then we were surrounded by icebergs. We were caught up in a force eleven gale, which was screaming through the rigging. Even without the engine we were travelling at twenty-five knots with little chance to manoeuvre away from the icebergs. We could take down the sails of course, thus slowing us down, but by doing so we would lose any control over our direction. We were like a motor car speeding down a hill without any brakes.

We spent the best part of the day discussing the problem. The experienced sailors managed to sail us past each iceberg, but we all knew that sooner or later our luck would run out. Unless someone came up with a brainwave the trip was over. We could not even start the engine because the propeller was jammed. We got to within three miles of Boat Harbour at Commonwealth Bay on the Antarctic coastline and threw the storm anchor over-board, in huge swells, to keep us relatively stable. As we all sat down to discuss the matter, Ez was in tears. She blamed herself for an error that had now placed our lives, let alone the trip, in some jeopardy. Outside, the sea temperature had now dropped to − 1°C.

Nig told us that we would try to find a big enough iceberg to draw up to in order to be sheltered from the worst of the waves. Once we had achieved this a crew meeting was called. The skipper explained that we had to detach the rope from the propeller. Even if we succeeded here, we were not to know whether the propeller had been bent and broken by the rope, but unless we used a diver to cut the rope and inspect the damage, we would never know. The alternative, he added, was to set off back to Hobart through everything the Southern Ocean could throw at us without the use of the engine or propeller.

We looked at each other and waited for the next question. 'So,' Nig began. 'Who's going to volunteer to dive over?' We were all sitting in a circle drinking hot coffee. We all heard the question and within a split second eyes were darting all over the cabin at each other before universally turning to Pete Bland, the youngest and fittest among us. He looked at all of us, gulped, and then said, 'Well, it looks like it's me.'

Within twenty seconds Becks was tearing off his clothes and we were getting him into a wet suit and preparing his snorkel. While someone sharpened a knife, I gave him another cup of coffee. Someone brought a video camera out and Pete asked if it could be caught on film for his mother back in Melbourne. We then helped him to get his flippers on, which would help him not to drift away from the yacht. His hands and neck upwards would be exposed to the water. He would only be able to last in it for a matter of two or three minutes. As he prepared himself to leap overboard I looked down into the sea. There were bits of ice floating everywhere, and even though in the lee of the iceberg the waters had calmed down considerably, the waves were still uninviting and dangerous.

We all gathered on deck and watched as he slipped over the side. As Pete hit the water you could see quite clearly how the numbing cold took his breath away. His eyes suddenly stuck out of his head, he looked up so that the whole of his face stared towards the sky, and he just let out an 'aaaarrrrgh' noise before flipping over and diving down into the sea.

The whole trip, and quite possibly our lives, depended

on the next three minutes and the bravery of this remarkable young man. The rest of us stood there thinking the same morose thoughts. Not a word was spoken. All that could be heard was the slapping of the waves against the yacht and the whistle of the icy wind.

SUCCESS IN THE NIGHT

The silence was shattered after a couple of minutes by a great whale of a kick of flippers and a spout of water. Pete emerged, gasping for air. We all started shouting, 'Well, how did you do?' Eventually Pete yelled back, 'I didn't do it, I didn't do it.' I don't know about the others, but having felt so sorry for him just a moment before, I was now thinking, 'Well get back down there again.'

Nig leant over and asked what the problem was. Pete explained that the rope had become wrapped four times around the propeller, and that he was going back down there to try to cut it free. I told him to get a move on before he got too cold, and added that I would buy him a pint of Stella Artois back in Hobart if he succeeded. For a moment he stared back at me with a look that said 'Screw the Stella' before he rose once again from the water and flipped down below the surface.

The silence returned for what seemed to be twice the amount of time he had previously spent under water. A good three to four minutes later he emerged again with a broad grin on his face. This time he shouted up, 'No problem, I've cut the rope.' In fact he had to cut the rope in three places before seeing that the propeller was not damaged. We all cheered and clapped. As Pete hauled himself back on to the boat Becks leapt at him again to rip off his cold and wet clothes and bring him downstairs. I made him a hot drink and as he sat in the cabin lapping up the adulation he was as proud as punch. We caught the moment on video, and ended the short film by saying, 'Well Mrs Bland, your Melbourne Grammar boy did well today.'

With the trip well and truly back on again we set our sights on Antarctica. I was really excited about the prospect, even though I had only been there six weeks before, and the others couldn't wait for their first sighting of the continent. The plan was to sail to Boat Harbour in Commonwealth Bay, where we would land, have a look at Douglas Mawson's hut, take a few snaps, and then return to the yacht. We sailed to within three miles of the harbour when Nig announced that there was no way we could get ashore in such windy conditions. The catabatic winds had swept across the whole continent before reaching Commonwealth Bay, the windiest place on earth, and it was just too dangerous to attempt to land in ninety-knot gusts.

We had no choice but to wait for the weather to subside. Drifting twelve miles during the night of the fifteenth, we had one person on deck the whole time filling hourly shifts on the look-out for icebergs. It was a delay we could have done without, but the unanimous view on the yacht was still to set foot on land. I thought it would be sad to bring all the team down to the southernmost parts of the Southern Ocean and not actually experience Antarctica. Okay, they would be able to see it from a few hundred yards out, but that would be like orbiting the moon without setting foot on the surface.

Settling down for the night I was reading in my bunk when, suddenly, there was a huge bang and shudder on the side of the yacht just, it seemed, the other side of where I was lying. Roy happened to be watching me at the time and he said that I was out of my bunk and changed from a horizontal to a vertical position in one rapid movement, like a penguin leaping out of the water. I all but jumped into Roy's arms.

Once everyone had stopped screaming 'What the bloody hell was that?' Nig looked over the side and saw a massive dent in the hull, courtesy of an iceberg whose tip barely emerged from the water's surface. It could have been extremely serious for us all but, thankfully, the thin layer of aluminium hull was strong enough to take it. Even so, we were all pretty disturbed by the accident, and the consequences if the iceberg had cut through any more of the hull. We decided to christen the iceberg 'Ollie's Iceberg' after that because he happened to be at the helm at the time. Ollie was pretty embarrassed and apologetic, especially when Nig told him to put his glasses on in future. Ollie agreed and immediately went to find them.

By that time ice was becoming permanently encrusted on the deck, mast and sails. Some of us spent nearly all our time scraping off the ice, but with spray freezing within minutes the chances of job completion were as likely as painting the Forth rail bridge quickly enough to avoid having to start all over again. We understood that we really did not have too much time to muck about being blown along the Antarctic coastline, and that if the winds proved to be too strong we would just have to give the mainland a miss.

On the sixteenth the main sail, under the weight of ice, finally ripped. Now we knew we had to anchor near the shore in order to stitch it up, not just for the vast majority of the crew to visit Antarctica. Later that day the winds, although remaining very strong, abated sufficiently for Nig to decide to go for it. It proved to be a dangerous exercise, partly because of the hundreds of icebergs, but also if we grounded we would all be in serious trouble.

The skipper had the engine on full belt, constantly looking at the depth sounder as the equipment revealed we were fifty feet, then forty feet, then thirty-two feet and so on from the bottom of the sea. Just a few yards from the shore we dropped anchor. As it was late we would be venturing ashore in the morning, but we were at least able to enjoy a great night's sleep because, for once, we were not being tossed all over the place by the angry waves further out to sea.

We woke up the following morning to a fine view. Apart from the sight of the coast just a few yards away, we were able to enjoy a welcoming party of thousands of penguins darting through the water before bouncing out of the sea and landing, rather clumsily, on the ice. The only other time I had seen a penguin was in London Zoo so I found the whole show wonderfully exciting. At times the birds were no more than six feet away from us, so cumbersome on land but so naturally developed for swimming under-water in the sea. You could smell the bird shit all around you, and see the odd seal moving slowly through the water, whiskers appearing above the surface, on the look-out for any stray penguins.

Before actually going ashore we had work to do. For a start, we had to hack off all the ice on the sail before taking the main off in order to sew it back into one piece strong enough to get us back to Hobart. Then we had to thaw out our water after discovering that all our water tanks had frozen. We resorted to taking plastic containers down into the galley in order to turn the ice back into water.

What appeared to be our biggest potential problem was the fact that after tests we discovered we had another earth leakage. Holes were beginning to appear in the soft metal of the hull, devoured by electrolytic corrosion, which made the bilges start to fill with water. Ollie and Pete were trying out a whole host of different vault meters to check where exactly the earth leakage was coming from, but all their efforts were in vain. Roy, in particular, spent hours and hours on this. In fact, the commonest sight of Roy throughout the trip was his arse hanging out and his head down the engine hatch surrounded by a horrible stench of diesel. How he was not sick I will never know.

Even Julian had stopped throwing up by now. Mind you, he had received so much stick from Nig that this provided the necessary motivation to stop. Nig would sometimes sit right next to a vomiting Julian during meal times. When Julian started up Nig would eat a mouthful of food, look across disdainfully at Julian and say, 'Stop chundering, Julian, I'm trying to eat my dinner here.' Another time I complained about the fact that for a number of days we had eaten nothing but lamb for breakfast, lunch and dinner. Nig turned round and said, 'Look at old Hempy, he must be a fucking vegetarian!' Like I said, Nig was a character.

On the seventeenth we finally set about getting ashore. We took our emergency kits, sleeping bags, stove, and all our cold weather kit just in case we became stuck on land, and then, making sure we were clipped on to prevent us from shooting off into the Southern Ocean, we paddled ashore in a small dinghy in three separate journeys.

Standing in front of us was Mawson's Hut, a large wooden building constructed during the Australian explorer's 1912 research trip to Antarctica. He actually claimed this part of the continent for Great Britain and the Commonwealth, but the British, in their infinite wisdom, decided that they already owned enough land and that Mawson could keep the ice and the cold for himself. So Mawson claimed it for Australia, which is why, to this day, Australia owns vast stretches of the Antarctic continent.

It was wonderful to see Mawson's Hut because here was history left untouched for the best part of a century.

I have two volumes of Mawson's work back home but it was much better to see the hut for real. There were these wonderful souvenirs left outside the hut, from old leather boots to packing cases, even old Colman's mustard jars, but there were two very good reasons for leaving them exactly as you found them: first, it is against the law to remove anything from Mawson's Hut; and, secondly, it is a polar tradition that if you ever took anything then you would never get home safely. I don't know how true this threat is in reality, but it would take a brave man to defy it.

Just over the headland stood Don and Marge McIntyre's hut. While Mawson's wooden hut had withstood the ice and the wind for over eighty years, Don's contraption, in contrast, had been there for a year. It was tiny in comparison, and boasted high-tech solar panels and a weather vane, all held down by steel guidelines. I looked at both and decided that I would prefer to live in Mawson's construction.

Ron, meanwhile, was in his element, brewing up tea for everyone inside one of the two tiny scientific huts adjacent to Mawson's, courtesy of the food, drink and fuel left for any passing adventurer. As they are as common as a comet in the sky there is little danger of resources running low, nor indeed of theft. Mawson's Hut has an open house policy, in keeping with just about the last unspoiled environment on the planet. We had a quick peer through the windows inside, where snow had covered up most of the equipment, took a few more photographs, and then rushed back to the dinghy in order to return to the yacht. We had, in case anyone had temporarily forgotten, a mission to complete.

Even slopping about in the waves during the short journey back to the yacht was, at least for me, a scary experience. I kept looking down at the cold, almost black, and definitely uninviting waters and thought to myself, 'If this thing tips over ...' It was therefore a huge relief to get everyone safely back on board.

Time was getting on, but we still needed to mend the main sail. Adopting a rota system, we stayed up until five the following morning sewing the tear until it was ready once again to hoist up on to the mast. Finally, at midday on the eighteenth, we upped anchor in readiness to set off on the last leg of our journey to the Magnetic South Pole. In doing so, we very nearly lost Graham Hoyland.

As the anchor was raised we noticed that a large block of ice had stuck to it. Graham, a fellow Everest climber, produced his ice axe. Whenever a climber uses one of these, he always makes sure that the accompanying loop is fixed firmly around his wrist in order to prevent any chance of losing the axe. Graham attached the loop around his wrist, and then started to hack away at the ice.

Suddenly, just as Graham's axe lodged firmly into the ice, the anchor began to drop back into the sea. Graham tried to wrench the axe out of the ice, but it was lodged too firmly in the block. In a split second his body was hoisted up and almost over the side of the yacht. He could not release the axe because the loop was tied firmly round his wrist, and he was about to be dragged down below the surface of the icy water with the anchor. Whether drowning or hypothermia would have killed him first is questionable but, thankfully, I was able to grab hold of his legs while someone else grabbed hold of me. Roy and Ollie got hold of the anchor chain and, between us all, we managed to drag both Graham and the anchor back over the right side of the yacht.

We all flopped down on the deck pretty shaken by what had almost happened. There is no doubt that Graham was within seconds of plunging to a certain death, and nobody knew this more than him. Becks was all over him, of course, while we made Graham a consolation cup of tea. Within minutes it was back to business again. If Graham had been really scared he did not show it. But he has climbed Everest, don't forget, and after an experience like that you become accustomed to near misses.

Later that day, as we steamed closer and closer, a combination of the weather and the scenery provided one of the most breathtaking sights I have ever experienced. The skies were a mixture of red and pink, while all the icebergs reflected in the sun. I am not the most romantic of people, but I really wished that Claire had been with me on that day to share the moment.

Everyone commented on how nice it was, but one could hardly have sidled across to someone like Nig and talked about how beautiful the skies looked. Besides, Nig was looking at his charts and asking me if I would settle for sailing to within ten miles of the centre of the Pole, because its circumference is quite large and shaped like a rugby ball. He was also thinking about the hassle of changing tack in order to sail to the very centre. I became quite agitated about this. I told him, in no uncertain terms, that we had come all this way, through immense danger and discomfort, and we should be prepared to spend another three days if we needed it to ensure we sail across the exact position of the Pole. As far as I was concerned, anything else was not even an issue. I had to be a little wary because, although I had set up the whole expedition, Nig was the yacht's skipper, and if he said it was too dangerous, or that there was an iceberg in the way, then I would have to accept his word. To his credit he understood my point and started to plot the final course to the Pole. It had passed midnight, and we were sailing in the early hours of 19 February.

As the GPS confirmed that we were edging closer and closer to the Pole the excitement on the yacht grew. We produced some crisps and lagers, and prepared ourselves for a champagne celebration. With less than an hour to go Nig told me to go up on deck and be the person in the crew to sail the yacht across the Pole. I refused, arguing that I was a big boy, I had done enough in my time, and that if anyone deserved to do it then it should be Pete Bland for saving the entire trip.

Pete refused point blank and agreed with the skipper that I should be the one to place the final piece in the jigsaw. I said to Pete that it would be sad if nobody did it, because I was set in my ways and I was not going to be the one to steer us over the Pole. That did the trick. Pete took the wheel, while the rest of us fixed our eyes on the GPS. As each mile was notched up we cheered in celebration, ten, nine, eight, seven, right down to the last mile, when we had to bark up instructions to veer two degrees to the west. Eventually it boiled down to metres. The GPS was rotating with the variation of the tracking until, finally, it flipped up to tell us that, after a fortnight's hard and frozen sailing, we had reached the Magnetic South Pole, about thirty miles off the coast of Antarctica.

In the southern hemisphere winter months, of course, the area of sea we were sailing on would all be iced over, but right now it was perfect, if still distressingly rough. I stood up and delivered a quick speech, thanking everyone for their efforts and adding that the achievement was a collective, team performance. Everybody shook hands, hugged and kissed each other, drank champagne and felt extremely pleased about themselves before, elated but tired, all but the night shift flopped into their bunks. In the back of my mind, as I sunk into a deep sleep, I remembered that we still had to sail all the way home again, and to meet the ferocity of the Southern Ocean once more. We had problems with the generator by now, the main sail had only been patched up and could not guarantee holding out through the terrifying winds it was about to face, and the boat was slowly dissolving. Climbing Everest had taught me the adventurer's caution: any trip is never completed until you have arrived home safely.

The next day, 20 February, proved to be kind to us, and the *Spirit of Sydney* made good progress away from the Pole back out into the main ocean. I was beginning to carry out more and more helming duties, and a dinner of steak and risotto rounded off one of our better days. I phoned home to tell Claire that we had made it to the Pole and, would you believe it, got the answerphone. This time I left a message, cursing to myself that every time I ever reached a significant point of the globe, my wife was out.

The next morning, in comparison, brought a terrifying wind and, with it, equally fearsome waves. When faced with such conditions I, for one, experienced mixed emotions of terror and exhilaration. You can see the fifty-foot-plus waves heading towards you from the horizon like an express train. As they pass through you the boat is lifted up high and almost dry, before being hurled back down into the remaining sea abyss. You peer over the other side of the yacht and the same wave continues its journey, its enormous energy seemingly unspent and its wanderlust yet to be satisfied. Even when it reaches the other horizon you can still see the white-caps foaming at the summit of the mountainous water.

I was given the dubious honour of helming once in such conditions and, frankly, found the solitude and more obvious vulnerability unnerving. The door down to the cabin is locked so you are very much out there on your own, expected to meet the challenge. It really is, literally, sink or swim time, and while you battle to keep yourself and the yacht upright, you become permanently drenched.

The exhilaration, however, comes as a direct result of this danger. When you are at the helm during a sixty-five-knot gale, careering down the backs of fifty-foot breakers, you find yourself almost experiencing this in slow motion. You are cold, you are wet, and you are very, very scared, but at times such as this there is nowhere you would rather be in the world. It makes you feel so very alive.

Mind you, it also gave me a headache, or two to be precise, after the force of the waves twice caused me to crack my head on the ceiling above my bunk bed. I can safely say that this is the only time I have ever sustained an injury while lying in bed. Of course, when Jock Wishart got to hear about this he grew even more surly with me over the radio. He had his point. He was finalising plans for the Ultimate Challenge in the fear that at any time I could injure myself badly enough to postpone the whole trip. By doing so I would be letting down a great deal of people.

On the morning of the twenty-third we woke up to discover that during the night the combination of a force ten gale and the savage sea had ripped away our second, and last, life-raft. A wave had powerfully invited itself aboard, cut away the ropes, and disappeared into the night with the raft without leaving a sign. We now had no life-rafts on the yacht. You did not need to be a genius to work out that if the boat tipped over that would be it. We had the dinghy, of course, but that could only hold a maximum of four people and would not last ten minutes in the full force of the Southern Ocean. The only saving grace was that the person who was helming at the time had not been smacked in the head by the fugitive life-raft, which was encased in a plastic container and therefore extremely hard. Everyone who had been at the helm during the night swore that they had not heard or seen the raft go, but this was not too surprising bearing in mind the noise of the waves crashing into the yacht. It prompted Nig to give us all another safety lecture. He kept reminding us to clip in at all times. There was a danger that we were all becoming a little complacent as time passed by, but the sight of the empty space where the life-raft had been the night before, plus Nig's serious tone, did the trick.

Later in the day the colour of the sea changed from a dark, almost dirty shade of brown to a turquoise blue you normally associate with the Caribbean. As with the weather conditions, it had changed with no prior announcement. This new colourful sea was also friendly to us that day, and made me begin fully to appreciate the environment. We all seem to live in an unbelievably congested world, and yet for the best part of a month I did not see a solitary yacht. People kept talking about depleting fishing stocks, and yet down here we have one of the biggest oceans in the world bursting with fish and untouched, which is the way it should be. We saw no petrol cans, oil pollution, or any rubbish whatsoever. It remained clean and pristine.

On such a beautiful day we first noticed how the temperature was beginning to warm up. The ice was melting off the mast and main sail, we could feel the sun on our faces, and the whole mood of the boat seemed to pick up. We were on our way home, and about to experience the most wonderful thing any of us had ever witnessed.

On the night of the twenty-fourth I first saw the Southern Lights. It was a Saturday night, and for me the show put on in the sky above by the aurora australis will live for ever in my memory. An aurora is a high-altitude, many-coloured luminosity visible in night skies of polar and, occasionally, temperate zones, thought to be caused by the capture of charged particles, especially ones of solar origin, by the earth's magnetic field. The best chance of seeing them would be in close proximity to a magnetic pole. The lights looked like a large green ghost covering the sky, with smoke changing in depth and colour, swirling round and round the yacht. The stars seemed as near and as clear as they do on the summit of Everest, huge chunks of them, sending out slivers of shining light and surrounded by a beautiful fountain of lights almost dancing to a tune like a ballet dancer engulfed by dry ice. All the crew were on deck, staring up at the sky, entranced by the vision. Most of us shed a tear and later admitted to finding the whole experience intensely spiritual.

It also reminded me, once again, of how insignificant the human being really is. We see ourselves as the dominant, superior being on planet Earth, but when you experience the winds and the ice at the top of Everest, the 100-foot waves of the Southern Ocean, or the aurora australis, it only serves to remind you that your power is negligible compared to these almighty entities.

Only Nig had seen the Southern Lights before, and even he admitted that this was the most beautiful sight he had ever seen. I thought of Claire again, and how I would have loved to share the moment with her. And then I decided that if spirits really exist, then this is how I think they would manifest themselves. Although I had achieved my aim of reaching the Magnetic South Pole and seen many sights on the way, looking up into the night sky and witnessing the Southern Lights was the highlight of the whole adventure.

It also signalled the beginning of the end. That night, I felt, was the peak of the crew's camaraderie. We had become very close-knit, and had shared experiences about which all of us will tell our grandchildren. But after the Southern Lights, the finale of the trip, everyone started to look ahead to home and the next challenge. Graham talked about the Himalayas, while Nig and Ez decided to take the boat back up to Sydney for repairs. Ron was now keen to get back home, while Julian was going to make his way to Japan.

I also felt that the comradeship between us was just beginning to become a little strained. Ron, for example, wouldn't talk to Ez. Everyone felt she was too blunt for her own good, and she was always trying to run down Ron, Roy, Julian and especially Pete, because he had been educated at Melbourne Grammar. I was able to silence her instantly just by saying 'Shut up, kipper knickers.' For some reason this always seemed to work, but it hardly helped the atmosphere. Nig used sometimes to go a little too far in winding up people, especially those whom he felt were the weaker ones among the crew. On a couple of occasions I had to tell him to be quiet when his mocking was bordering on bullying. To his credit, he would never take it any further.

By 26 February we caught sight of the first seabirds. Now we knew land was not too far away. This also signalled the time to turn back on our steaming lights and to start looking on our radar again for other vessels. For some reason that day the weather was calm, there was hardly any wind, and the great Southern Ocean was, by its standards, flat. As we bobbed in the water the *Spirit of Sydney* resembled a Chinese junk. Everyone got the sleeping bags out on to deck and then produced clothes either to wash or dry. It was a bizarre sight to see socks hanging over the rails and the rest of the boat festooned with our washing.

The next day we saw our first fishing boat. It felt like a long time since we had seen our last and, although in one sense it was good to start returning to the living world, it was sad to see visible signs that our adventure was coming to an end. The trip back, apart from a few hairy moments, had been considerably easier than the trip down to the

Magnetic South Pole. We were covering more miles each day for a start, we were not being so cautious, having grown well-used to the conditions, and we were a happy crew, having achieved our aims. I am sure if we had failed to reach the Pole for whatever reason, we would have limped home slowly in a sorry state.

As it was we steamed into the Hobart Sound, past the point where we had thrown the rhododendrons into the sea, and soon were able to see the little village of Dover on the coast. By most people's standards the water was still pretty rough. I remembered leaving Tasmania and how frightened I was when we hit the Southern Ocean swell. I could hardly call myself an experienced sailor, but I could laugh at these conditions now because they had been nothing compared to the savage seas I experienced down in the fifties and sixties.

As we sailed up the Derwent river on the morning of 29 February, Leap Year Day, Don and Marge had driven down the coast to see us complete the final stage of the journey. In the last few hours we indulged in a porridge and champagne breakfast and took photos of each other up the mast. By the time we arrived at the marina in Hobart at two that afternoon, they had rushed back up the coast to be there to welcome us home. We did not expect any kind of reception, but people seemed to be there in droves, either from the marina, the general public, or the Australian media. Pete was basking in his new-found glory now, telling anyone who cared to listen that his name was Pete Bland and he had saved the whole trip. I laughed at his energy and enthusiasm, even when asking photographers if they would like to take a picture of him.

Don must have been pleased to see us because he did not utter a word about the condition of his boat. We returned it to him in a right state. The earth leakage needed to be looked at, the main had been ripped, there was a dent in the side of the hull caused by the iceberg, and his once proud yacht now looked more like a floating bucket. But Don was happy, and had laid on food, drink and shower facilities for us all.

That night most of us went out for our last communal meal before going our separate ways in the morning. It was here, back on dry land, that the comradeship of the yacht finally fell apart, and when Graham nearly had a massive bust-up with Pete over Becks. While Graham sat next to me and opposite his girlfriend in the seafood restaurant, Becks and Pete sat together and spent the whole evening flirting outrageously. I could tell that Graham was growing angrier and angrier by the minute. He was talking to me, but had half an eye on the happy couple opposite, and was absent-mindedly bending his fork with so much ease that he would have earned Uri Geller's respect.

When the meal was over there was a detectably sour atmosphere within the party. I pulled Pete aside and told him he had been out of order, and that if he wanted to flirt with Becks that was fine, but not if it meant humiliating Graham in front of everyone else. At first Pete did not see the problem, claiming that Becks was equally at fault. I replied that he was being childish, and if he wanted to carry on then that was up to him, but he could not expect ever to go on a trip with me again if this was going to be his attitude. He thought about it for a while and then trooped off to a less-than-happy Graham.

Meanwhile, we said our farewells to Nig and Ez. I had a begrudging respect for Nig. He had been hard work at times, and would struggle ever to be a success in the diplomatic service, but he was a bloody fine sailor and I would be more than happy to carry out another adventure with him. The same can't be said for his girlfriend, however. I quickly shook Ez's hand but was not too sorry to see the back of her. Looking at the crew as a whole, I think I would be happy to spend time, and maybe another adventure, with any of them, except for Ez.

As she trudged off, and while Pete was apologising to Graham, I looked at the situation in front of me. There I was, having just sailed for thirty days with these guys over 3000 miles in the roughest conditions possible without hardly a hint of trouble, yet within an hour or so of returning to Hobart the crew had fallen apart, with two of them at odds over a woman.

It was time to move on. After a couple of days in Australia, and then a quick stop in Jakarta, I finally returned home on 9 March. Once again I was almost knocked over by three little girls as I walked into my own hall safely returned from an adventure which I presumed would be a doddle after my South Pole trek, but which turned out to be just as dangerous.

Even on the plane home my thoughts had turned to the Ultimate Challenge. I would be leaving in just four weeks, this time for the Arctic, and whereas on the *Spirit of Sydney* I could hide behind the fact that I was a novice sailor, this time, trekking through polar conditions I was familiar with, I would be in charge.

It was a daunting prospect. It is, after all, one thing to walk solo in polar conditions, with only yourself to be responsible for. Now I would have to make life or death decisions for a group of wide-eyed novices dependent on my skills and experience. This, I thought as I focused my attention on the Magnetic North Pole, really would be a true test, not only for the fresh-faced team I was taking, but also for myself.

BREAKING ICE

The Ultimate Challenge, April–May 1996

The preparations for the Ultimate Challenge had been made while I was off trekking to the South Pole and sailing to the Magnetic South Pole. It was a once-in-a-lifetime opportunity for a group of would-be adventurers, provided they could pass the selection process and find a way of paying £15,000 towards the costs of the trip. Each applicant was asked to attend an interview and a full medical including psychological assessment before the team was selected. They all underwent a series of physical tests, and the final choice of personnel was made on the basis of overall suitability rather than experience.

By the time I could finally turn my full attention to the Magnetic North Pole the team of novices had not only been selected, but trained. All the members of the team had their own responsibilities on the forthcoming trip, from shooting to medical courses, dentistry to navigation. It was important that the Ultimate Challenge was not going to be a case of everyone holding my hand for 350 miles. They would have to learn to fend for themselves as much as possible. At the same time, however, the majority of the team would still be novices. It became clear when I was finally able to meet up with everyone that, in my absence, the team very much had their own ideas of how the trip should be done. A little knowledge in a place as uncompromising as the Arctic can be dangerous.

I knew that by the time we were ready to set off from Resolute airport on the south side of Cornwallis Island in the North-West Territories of Canada, everything would be sorted out. But I realised that it had got completely out of hand when, during another short break in France, I made the trip over to London at the beginning of April for just one meeting with some of the novices. In my absence they had become a close-knit group, which in some respects was extremely healthy, but it also made me feel like an outsider which, bearing in mind I had not only set up the trip but was about to lead it, made me feel slightly ridiculous.

I sat quietly at the meeting at first and listened to everyone's contributions around the table. Every so often I had to point out that the idea just suggested would not work. In the end I grew impatient and said that I would like to speak. John Simnett, one of the novices who chaired the meeting, turned round and told me that I could only have five minutes because he wanted to carry on with other business. I was taken aback. These guys had never been in polar conditions, and they were telling me, someone with twenty years of polar experience, that I had just five minutes to talk.

I knew that once we were out in the cold and facing the constant threat of polar bear attacks and open water, the buck would stop with me. I also knew that if the trip failed or, even worse, if there was a serious or fatal accident, then it would be me who would have to answer for it, and nobody else. Yet I was sitting at this meeting listening to plans which were crazy. It ranged from minor, but still important, aspects like taking fifty pairs of socks to keep on the sledge, to acquiring navigational equipment that would not have worked. They were also telling me how the day would pan out. They had made up their minds about the tent plans, when the tea breaks would be, how long it would take each morning to break camp, and how many hours each day they would walk.

That night I telephoned Neill Williams, who would be accompanying me to the Magnetic North Pole, and 'Mitch' Mitchell, who was helping out in the planning and preparation. I told them that I wanted no part on the trip. It was not looking good, and I couldn't see it working. The guys, although quite exasperated with the novices' attitudes, talked me out of my mood.

Then I reminded myself of Margaret Thatcher's quotation which I had put to such good use at the South Pole. I had, after all, started the Ultimate Challenge bandwagon, so I may as well go on and finish it. Mitch, a British army officer, reminded me that in the army if you don't like something it's tough, you just have to get on with it and solve any problems in the best manner you can. Besides, when it is really cold in the Arctic and the shit hits the fan, the novices would adopt a different attitude and look towards me. I reckoned this was good, sound advice, and decided to go ahead. The team never knew I was close to pulling out.

Claire was once again resigned to my absence. In the sixteen years we have been together I have never been away for more than three months in a year, except for 1996. We talked long and hard about what the three trips would entail, and the actual time span of the expeditions and, although Claire was hardly ecstatic at the thought of my risking my life over six months, she was completely supportive of my efforts.

The day before I left for Canada, on 8 April, Borge Ousland came to stay at my house in Lacock. As he had helped me get to the South Pole I had vowed that on my safe return I would buy him lunch at Simpson's-on-the-Strand in London. This was going to be my big meal before leaving for the Arctic. The following morning we set off. Borge, a father himself, knew what I and my family were about to go through, so he tactfully went outside and waited in the car.

Claire was fine, but we could not find Alicia. Eventually, we discovered her in her bedroom. When I asked her if she was going to give me a cuddle she burst out crying and told me that she didn't want me to go. I looked at her beautiful blue eyes, wet with tears, and felt absolutely dreadful. The past four months had finally caught up with Alicia and, in my own selfish way, I only then understood how much my absences were affecting my children. I tried to appease Alicia by telling her that I didn't really want to go at all, but she just turned round and said, 'Why are you, then?'

I sat down for half an hour with her and Claire and tried to explain that it would not be for long, and this would be a one-off year, and that I would never be away again for so long, but none of it seemed to make a jot of difference. I even tried to cheer her mood by promising presents and chocolates, but then felt immediately ashamed by my pathetic attempts to appease her. Borge sat patiently in the car, but I knew I had to get going. I promised I would phone every day and walked to the car, once Claire had prised Alicia's arms from my legs.

I drove away with a large lump in my throat. For half an hour there was complete silence in the car. Borge has a young boy and has been through the exact experience himself. In fact, we both get our children to paint pictures on our skis so that we are constantly reminded of them when trudging through polar conditions. Just as I was passing Swindon Borge finally spoke. 'Okay, you've had half an hour,' he said. 'We both know it's tough, but you've got a trip coming up so now it's time to snap out of it and go for it.' It was just what I needed to hear.

Even so, on reaching Simpson's I was straight back on

the phone to see if everyone had calmed down a little. I then treated Borge to a slap-up meal in keeping with the time-honoured tradition of polar explorers. Scott, Shackleton, Wilson, they all ate at Simpson's on their return from the poles, and even wrote in their diaries of their longing to taste the food there. Then it was off to Heathrow, where Borge caught the flight home to Oslo and I left for Toronto.

On arriving in Canada I was driven to Ottawa to meet Dr Larry Newitt, the man who actually tracks the Magnetic North Pole. I had promised to carry out extensive scientific research for him during the trip. Because of cutbacks Dr Newitt's geomagnetism group could only afford to study the magnetic movement of the Pole every three years, but now I was going to provide him with specific, daily details of the Pole from Resolute airport right the way to the final destination. It meant that for three long days I was subjected to what seemed like a physics degree, armed with a sextant, a theodolite and a proton magnetometer.

On the third day Jock phoned up from England. I had sent back to the office details of the insurance for all the scientific equipment. The cheapest I had found was a thousand pounds. Jock said there was no way we were going to pay for the insurance. The doctor had gone out on his arse to obtain Canadian equipment for a British team. The four novices chosen to do most of this work, once trained by myself up at Resolute, were all tremendously excited by the prospect. I saw it as a good way of keeping them busy on a trip which would test their mental strength. It also provided tremendous kudos for us to be carrying out such research. I was furious and, deciding to pay for it myself, I felt that there was no way we were not going to carry out the experiments.

It really was not looking at all good. On the flight I

decided to calm down and to take firm control of matters once the whole team had assembled. I arrived at the hotel in Edmonton at the same time as the BBC crew who would be accompanying us and the rest of the Ultimate Challenge team. The sight of bags and cases filling up the entire reception area hardly made me feel any more confident. On this evidence we would not even make it to the end of the first day of the trip. I decided it was time to take the bull by the horns.

Upstairs Neill, Jock and myself staged a quick meeting. I thanked Jock for his efforts but told him from the moment we reached Resolute I would be in sole charge of the operation. We were responsible for ten novices who had paid an awful lot of money for the adventure, plus a BBC crew who could provide positive or negative pictures back home. It was up to us to ensure that the trip went as smoothly as possible for everyone's benefits.

The news we received later that Rupert Haddow had failed in his solo walk to the North Pole, after covering only two miles in four days, helped my cause. He had been unlucky in breaking a ski which, obviously, made his plans impossible to complete. It made the novices realise, possibly for the first time, that if Haddow could not muster more than a couple of miles, then the forthcoming trip was going to be anything but a picnic. They all wanted to have their sleeping arrangements confirmed, but I told them they would only find out at the last minute to avoid any cliques forming. We needed to be a complete team, not a set of small groups.

The mood swing continued in my favour on the flight from Edmonton to Yellowknife, where our 737 would refuel. As we ventured further and further north so the climate grew colder and colder. I studied the faces of my team as they clambered off the plane at Yellowknife to stretch their legs. The temperature was $-10°C$, which was pretty cold, but nothing compared to what we would be facing. At least there were still trees here. As we continued on our journey the trees and foliage disappeared completely, to be replaced by tundra. By now you could have dropped a pin in the aircraft. Even the extrovert novices, like Julian Johnson and Paul Kiss, had gone quiet.

By the time we reached Cambridge Bay for a second refuel the temperature had plummeted to – 20°C. As we walked along the small runway Neill and I, who were both used to such conditions, chatted merrily away to each other, but the rest of the guys remained silent. They were quite clearly shitting themselves, and it was at this point that I knew all the pre-trip confidence had gone. Now they would be listening to me. As I clambered back on to the plane for the last leg up to Resolute, I knew I finally had them in my grasp.

Resolute is the small village on the south-western coast of Cornwallis Island where I had stayed prior to each of my previous trips to the North Pole. Everywhere around was frozen over. I had been told that there was some open water nearby, but having sat in the cockpit of the plane to look out for it, I could only see the frozen wastes of the Arctic Ocean, stopped in its tracks by the power of ice. Even the polyanas (small areas of the sea which remain unfrozen all year and provide breathing holes for whales and seals) were frozen up. Resolute boasts a small cinder runway and a shack, which they call the terminal. The actual village is five miles away, and is inhabited mainly by Inuits. They get a social security cheque from the Canadian government, and have a Co-op, small hospital, a dentist's and a school, but that is just about it. In the summer the terrain is just a horrible brown rock. I have often wanted to re-enact here the final scene in the film *High Plains Drifter* where the character played by Clint

Eastwood crosses out the name on the town signpost and in its place writes 'Hell'.

Terry Jesudason was now in charge of High Arctic International at Resolute, providing a boarding-house, fuel, resources and sledges for Arctic expeditions. The local police even carry out a polar bear patrol on your behalf, in case the creatures have travelled this far south. Anybody who goes to the North or Magnetic North Pole would virtually have to go through this place. Terry's husband, Bezal, had died in 1994 and so, in his honour, I brought with me a large bunch of flowers for her. Surrounded by either white in the winter or rocky brown in the summer, some of the local kids were amazed to see so much colour in a bunch of flowers.

We would stay here for three days before setting out on to the frozen ocean to begin the expedition. During this time we would all get to know each other a great deal better, and prepare and rehearse various aspects of the trip. It was also a chance to meet up with Geoff Somers, who had manned the radio for me at Patriot Hills during my South Pole trip. I had asked Geoff to join the party and he had travelled up early to Resolute together with two of the novices, Sue Stockdale and Simon Michlmayr, to prepare for the big group arrival.

Geoff, Neill and myself would be the tent leaders, with four of the novices housed in my tent and three each in Geoff's and Neill's. There would be a fourth media tent for Jock and Ian Howells, the BBC engineer, who were going to film the expedition and send back the pictures to London. This disposition of the group members would remain the same until we reached Polaris Mine, an estimated seven days into our expedition. This is where I would swap the team around a little and, if necessary, tell people whether I felt they could carry on. I made a point of making it very clear to the team members that if there was going to be any mucking about from any of them they would be straight out. There would be no arguments or discussions about this, because they had all signed a contract. As we sat round a coffee table in the Resolute boarding-house everyone nodded their heads. By this time they had come to understand that what lay ahead of them was serious.

Each sledge would weigh 40lb. This, even for the two girls on the trip, would be easy to pull when you consider that I was dragging nearly 300lb of weight on my sledge down at the South Pole. The rest of the equipment would be carried on snow mobiles driven by a couple of Inuits called Samson and Berry, who was later nicknamed Delilah. Jock and Ian Howells would sit on the back of these snow mobiles. Having obtained the necessary film for the day they would shoot off back to where we had set off each morning to send their coverage, via satellite, back to the BBC. They would then enjoy some extra sleep before catching us up at the end of the day.

I felt it was important for the two girls to be together to begin with. Sue Stockdale is a small Scottish girl in her late twenties, a former athlete and a computer expert who used to work for the United Nations. She was determined but probably the smallest member of the group. In contrast, Susanna Wickman, a blonde-haired Swede also in her late twenties, was as strong as an ox and, as befits a ski instructor, the best skier in the party.

I decided that Neill should look after them. There were eight other novices on the expedition. Julian Johnson was a rugby-playing stockbroker who, although a little crude at times, was an extrovert and became the life and soul of the party. An old friend of mine, Rikki Hunt, who was a director of Swindon Town FC and used to run Burmah Fuels, came along after my invitation. As a result he underwent the most rigorous testing to ensure that there were no claims of favouritism. Simon Michlmayr was a watchmaker from Norfolk; although small, he was also stocky and a good all-rounder. Susanna, who was into nicknames, decided to call him 'Little Bull', and me 'Big Bull'.

Andy Higgs was an old friend of Jock's from university days. He was a lawyer by trade, and a big guy, but of all the team he was the most hesitant, mainly because he was neither a natural outdoor nor team man. He had reached his mid-forties and wanted to do one trip like this before, as he saw it, he got old. His wife, a doctor, could not understand him at all.

Mark Kearton was an ex-paratrooper who was, not surprisingly, strong, fit and confident. Now a policeman in the Metropolitan Police Force, he was one of the few members of the team who did not have a problem during the trip. Then we had Mike Hughes, a Territorial Army officer, who was a printer. If you did not know what he did for a living you would guess that he was an army officer.

In contrast, Paul Kiss was a company director of Abbey Underpinning, a very successful London-based construction company. He would always come up with new ideas for absolutely anything. He'd find a different way to put his underpants on if he could. John Simnett was the oldest member of the party. He was a confident guy, with a big grey beard. Interestingly, after the team had undergone psychometric tests, I was told to watch out for John more than anyone else because he was described to me as potentially manipulative. It transpired that there was no reason for any such fear.

The two Inuits, Samson and Berry, completed the team. They were both in their early twenties and considered the whole trip to be a total hoot. They were both small with accents that made their English difficult to understand, but they were great fun and clearly enjoyed themselves, especially when they could rev up their snow mobiles and scurry along the ice.

On 14 April, two days before leaving, we heard that both a Dutch and a French team had failed in their bids to reach the Magnetic North Pole. If anyone on the team still needed reminding that this was not going to be a pleasant walk, then this news did the trick. All the Boy Scout stuff they were talking about in the middle of London had long been forgotten now that we were in the High Arctic in extremely cold conditions. I was also pleased to see how everyone was now listening attentively to advice and instruction. During the day I gave them a long lecture about polar bears. Having seen quite a few in my time I was able to convince them that they are far from cuddly white teddies, rather highly skilled hunters who appear from nowhere in the wind. The team had to be on guard at all times.

That night we went through a trial run of putting up tents, cooking inside them, and then settling down for the night outside the boarding-house. The temperature was recorded at – 30°C. Of course, they all could put up a tent, but appreciated the various tips provided; for example, how to take your shoes and boots off inside the tent, how to put the carry mats and thermo mats down, and never to leave a shovel near the tent just in case you rip the material.

The BBC team was filming our training and acclimatisation in Resolute before flying back to London with the material. We hoped to see them later at the Magnetic Pole. The reporter, Charles Rhodes, pulled me aside one morning to say he was worried that Ian Howells, who would be travelling with us, would find it impossible to film, operate the satellite equipment and look after himself with just Jock to help him. I had no option but to ask

Mark Kearton to join Jock and Ian in their tent each night. The following day Mark sought me out. He told me that he was not paying £15,000 to look after Jock Wishart, and added that he wanted a categorical assurance from me that when we reached the Polaris Mine someone else would take over in Jock's tent. I gave him my word.

Finally, on 16 April, we were ready to begin. The equation was simple: we had 350 miles to cover in thirty days. If we were any slower than this we ran the risk of facing rapidly melting ice and open water. On reaching Resolute airport, our starting point, I delivered a final speech. I told the team that we were all in this together, and if there was any falling out then those involved would be on a plane home once we reached Polaris. Some people would have good days, while others would have bad days. Those having the bad days would need help and encouragement, because we were all bound to experience them at some point.

I asked John Simnett, as the oldest person in the party, to lead us out in single file on to the frozen sea. We were a convoy of thirteen people, stretched out into a thin line. John was under orders not to go too fast. Again, as with the South Pole trip, I did not want my team to burn themselves out too soon and so, at least on the first day, I did not want to walk more than four hours, building up the length of time out on the ice as the week progressed.

In the middle of Allen Bay we practised our marksmanship with the rifle, just in case a polar bear wanted to get to know us. Having served in the Falklands, Mark Kearton was our obvious firearms expert. The rifle given to me seemed to be jammed. I took it over to the Inuit boys who played around with it before insisting it was okay. Placing the butt next to my shoulder I pressed the trigger just as a precaution, to make sure there was nothing inside it. The resulting boom nearly took my shoulder off.

I could not believe that a live bullet had been left in the rifle. I could, of course, have killed anyone at any time.

Still, at least we made eight miles in four hours on the first day. Bearing in mind we were taking it easy, it was a pace I was more than happy with. It was amusing to see each member of the group, except for Neill and myself, wander off into his or her own little corner to pee into the ice, until I remembered I did exactly the same down in the Antarctic. That night both Andy and Rikki were a little quiet in my tent. I felt they were suffering a touch, and decided I should go round the troops just to rally them a bit.

I was even happier with the team by the evening of the third day. We had stepped up the pace to six and a half hours, which translated into fourteen miles. I still had reservations, but saw no reason, barring ill luck or accidents, why we could not succeed in our mission. During the course of the next day we had to struggle through icy rubble caused when pans of ice hit either land or each other. By now Julian, Michael and, in particular, Susanna had cold burns on their faces. They are not dangerous, but uncomfortable, and if not looked after can develop into full-blown frostbite.

The weather up to this point had been kind to us, and yet still three members of the party had been affected. I told them that if their conditions grew any worse I would have to consider withdrawing them at Polaris. The boys, less used to the cold than Susanna, were more bothered about their condition. On day five the weather finally turned a little on us. There were gales up to twenty knots and I decided, having consulted with Neill and Geoff, that it would be too risky to expect the novices to get away from camp without any hiccups in such conditions. Besides, it would be a good idea to give those with cold sores a day to relax in the warmth of their tents. Instead we slept, read, and played games, notably 'Two Pigs', which basically meant throwing two colourful pigs on the floor like poker dice. If they landed on their noses you obtained a certain number of points, or on their feet, or if one landed on its feet and the other with its legs up in the air. It was amazing to see company directors throwing themselves so enthusiastically into such a stupid game in the middle of nowhere on top of the Arctic Ocean.

It was still a bit windy on day six, but we got going, with Geoff out in front. After a while Neill's tent was given the lead, while Geoff lagged behind, occasionally doubling over his course. After a while John Simnett approached me and said that he was extremely worried about Geoff. He reckoned that Geoff was struggling with hypothermia, or perhaps the going was just a little too tough for him. He added that I should go over and have a word with him.

I could not believe what I was hearing. Of all the people out here in the high Arctic, the very last person I would expect to be having difficulties would be Geoff Somers. Yet here was a guy who had the total sum of five days' experience in such conditions expressing his doubts over a colleague who had spent the best part of thirty years at one pole or the other. I was pleased that my talk about instilling teamwork and looking after each other had clearly sunk in with John, but I felt this was pushing it a bit far. There was no way I was going to insult Geoff by asking him if he was coping all right. If Geoff had a problem, he would be the first to tell me. So instead I went back to Geoff and asked him if he wanted some salami. He turned round and said, 'I've got a real problem here.' I asked him what it was. 'It's just that we're going so bloody slowly that I've got to exercise my legs more, so I'm doing triple the distance just to keep me interested and warm.' I left him to his own devices.

That evening I stressed to everyone again that they had to look after themselves, and that if they failed to cover up their flesh then they would pay for it later. Susanna was the worst when it came to this. Although she was the most experienced novice in the cold weather, she just would not listen, and kept skiing with her face exposed to the biting cold. I first asked Neill to give her a quiet lecture, but when it became clear that the advice had been passed up, I took her to one side and told her that unless she did what she was told she would be off the trip on arriving at Polaris. She turned round and said there was no way I would carry out my threat. I told her that she should not think I would not do it because, with less than a third of the trip completed, I could not think twice about her safety.

On the morning of day seven we could see the Polaris Mine on the coast of Little Cornwallis Island, just a tiny dark speck in a sea of white. As we ski'd closer and closer so the speck turned into a building. Polaris is the most northern mine in Canada. Canadians live here, mining for zinc and lead. During the summer months barges take the mined substances back to the Canadian mainland.

By reaching Polaris we had covered fifteen and a half miles which was by far our best day of the trip to date. Here we obtained new munchy bags, a new set of clothes, and sent off mail. On putting up our tents I announced the new changes of tent personnel in front of an anxious sea of faces, as if I was announcing the school's rugby first fifteen. I had Susanna in my tent so that I could check on her face and, if need be, give her a hard time.

During the last few miles before reaching Polaris virtually all the team were coming up to me and asking if I had decided who would be the one to share with Jock. Michael Hughes started offering me his bars of chocolate. He asked me about my children, before coming out with the real reason for being nice to me: 'Have you chosen who's going in Jock's tent?' I told him I had not. Michael then begged me not to choose him, and offered me some more food. Simon Michlmayr also made it clear that he would be far from happy if he was asked.

I had a problem here. Nobody wanted to share with Jock. Even Ian Howells, the BBC cameraman, was sending e-mails back to London saying that he did not mind the cold, the ice, the hardship or the work, but he drew the line when it meant having to look after one of the so-called experts. In the end I went over to John Simnett. Rather tentatively I asked him if he minded sharing with Jock. John immediately agreed, which was a huge relief. Just before reaching Polaris, Andy Higgs had come over to me. He admitted that he had been close to pulling out after a couple of days. He really did not think he would be able to carry on. He then added that he had now come through his personal anguish, was looking forward to the rest of the trip, and was more than willing to help out in any way he could. As I ski'd back to my place in the convoy I reflected on how hesitant Andy had previously been, and how much he had grown in stature over the past couple of days.

On day eight the plan was to ski across Crozier Strait and up to Kavalik Island. Half-way through the day John suddenly went downhill. I asked what the problem was and he admitted that, through sharing with Jock, he had not managed to have any breakfast or, for that matter, an evening meal the night before. Jock was supposed to be in charge of the cooking, but they ended up eating ginger biscuits. John, it transpired, did not want to rock the boat with one of the tent leaders. I provided him with some Mars bars, and told him, if need be, just to cook for himself and leave the others in his tent to their own devices.

On the ninth day we passed by Black Point on the edge of Bathurst Island. This is an area I am unlikely ever to forget, having had a close shave with a polar bear there during my 1984 trip. It reminded me that we were venturing into the very north now, and that we were drawing ever closer to the dreaded Polar Bear Pass. Reminded of my frightening encounter last time round, we all spent the day looking nervously over our shoulders. The sight of large bear prints only served to intensify the group's anxiety.

As we woke on day ten we all knew this was going to be one of the most dangerous days of the whole trip. This was the day when we would attempt to walk straight past Polar Bear Pass. Polar bears have an unnerving knack of emerging from their hibernation and hunting people with amazing stealth. I was bloody scared, partly for myself but also because I kept thinking of the nightmare scenario of one of the novices being picked off and mauled to death by one of these beautiful but deadly animals.

As the day went on matters grew increasingly worse. Rubble reappeared, and this time we encountered blocks of ice the size of houses. Worse still, conditions deteriorated until we had a white-out situation. Now, although a white-out may mean that a human cannot see ahead more than a few yards, a polar bear is in its element. The wind was also beginning to pick up. In fact the only thing we could see were bear prints, and these came virtually every one hundred yards.

If you think our plight could not get much worse, then think again. In such conditions our snow mobiles were unable to find us. We were in the middle of large blocks of rubble surrounded by a white-out and, no doubt, hundreds of polar bears. Two thoughts immediately crossed my mind. First, it would mean that we would have to camp in just about the worse place possible, right next to

Polar Bear Pass. We had just provided a drive-thru fast-food service for the bears. Short of setting up flashing neon lights, we could not have advertised ourselves any more clearly. Secondly, if the weather conditions stayed as they were for five days, which was highly possible, then the snow mobiles would not find us and we would run out of food. The trip would be over and, more worrying still, our lives would be in some danger.

As I surveyed the situation I kept my thoughts to myself. After all, I mused, I was sure the rest of the team would not particularly like to choose between slow starvation and death by polar bear.

IN THE NICK OF TIME

The situation that confronted us that night in Polar Bear Pass is as good an example as any for why I sprouted more grey hairs on the Ultimate Challenge than on any of my other polar expeditions. Ahead of us other trips had either failed or were in desperate trouble, and none of these comprised mainly novices.

I had been told there was a great deal of rubble ahead, quite possibly too much for the snow mobiles to handle. I sat down in my tent and began to work out the possibilities. If we never saw the snow mobiles again we would, after five days, have to go on to half rations. Alternatively, we could just keep on going ourselves by loading up everything on to our sledges, but that would prove too demanding for some. Then another thought entered my increasingly concerned head: maybe I should forge ahead with half the team, leaving the remainder behind to be picked up and flown back to Resolute. At least then some of the team still stood a chance of making it to the Pole. But how would I be able to make the selection? And what would I say to those who would be left behind?

I went for a quick walk around the tents. Each had a rifle in readiness for a polar bear attack. Rikki Hunt's knees were beginning to give him some grief now, even though he would try his hardest to disguise the fact. 'You okay, Rikki?' I used to shout over to him from time to time. He would always put on a cheery smile, grit his teeth and answer back, almost too assuredly, that everything was absolutely fine.

Once again I felt guilty. On previous trips my guilt had always been directed towards my family back at home, wondering how I was faring and trying to face up to the daily possibility of bad news. But this time, as I trudged through the ice past each tent, I thought about the novices. All of them were so determined to make it to the Pole and enjoy what for most would be their trip of a lifetime, that perhaps their enthusiasm and determination had blinded them to the stark realities of the trip. Maybe I, too, had forgotten that while the likes of myself, Geoff and, to a lesser extent, Neill had vast polar experience, these members of the public had none. Had I been totally irresponsible?

This thought process would probably have continued for quite some time had the eerie silence not suddenly been shattered by the glorious sound of snow mobiles. Everyone emerged from their tents, waving frantically and blindly through the pea soup of the white-out and towards the noise as it grew louder and louder. Eventually the boys emerged, smiling and waving back at us. I don't think Samson and Delilah have ever received such a reception before in their lives, but that night in Polar Bear Pass they were treated like heroes.

Mind you, they had their own agenda here. Having set up their own company, Hunters and Trackers, its prestige and reputation were on the line. They realised that it was almost as important for them to make it as it was for us. Consequently, they had been working their butts off all day, dodging in and out of rubble, and feeling their way through the white-out.

This was one huge problem removed, but the time was so late now that we still faced a night spent in the middle of Polar Bear Pass. How no one blasted the shit out of a colleague I'll never know, because everyone that night tossed and turned, forever with one eye on the tent door and the other on the rifle. As a precautionary move we loaded the guns with plastic bullets, partly to scare and not kill the bears, but also to make sure that if, for whatever reason, an accident took place, it would not be a live bullet. We also had a slug called a cracker, which was pretty harmless but made a hell of bang. Again, this was designed to scare any bear away from us.

I had also prepared some food for the bears which was placed on our sledges some distance from the tents in the hope that if they came to scavenge they would settle for the sledges and not the humans. In the morning, having first ensured that none of us had been a bear's dinner, we inspected the sledges and discovered, to our surprise, that they were untouched. We had been lucky. The local bears had obviously had their fill of seal that night and had decided to leave us alone. But none of us was under any illusions. The bears knew we were there all right, even if we were not as certain about their whereabouts.

That morning, on day eleven, I saw my first rooks, back from their winter vacation in warmer climes. This confirmed my fears. The Arctic summer was now not too far away, and the team really had to get moving. I was very keen to get to the actual coast of Bathurst Island because I had been told that some open water had been seen nearby in the sea. I therefore decided to find ways of reducing the loads each team member was pulling on his or her sledge. This, as you have read elsewhere, is a familiar and almost necessary ploy of mine in polar conditions and here, edging closer to the Magnetic North Pole, was no exception.

The worst culprit was Paul Kiss. I did not realise until close inspection that he was pulling at least ten extra bags of gear, much of which could go. In particular, he had sewing equipment and badges of his various sponsors. He was supposed to sew them on to his clothes before leaving Resolute, but ran out of time, and therefore intended to finish the job en route to the Pole. This was the first to get slung out, followed quickly by his spare bowl until, at the end of the purge, I had reduced the weight of his sledge by 30lb. After that, he was flying on the ice.

Towards the end of the day's walk Jock provided an unintentional cabaret. Everyone had completed seven hours' walking by the time Jock arrived on the back of the snow mobiles and decided to walk the final hour or so with us. He leaps off the snow mobile, as fresh as a daisy, and ends up half buried in a deep pile of powdery snow. What was interesting to notice was how each team member merely carried on with his or her weary plod, leaving Jock, with just his upper chest and head showing, to get himself out of the problem.

Day twelve proved to be one of the most critical days of the whole expedition. It was extremely cold, made worse by the windchill factor caused by the thirty-knot winds, yet by now the team had grown confident enough to carry out its business as usual. Three of the four groups (Jock's tent would follow on) seemed ready and willing to get going that morning, except for Geoff's contingent. He was supposed to be taking the lead to begin with that day, but something seemed to be holding his lot up. After another ten minutes of hanging around in the cold I told Neill to go on ahead and take over the lead. We would catch them up shortly.

I then went over to Geoff and found an extremely cold Rikki looking a little glazed. I could immediately see that something was wrong. I asked him what the problem was and, predictably, he insisted there was nothing wrong. But this time I could quite clearly see that there was. I felt his hands and they were frozen. I placed them under my armpits and realised that they were on the brink of frost-bite. The subsequent warming-up operation would take some time, and Neill's group was already a distant blur. The longer we stayed behind helping out Rikki, the further Neill would trudge, fully expecting to be caught by us later that morning. He had no idea that we were still rooted to the camp. Worse still, the conditions were rapidly deteriorating. The wind was really blowing by now, and the visibility was fast becoming non-existent. It was looking as though another white-out was forming.

The only tent still standing was Jock's. He and Ian Howells would be joining us later with the snow mobiles. Even at times like this there was an amusing episode in the midst of the cold, the winds, and Rikki's dangerously cold hands. While the rest of us were very casual about having a shit outside in relative company, Jock liked to wait until the rest of us had got going on the morning's walk before retiring to his tent to carry out his movements in peace and solitude. He was totally unaware of the drama that was unfolding outside. Under such cir-cumstances there was nothing for it. We all burst into Jock's tent in order to speed up the warming process of Rikki's hands, to discover Jock squatting down in a corner. Poor old Jock leaped a mile, but before he could really start complaining about our intrusion Geoff told him, in no uncertain terms, that we were going to use his tent whether he liked it or not. Slowly some colour returned to Rikki's hands.

A further fifteen minutes later, with Rikki's hands back to a relatively normal temperature, we set off in search of Neill's group, hoping to stick to the ski trail. Luckily for us, Neill had shown tremendous initiative. Guessing that there must be something up, he had decided to turn his group round and head back from where they came. I was therefore doubly delighted to see them all, firstly because it allayed fears that we might lose them, and secondly because it showed how much we were all now working as a team. Buoyed by this sense of togetherness, we made good progress for the next day and a half until, by the morning of day fourteen, we were fewer than 150 miles from the Magnetic North Pole.

At this point we came to a place that meant very little to everyone else on the trip, but a great deal to me. Unbeknown to my fellow adventurers, I had my own personal battle to overcome. It was here, at Cape Kitson near the Organ Heights, that I nearly drowned, or died of hypothermia, depending on which means of death would have taken place first. Back in 1984, during my ultimately successful solo walk to the Magnetic North Pole, I fell through the ice at the exact spot at which I now found myself. I was lucky, as I explain earlier in this book, to escape from the icy clutches of the water back then, and I knew it. But there were two factors that now made me very scared indeed.

We had just heard on the radio that a Swiss team had given up on its attempt to reach the Magnetic North Pole after its snow mobiles and dog sledges went through the ice at Cape Kitson. This did little to improve my nerves which were already frazzled by nightmares recalling my own dice with death. Although their regularity had decreased, I was, and still am for that matter, troubled by the same recurring nightmare. I see myself, quite vividly, plunging feet first through a small hole that has suddenly opened up in the ice to reveal water. My arms are flaying wildly as I lose my balance and try desperately to grab on to something. But my hands slide limply across the ice as my sledge follows me into the water and drags me down beneath the surface of the sea to what, I assume, is a watery death. Returning to the very same place again, even after all those years, was very difficult to take.

I decided, primarily because of the open water the Swiss encountered, to make a beeline for land and crack on up the coastline of Bathurst Island. It was not the most direct route, but it was a great deal safer than attempting the open water of Cape Kitson. We hit land at Greenwich Hills and continued heading north towards the tip of the island. Across the sea you could see, quite clearly, the beautiful mountains on the Brunel Peninsula of Devon Island. They may have been twenty-five miles away, but the snow-capped peaks were crystal clear on one of the most beautiful days of the trip. It was, in fact, a typical day in the Arctic, one dominated by breathtaking scenery but always with the potential of extreme danger in the background.

At the camp site that night I decided to call a meeting between the tent leaders. In another two days we would reach the northern tip of Bathurst Island and would then be facing yet more, and this time much bigger, rubble. We needed to discuss reducing the weight of the sledges by a great deal in order to get away with not using the snow mobiles. I told the guys that I was concerned about Sue, John and Rikki. We were taking off some of Sue's load already to ease her burden, while John was suffering with eczema. Rikki's knees, meanwhile, were still causing him problems.

I then called everyone else in. The consensus of opinion was that we would try to go as far as we possibly could with the snow mobiles before loading up the sledges with as little as possible. If we struggled after that, then the possibility of ditching people, who would be picked up, of course, by a plane, would come into play. Although we had become a great team by now, it was interesting to see how the determination of some to make it to the Pole created a dog-eat-dog atmosphere. A couple of the men brought me aside later and said that they would prefer not to offload the scientific equipment, and suggested getting rid of one or two of the team instead. They had it all worked out. 'If you get rid of her, we'll still be able to take the rest of the gear with us,' or, 'Sod him, he's an old bastard,' were the general sentiments. Some of them repeatedly told me how well they felt, as they were worried that they might be in the firing line.

It reminded me a little of that Monty Python sketch where the four shipwreck survivors are floating in a dinghy on the sea, and holding a discussion about which one of them they should eat first. What was really interesting about how the team reacted to the threat of being dropped was that, prior to the start of the expedition, Jock had given me a piece of paper providing details of who wanted to share with whom in the tents. I refused to use this because I wanted to select the tent personnel and avoid establishing cliques, but when I looked at this list again I noticed how the very same people who wanted to share were now secretly sticking the knife into each other. Funny animal, the human being!

The following day, as we ski'd around the top of Bathurst Island and across to Lonely Island, I introduced a series of lists for people to think about and debate. For example, all of us had to come up with our ten favourite songs of all time, and explain why. Apart from it being quite good fun, it helped to alleviate either the monotony or the pain experienced by most of the team. It got people thinking for days. Then we moved on to films, which caused great argument. One of the guys would choose *The Right Stuff*, for example, which did not go down well with Susanna, who plumped for sloppier stuff starring people like Clark Gable or Audrey Hepburn. Neill and Rikki spent more and more time discussing the FA Cup final which would shortly be staged at Wembley. As Neill's Manchester United and Rikki's Liverpool were playing, it provoked much discussion about the teams, the tactics and, of course, the predicted result.

Just off the coast the following day we passed Cape Lady Franklin, which in itself provides a classic story of the Arctic and a reminder to all of the dangers constantly surrounding us. In trying to find the North-West passage in 1847 the British explorer Sir John Franklin disappeared. Lady Franklin sent numerous expeditions to try to find him but his body was never recovered. There have since been countless trips to try to discover what fate befell the great man, and as many books, but his story remains a mystery. The actual Cape Lady Franklin is a spot of breathtaking beauty, but also one of the most barren places on earth. As I stood there and looked across the sea towards Mount Percy, I found the Franklins' story quite sad, but also romantic. In their honour the Canadians named a whole district of the North-West Territories after them, comprising the islands of the Canadian Arctic and the Boothia and Melville peninsulas.

We would not be walking on land again until we reached the Magnetic Pole itself. As we ski'd across the ice now edging further and further out to sea, we came across what were the remains of a musk ox. It looked as if four bears had got hold of this great big shaggy animal and ripped it to shreds. All that was left, sprawled out on the ice, were bones, fur, and a mass of blood and guts. I noted with interest how each and every one of the party skied slowly past the remains without saying a word. It was a reminder, as if we needed one, of what a polar bear would do to us given half the chance.

Eventually the conversation piped up again. Which were the ten best restaurants everyone had eaten in, and why? What's the best meal you could possibly make for someone? Here Paul Kiss came into his own describing, in graphic detail, the exact ingredients needed, and how to slice or chop them up, for a starter, main course and dessert. After a while, as we looked forward to our dried chilli con carne that night, we realised we were being masochistic, so we changed the subject. When did you lose your virginity? Everyone owned up except Susanna, despite general harassment to reveal all. Then we realised that this, too, was an area in which we had been missing out for the past three weeks.

Day nineteen was 4 May, and a day that everyone was looking forward to. A plane would be coming in to remove a lot of the now superfluous weight, such as a generator, and to bring in new food supplies and, of course, munchies for our individual munchy bags. We all saw this also as the end of the second third of our expedition. There was no way I was going to ditch anyone at this stage, even though some were clearly struggling. It was also the time when I would be swapping tents around, which meant that everyone was trying to avoid Jock yet again. The bribes had by then increased from a chocolate bar to, in the case of Michael Hughes, a meal on him at the RAC Club and, in Rikki Hunt's case, a free day at the British Grand Prix at Silverstone, including free transport, lunch and corporate hospitality.

They were making it very hard for me. I did not think it would be fair for the girls to go in with Jock, so I turned to Andy Higgs, his old university friend, and asked him to share for the next five days, with Simon Michlmayr then taking over for the following five days. I was rather hoping that we might still be some way off the Pole by then, which would enable Michael and Rikki to up their offers even more.

The plane needed to land on skis, and therefore required a flat surface. It took some time to find a suitable spot, circling round and round above us in the sky. For a moment I feared there would be too much rubble, which would have forced the plane to turn round and head back to Resolute leaving us in dire straits, but the plane eventually landed a mile away from us. The snow mobiles shot off over the ice to collect the treasure that had been brought out to us. On returning, we were presented with a veritable feast of goodies ranging from biscuits and cakes to apples, oranges and cans of Coke. Our sledges also became much lighter with the removal of much of the BBC kit.

All this time reports and pictures had been sent back to London, via satellite, following our progress. The small films were mainly shown on BBC *Breakfast News*, but also appeared frequently on the lunchtime and early evening editions, plus BBC's *Newsround*. Obviously, though, the films stuck to the physical challenges and showed little of our lives in the tents, which is just as well bearing in mind how much we had all degenerated. There was, however, one exception. Having told everybody else to have a thorough dental check-up before leaving England, I was eating one of my beloved pork scratchings when a side of my tooth fell out. Paul Kiss, who we nicknamed Doctor Death, had medical and dental training and immediately got to work. While I was laid out on my back Michael Hughes shone a torch inside my mouth, Susanna poked away with various metal implements, as if administering torture in a James Bond film, and Kiss filled the gaping hole with amalgam. Ian Howells filmed all this which, amazingly, made all the BBC news programmes that day.

The environment and the sense of danger that one feels in polar regions, really do remove any self-consciousness. The human is cut away in such conditions until all warts are on show. Three weeks earlier none of us really knew each other. We were hesitant in each other's company, and felt that there were certain things a human does each day which remain private. Well, once you've been out in the ice long enough all of that dissipates into the cold air. So, for example, on receiving my new personnel for the tent I instructed them all that in my tent there were three rules strictly to adhere to: one, there should be no belching; two, no farting; and three, under no circumstances should there be any wanking.

It was impossible to imagine my saying that to ten strangers three weeks before at Edmonton airport, yet by that time on the trip we had not only grown utterly accustomed to each other, but had been almost forced by the conditions completely to open ourselves up for general scrutiny. This is what a trip to a pole will do to people who will return to their old ways, of course, on returning to normality back in England. Out here, surrounded by nothing but white, the human reveals itself to be just another animal.

On the twenty-first day since leaving Resolute we finally saw a polar bear. He was the biggest one I had ever seen, even from 300 yards away. He was tracking, pausing every so often to cast a quick glance at us, before continuing on his way. He was not interested in eating any of us, which was rather good of him. Even so, we were all poised with our guns, just in case. Most of the novices were snapping away with their cameras, excited by such a beautiful vision. Despite the obvious danger, seeing a fully grown male bear with King Christian Island behind him provided one of the most amazing sights on the whole trip.

Samson and Delilah wanted to shoot off on their snow mobiles to try to make the bear come a little closer, but the general feeling within the group was that we were happy with the current situation. Still, at least they went off and shovelled up a piece of frozen polar bear shit for me to post back to Mitch in England. I had promised him a souvenir, and thought he would see the funny side of opening up a parcel all the way from Resolute to discover a rock-solid bear turd inside. Well, he would see the joke eventually!

Andy Higgs, the one novice I was perhaps most concerned with at the start of the trek, was now really coming into his own. Andy became an excellent navigator and basically took over these duties. As we ski'd closer and closer to the Pole, he would be shouting out instructions to the rest of us. 'We need to be two degrees over to the east,' he'd announce, and so accurate were his findings that we all grew to trust totally his navigational decisions.

This was also the time, with less than a week to our goal, that I saw signs of the team beginning to fall apart. There was nothing sinister about it, and it certainly did not affect performance one iota, but I could tell that quite a few of the novices realised that quite soon the whole adventure would be over, and they would be transported back to their previous lives. This I found to be quite sad. When you are skiing all day in single file it gives you plenty of time to think. There is no doubt about it, skiing to the Magnetic North Pole or, for that matter, circumnavigating the world in a yacht is an escape from reality. Out there in the middle of absolutely nowhere, issues such as paying gas bills, speaking to the bank manager and so on become not only totally unimportant, but almost farcical. Once again I was reminded how much of an irrelevant speck I was on this planet, surrounded by terrain and elements far more powerful and significant than me. In this context, do the daily hassles of everyday life back in what we like to think is civilisation really matter?

Of course, back in normality such problems are crucially important, but in the Arctic all you have to think about is skiing, mile after mile, day after day. Although he was a friend of mine, for example, it wasn't until nearly the end of the expedition that I discovered that Rikki Hunt had just split up from his wife. With the end of the trip now looming, a time which should be of great joy for succeeding in our mission, Rikki was beginning to ponder whether his marriage would be saved or not. Michael Hughes was having problems with his company, while his wife was heavily pregnant. I could tell that these dual pressures played heavily on his mind towards the end. Andy Higgs's wife had told him before he left for the Arctic how opposed she was to his participation on the trip, while John Simnett and Paul Kiss were both worrying about their girlfriends. And so on. I used to keep skiing up and down the line of novices, just to make sure that all was well. I could tell almost immediately which ones were happy to talk and which were alone in their own thoughts.

By day twenty-five we recorded an inclination of 89°40'. Now we knew we were drawing close to the Pole. Neill's tent took the lead that day and recorded the best mileage of the whole trip, some eighteen miles. Everyone seemed to try their hardest for Neill. Despite his shyness and quietness, or maybe because of these characteristics, Neill had proved to be an extremely popular figure on the expedition.

The Inuits, meanwhile, decided to go out and shoot a wandering caribou. On returning to camp that night they proceeded to skin this poor animal before chopping it up into steaks. Samson and Delilah were extremely proud of their catch and insisted that we all came and joined them in eating the caribou stew they subsequently cooked. I tried to advise the team not to because they had been eating nothing but dehydrated food all trip and would have bowel problems if they started to eat something as rich as caribou. I knew I was fighting a losing battle as soon as I smelled the cooked meat. One by one they filed past the camp fire and, two hours later, one by one they disappeared into a distant corner for a prolonged squat.

By the end of 11 May we all knew we were going to make it. The rubble was proving a difficult obstacle to get over or round, but there seemed to be a steely sense of determination to finish the job, no matter how hard it was becoming. Neill was in a particularly good mood that day, having just discovered, courtesy of a radio call, that Manchester United had beaten Liverpool 1–0 in the FA Cup final, with Eric Cantona scoring the only goal. Rikki, therefore, was not so bright that day, although he was later cheered by the news that his good friends from their Swindon Town days, Glenn Hoddle and John Gorman, had just taken over the England football team.

Neill was pretty ill the following day, day twenty-seven of our trip, and our penultimate one before reaching the Magnetic North Pole. To be a little more precise, he was acting as if he had eaten the whole caribou himself. The rest of the team split up the contents of his sledge and shared the pulling of his load. I told him to grab a lift on one of the two snow mobiles, but he turned round and told me where to go. 'There's no way I'm getting on a snow mobile for the last day after all the walking I've done, even if I shit myself all day,' was how he put it.

We came to the Noice Peninsula where, further inland, the Pole would be found. Standing back on iced-over land, one could look back over where we had all come and see the most staggeringly beautiful sight of the frozen ocean behind. Ahead lay terrain not dissimilar to somewhere like Dartmoor, with tors and geographical outcrops sprouting up everywhere. That night there was a party atmosphere in the camp. We all knew that the following day we would achieve our goal.

Some of the guys decided to go for burn-ups on the snow mobiles. I grew very nervous about the very real possibility of one of them having an accident and breaking a leg which would immediately end his trip. I thought that we had gone all this way and here they were risking it all, but I also felt that I had shouted and barked out enough orders over the past month. Sure enough, John Simnett got his leg trapped in one of the tracks and was lucky to escape with nothing more than bruising.

Everyone was up bright and early on the morning of 15 May. I suggested to Neill and Geoff that on this, our final day, we should let the novices go on ahead of us to find the Pole first. They were virtually their own bosses now in any case, and I felt that they were not only capable of doing it off their own bats, but also deserved their moment of triumph. I put all the novices' names into a hat and asked Samson if he could lend us a hand. He pulled out Andy Higgs from the hat which, bearing in mind how much the man had grown in stature during the trip and how much navigational work he had put in, was rather fitting. He would therefore lead the team to the Pole, and when I announced this it was greeted with unanimous approval.

They provided a tremendous sight for the rest of us, skiing on ahead in a long, well-disciplined line across the ice. We decided to take photographs of them inching their way closer and closer to the magical moment when the GPS would verify their position to be the site of the Magnetic North Pole. Watching them forge ahead I felt a sense of overwhelming pride. Suddenly they started jumping up and down and waving their arms in the air in salute of their triumph. They started to take their skis off, and then proceeded to hug each and every one of the group. We were just a few minutes behind them but, having learned from my experiences at the South Pole, I felt it was only right that the novices should have their moment for themselves, before the so-called experts arrived. It was only after the Union Jack had been planted on a ski pole into the ice that we, too, walked the final few yards to the Pole.

A few of the team were in tears, and they all seemed to make a point of thanking me. The first person I thanked was, you may be surprised to read, Jock Wishart. I recognised all the hard work he put into the trip before we left, and all the first-class organisation. I told him that I knew we'd had our differences during the trip, and that it had been hard work, but I wanted to let him know how much I appreciated his efforts. The conditions were windy so we then quickly erected our tents and started to take readings for Larry Newitt back in Ottawa. We wanted to make absolutely sure that we really were at the Magnetic North Pole because our compass reading would change virtually every hour. When we recorded a position of 89°59.49', Dr Newitt confirmed by radio that as far as he was concerned this was not only the Magnetic North Pole, but that nobody else had ever gone so close to ninety degrees in history. This was therefore a proud moment, made doubly so by the fact that various geographical and geological groups over the years had been rather sniffy about adventurers carrying out scientific surveys on their behalf. I guess we had all just proved them wrong.

For the first time on the expedition we pitched up two tents together, and opened them up to create one huge communal area in which all seventeen of us crammed in. We poured out some tea and nibbled away at a packet of biscuits someone unearthed from a sledge. I thanked them all and congratulated them for their wonderful efforts. I added that never before had so many people made it to the Magnetic North Pole, let alone novices, and I also told them that we had recorded the closest position ever to ninety degrees. Sue Stockdale had become the first British woman to reach the Pole, while Susanna was the first

Swedish woman. I, in the meantime, had just become the first person in the world to reach both magnetic poles in the same year. We ended the meeting by saying three cheers for Samson and Delilah, who were happily waving and smiling away in the tent.

We were not totally out of the woods yet, however. We were running out of food and we still had to get to a place called Isaachsen, some twenty miles away, where an old airstrip had been laid many years before when a weather station had been inhabited. Bad weather was closing in and time was running short. So, the following morning we all set off on the snow mobiles through heavy winds and round and over fields of rubble. Camping at Camp Hazy that night we reached Isaachsen on 17 May in yet another total white-out. We knew that two planes were coming in for us the next day and prayed that they would still be able to do so in such appalling conditions.

At midday they duly arrived, complete with Franz la Rosee, the managing director of our main sponsors Breitling watches, together with his wife, Christine. Victoria, a Breitling girl, also emerged in her furs for photos with the conquering heroes, which would help serve the needs of the sponsor. I remember coming up to the woman to plant a kiss on her cheek. She recoiled in horror and said, 'Oh my God, you stink to high heaven!' She was right, of course, and neither of the girls would come anywhere near any of us. We all piled in to the planes and were taken back to Terry Jesudason's place at Resolute.

That night, suitably washed, shaved and better clothed, we had our last dinner together. The BBC had rigged up an interview between Andy Higgs and his wife. She, if you remember, had told him how opposed she was to his participation on the adventure. Now, however, she told him how proud she was that he had made it to the Pole. This cheered everyone up, and set the scene for a wonderful last evening together. A few made yet more speeches. I made a point of thanking Jock again, but the most poignant speech came from, of all people, Geoff Somers.

Geoff rose self-consciously to his feet, and began by telling people how he was not a man of speeches and did not like them. But he then went on to add that this had been the most enjoyable expedition he had ever been involved with, and wanted to thank each and every one of us for making it so memorable for him. Having known Geoff quite a few years, I felt a lump in my throat at this moment.

I sat back for a while and weighed up the trip. It was great, of course, to reach the Magnetic North Pole, but what I learned from it more than anything else were the lessons of man-management and teamwork. It was a fantastic exercise for all of us. Here were ten novices, from very different social and career backgrounds, who had never been out in the cold in their lives. It was my job, together with Neill, Geoff, Jock, and the novices themselves, to mould these people from nothing into polar adventurers who were able to take on everything the elements and nature could throw at them, both as individuals and as a team.

Undoubtedly the novices discovered a great deal about themselves, and unearthed hidden talents and characteristics which may well have remained dormant. But maybe it also provided a pointer to the human being. The novices had been specially selected for this trip, so we had a fair idea that they would stand half a chance of succeeding, both physically and mentally. Perhaps in the Arctic environment, if thrown into the situation, many if not most people would also learn to survive. It's the deep-end mentality, if you like, and I am convinced that those who feel that walking in such conditions day after day would be beyond them would surprise themselves if actually confronted with the opportunity.

We all flew back to Heathrow and to our previous lives. Bidding farewell at the airport, the novices all went their separate ways, much the better for their experiences over the past four weeks. No matter what else they may do in their lives, they can all look proudly at themselves in the mirror and say that they had what it took to reach the Magnetic North Pole.

As we were getting ready to return to England Geoff started talking to me about whether he should have a crack at the North Pole itself. He had never been there in his life and fancied the challenge. I was happy to think of nothing else but to return home, but then Geoff's comments touched a nerve. The North Pole! This, after all, had been my only failure in all my polar expeditions. But it registered as a big and painful blot in my book. The thought of another attempt at the Pole began to eat away at me, but Geoff had suggested it first and I did not want to queer his pitch.

Besides, I was on my way home. It had been an amazing past six months, a time when I had reached the South Pole, the Magnetic South Pole, and now the Magnetic North Pole. Now it really was time to go home and become a husband and father again. My brother picked me up from Heathrow and dumped me on my doorstep. The first thing the children wanted to know was whether I had brought them any presents. I told them the best present was that I was not going anywhere for a long time. I would be home with them, even at Christmas. And as I said this I felt extremely happy at the prospect.

Yet, at the back of my mind the North Pole began to niggle away. It seemed that my polar jigsaw was missing one piece. Despite everything I had achieved, the North Pole had beaten me. That's how I saw it. I took the fact that I had been hauled off the ice in great physical and mental pain some distance from the Pole very personally, even now, fourteen years on.

When Geoff phoned me up a couple of months later to tell me that he had changed his mind and would not be attempting a crack at the Pole, the coast was now clear. I didn't say anything to anyone right then, but I knew, even back in July 1996, that I would be returning to the Arctic again. It was a drug, I was clearly addicted, and it was almost as if the North Pole knew that one day I would be returning for the rematch.

UNLUCKY FOR SOME

The North Pole Expedition, 1997

Plans got under way in August 1996. My first decision was to find a partner for the expedition. The pain, fear and sheer mental and physical hardship of my solo South Pole trip earlier in the year were still fresh in my mind and, having failed to reach the North Pole in 1983, I fancied dragging someone along with me this time.

I knew, just by recent record, that the Arctic would still provide a huge barrier to break through. There had been nine aborted attempts previously by Britons. Ranulph Fiennes, of all people, had failed on four occasions, while Rupert 'Pen' Haddow had been unsuccessful twice. All this was pretty disconcerting, but at least my track record had been consistently good in the past and I saw no particular reason why, with luck, I should not succeed. Still, I was under no illusions. The North Pole is undoubtedly harder to reach than the South Pole, partly because temperatures start a great deal lower, but also because the Arctic has rougher terrain, drifting ice and open water to contend with. It took me fifty-nine days to walk the 680 miles to the South Pole, whereas this time I had worked out it would take me at least seventy-five days to traverse the 496 miles to the North Pole.

As a compromise for having a partner this time, I also plumped for an unsupported trip, partly because the 1983 effort was supported – I didn't want any similarities with 1983 at all – but also because I firmly believe that to succeed without any aid is always the greater achievement.

My next action was to telephone Borge Ousland, my Norwegian friend and fellow adventurer. Despite all the help I had received from him in the past, and all the times we had seen each other at our respective homes in England and Norway, we had never actually worked together on an expedition. Borge, as I have stated before in this book, has my total respect. He and his fellow countryman, Erling Kragge, walked unsupported to the North Pole in 1990, the first men ever to do so. As if this was not enough, Borge then took it upon himself to reach the Pole in 1994, entering the history books again as the first solo success. The Norwegians' success was in stark contrast to us Britons.

Borge's initial reaction, over a beer in London, was extremely positive. What particularly impressed him was the thought of a joint Anglo-Norwegian project. Virtually ever since Roald Amundsen pipped Robert Scott to the South Pole back in 1912 there has been an intense rivalry between the two nations when it came to polar exploration. None of this had ever bothered me. As far as I was concerned the hatchet had been buried between British and Norwegian explorers, especially as I realised that without Borge's help and equipment I would not have been able to walk to the South Pole. We both felt that the first ever Anglo-Norwegian expedition would break down the last remaining barriers.

There was, however, a snag. He had failed in his attempt to cross the whole of the Antarctic continent while I was 'merely' going for the South Pole. Borge, being Borge, meant that he was planning to have another crack at becoming the first man to achieve this feat later on in 1996. Despite this he was still keen to join me in the Arctic. 'Maybe I can get back in time from the Antarctic before you start your walk,' he suggested. 'Then we can go for the North Pole together.' Not content with walking over a thousand miles in appalling conditions down in the Antarctic, Borge was up for more misery on the other end of the planet.

We sat down and studied the dates very carefully. There was no doubt in my mind that Borge would, this time, succeed in the Antarctic. He was as strong as an ox, and doubly determined in his quest after his failure the year before. It was also technically possible for Borge to have a week's break before joining me in the Arctic. But neither of us could guarantee the state he would be in after such an adventure in the Antarctic. All it would need was a frostbitten toe and our joint expedition would be off. We both realised we could not take that risk.

I asked Borge if he could recommend a fellow country-man. He suggested either Torry Larsen or Rune Gjeldnes, both of whom had an impressive track record in polar adventuring. The two Norwegians made the Umanaq–Isertoq expedition across Greenland in 1994, an 870-kilometre trip which took them thirty-one days. This served as a training expedition for their 'G2' Greenland lengthways attempt two years later. Between March and June of 1996 Larsen and Gjeldnes completed the longest unsupported ski trek ever made. The final distance of 2928 kilometres was covered in eighty-six days.

These figures seemed pretty impressive to me. I tele-phoned Larsen first. He thanked me for my interest but explained that he was returning immediately to his duties in the Norwegian navy. I then contacted Gjeldnes. He had no pressing commitment, but seemed reluctant because he had just returned from his latest expedition and had to deliver a number of lectures. He just did not believe he would have the time to prepare for the North Pole.

I suggested that no decision had to be made immedi-ately; we should meet up first to see if we got on with each other. I flew to Bergen, courtesy of British Midland, who supplied all our flights, and we met in a bistro called Dickens. I would say that within a few minutes we had gelled. As the number of beers mounted we grew more and more excited about the prospect of walking, together, to the North Pole.

Rune, at twenty-six nearly fourteen years younger than me, turned out to be a delightful man. His main concern was that he felt it would be unfair for me to gain all the sponsorship and for him to join up at a later stage for the actual expedition. He just felt that he would not be pulling his weight. I had never come across someone before in my dealings who was worried about not working hard enough.

His other concern was over cooking. He told me that whenever he has been on polar trips before, he has always insisted on doing the cooking. He just did not like other people doing it. Would this be a problem for me? I looked at him and thought: 'Are you kidding?' I assured him that I had absolutely no problem with someone else doing all the cooking for me on the trip.

In return I expressed my only slight worry concerning my assumption that Rune might well be a great deal fitter and faster than me. I only had to look at his credentials to come to such a conclusion. Rune was brought up on a farm near the Trollheimen Mountains on the west coast of Norway; in other words, he was virtually born on skis. He spent much of his spare time mountaineering, kayaking on sea and river, and skiing both downhill and cross-country. He enrolled in the Norwegian navy in 1992 and completed a course to enter the Norwegian Navy Seals, becoming a career professional in the élite Marinejegerkommandoen later that same year. Here he gained considerable field experience during four years of service in the special navy units. This meant parajumping, diving, kayaking, skiing, mountaineering, and extensive field duties in Arctic conditions. There are only fifteen such men in Norway. Rune, in short, and behind his friendly almost boyish exterior, was a trained killer.

I explained to him that it was likely he would be a great deal quicker than me. I knew that a great deal of friction was created when Ranulph Fiennes and Dr Mike Stroud attempted their crossing of the Antarctic continent in late 1992/early 1993 because Stroud would often forge ahead leaving a huge gap between the two men. Rune insisted that this would not be a problem. We shook hands, promising each other that we would reach a final decision within a fortnight.

I returned the next day with a hangover. Claire was resigned to my intentions. She always knew I would not leave the North Pole with my wretched attempt back in 1983. She was not exactly ecstatic with the news, especially as I had been away so much during 1996, but she was at least pleased that this time I would be accompanied. She was even happier with the situation when she met Rune, who came over to Wiltshire to tell me that the trip was on. Despite his young age, Rune still has traditional values. He takes off his shoes at the entrance of our hallway. He brings our children presents, and writes a thank you letter to Claire for putting him up. He even takes his own plate and puts it in the dishwasher. In short, he is one of the nicest guys I have ever met.

He was still uncomfortable about what he perceived to be his lack of help in preparing for the trip. It had taken him and Torry Larsen four years to plan for the G2 expedition, and he could not quite understand how I expected to be able to do it by myself in just a matter of months. In fact, the preparation was remarkably easy.

For a start, I knew exactly what equipment we needed after my successful trip to the South Pole using primarily

Norwegian gear recommended by Borge Ousland. This served a double use because Rune, who was also concerned about having to make compromises over the equipment we needed to share, discovered that I was plumping for the identical equipment he was used to. It transpired that we used the same sledges, the same tents, the same skis and the same sleeping bags. Virtually everything was the same.

Most of my sponsors were old friends who were more than happy to come on board again with me. The whole trip would cost £80,000, with the major sponsor being Typhoo. Rune was a little surprised to discover how easy it had been to accumulate the necessary funding for the expedition. The Prince's Trust were delighted with the success of the Ultimate Challenge trip and pleased that we decided to call this adventure the Prince's Trust North Pole Expedition. The BBC also continued its interest in my polar experiences, asking me to help produce a video diary of the trip, and also agreeing to send up Charles Rhodes and the news team to film us in the Arctic prior to setting off.

Finally, to my amazement, I gained official approval from the Royal Scottish Geographical Society. I had never succeeded before in establishing a fruitful relationship with the Royal Geographical Society so, on the basis of nothing ventured nothing gained, I approached their sister organisation in Glasgow and was immediately approved.

We decided that the best time to begin the walk would be the beginning of March 1997. We would venture out from Ward Hunt Island, the northernmost tip of Canada and the nearest mainland to the North Pole, and would hope to complete the trip in seventy days. We knew that the conditions would not be exactly pleasant. The temperature would be desperately cold, and there would not be much more than a couple of hours of daylight, but we faced little alternative. If we started any earlier we would be catching the tail end of the Arctic winter, something nobody in their right mind would want to face, and conditions which would make landing an aircraft impossible. If we left it any later we would be pushed very hard to achieve our goal before the ice began to melt and the summer drift of the Arctic Ocean caused us to be continually sent off course by as much as ten miles in a day. At that rate we would never reach the Pole.

We left England on 24 February. Claire and the family seemed more at ease this time possibly than ever before. I put this down to the fact that Rune, in a very short amount of time, had already become part of the family. Claire trusted him and felt as if her old man was in safe company. I also felt remarkably stress free about the impending trip. The South Pole trip the previous year had been important for my credibility, while I did not fancy travelling down to the Magnetic South Pole again in a boat if we had failed in our mission. I also felt a great deal of pressure on the Ultimate Challenge because of the huge responsibility I had to deal with.

Yet I felt totally different before the North Pole expedition. I felt very comfortable with the Anglo-Norwegian concept, and I suppose the fact that everyone had failed before meant that success this time was not expected. I felt confident, of course, and would give it my best shot, but I knew that precedents had not been set.

We flew first to Calgary, then on to Edmonton, and finally up to Resolute, otherwise known as Hell on Earth. It was good to see Terry at High Arctic International again, and the rest of the people who remain out in this wilderness. The plan was to start the expedition after four or five days of acclimatisation, but the weather turned out to be far colder than initially expected. With a constant ten-knot wind, the thermometer sank down to as low as minus fifty degrees.

The other problem was that the world and its dog seemed to be at Resolute. Several expeditions were also booked in to High Arctic International, and were ahead of Rune and me in the queue to fly out to their respective starting points. A crew comprising two Koreans and a New Zealander was attempting the same trip as us, while another Korean was attempting the walk solo, but supported. An extraordinary American woman called Pam Flowers, who was barely five feet tall but as tough as they come, was also trying a solo but supported walk, as well as a Dutch team and an English team of women who would be walking to the Pole in a series of relay legs.

Rune and I managed to be third on the list of flights out of Resolute and up into the edge of the Arctic Ocean. We loaded up our freight on to the Twin Otter and discovered that the weight of our sledges came to 330lb, a heavy amount to drag by anyone's standards. We had catered for this and already knew that the first weeks would be extremely slow-going while we pulled such a weight through rubble and icy pressure ridges. As a result we had enough supplies to last us for eighty days, if necessary, hence the extra weight. We still felt, however, that it was a better system than the Koreans and New Zealander, known as the 'Polar Free', who opted for smaller sledges and backpacks. Our theory was that if they came to open water they would have to walk around it, while we would simply strap our two sledges together to form a boat.

It was five o'clock on the morning of 5 March when we left Resolute in the dark. Six hours later, via a fuel stoppage at the Eureka weather base, we arrived at Ward Hunt Island, landing in a light that was, at best, twilight. Rune and I were eager to get going so, after a few photographs taken by our photographer David Spurdens, who had flown up with us and would help to man the radio from base camp back at Resolute, we were on our way.

I always knew the start would be tough. I needed all my strength just to move the full weight of my sledge, and it was still desperately cold. For me the biggest difference about Arctic and Antarctic adventuring is that on a walk to the South Pole the sledge is at its heaviest when the temperatures are at their warmest, going to a lighter weight as it becomes colder in constant twenty-four-hour daylight.

That night, after a gruelling half day of walking, we had managed the princely total of two miles in distance from Ward Hunt Island. We were not even out to sea yet, but on the edge of the ice shelf. As we started to prepare for the night Rune suddenly announced that he had lost his blue bag, which contained, apart from his Walkman, tapes and cigarettes, a bible, photographs, a piece of embroidery from a family friend, and trinkets from his old girlfriend. It was clearly bothering him.

What had happened was that the pilot was in such a hurry to drop us off and get on his way back to Resolute before the weather closed in that it all became a little hectic. Rune's bag had been left on the ice and the pilot had placed it back inside the aircraft. I understood Rune's predicament. I always carried my own mementos, charms and trinkets on such trips, such as photographs of my family, a wooden cross given to me by a friend at Robnor, my 'Z' beads and, on this occasion, a lucky charm given to me by Rajiv Wahi, the managing director of Typhoo.

Rune said that we should carry on regardless, but I saw that it was disturbing him and insisted that we should stay where we were until the next day, when a Dutch team flying up for their own expedition would be able to give us the bag. One more day would not make any difference to us, I reasoned, and I knew that if I had lost such a bag

I would have felt uncomfortable venturing out on to the sea. Rune agreed, but admitted he owed me a case of beer for the inconvenience.

The one day turned into a week. The Dutch were unable first to get out of Resolute because of bad weather, and then could not land at Ward Hunt Island because of further poor conditions. The winds made the temperatures appallingly low, and on a couple of days we had white-out conditions. There was nothing else we could do except sit in our tent and wait. As the delay continued Rune became more and more guilty about the situation, but I reasoned with him that we would not be walking in white-out conditions in any case, and that the Polar Free, who were out on the sea, had drifted two degrees in one night. At least sitting on the ice shelf we were not drifting off course.

At long last, on 13 March, the blue bag was duly delivered to us by the Dutch and we could get on our way. Rune cheered up at once as soon as he laid hands on the bag. Once we had walked two miles back out on to the ice shelf we hit some of the worst rubble conditions I have ever come across. Some of the blocks of ice were almost vertical, reaching ten to twelve feet in height. Trying to haul a sledge with almost 300lb of equipment over these proved a desperately difficult task, always with the threat of injury looming. After the first day we had managed to cover the less than impressive distance of one mile. The next day proved even tougher. All we could see in front of us was a sea of frozen rubble. Rune and I were out there on the sea for six hours that day, panting and gasping, and needing all our strength just to drag our sledges through, over and across these huge icy obstacles. After six hours we had advanced by two hundred metres.

This was very tough to take at such an early stage of the expedition, but at least we knew, having studied previous routes taken by the Canadian Richard Webber and his Russian partner Mikal Malankov, that we were likely to cover just seven miles in the first nine days. By day four, however, it became impossible to carry on. 'We'll have to start relaying,' Rune suggested to me. I nodded my head in agreement. 'Come on then,' I said. 'We'd better start.' We dumped half our equipment on the ice, took the remaining gear on our sledges over the rubble for a couple of hours, left the contents, and returned with our empty sledges for the rest. This, of course, was not exactly ideal. It meant that we were covering more mileage than we needed to, and if a white-out had suddenly formed we would have been hard pushed to find our equipment. If we and our tents had been parted, this would almost certainly have resulted in death. Still, it was the only way we could make any progress and, despite all the extra work, we found that we were just about keeping up to our schedule. Then, on our fifth day since starting out from the ice shelf, Rune suddenly shouted out to me. 'David,' he yelled, 'we've got a problem.' He was bending over his sledge and looking at a three-inch-square hole in the side.

Our first reaction was disbelief. We had ordered a Kevlar sledge which should withstand just about anything thrown at it. Kevlar is a very lightweight, high-impact resistant material which is used by the likes of Borge Ousland with great success. We'd both used such sledges many times before and therefore had no reason to doubt that we were using top-notch equipment this time as well. Besides, short of drilling a hole into the side of the sledge, it was impossible to tell by using the naked eye. Once the terrain had produced a hole, however, it was clear that the material used for our sledges was fibreglass.

The next thought to hit us was that our plans to use both sledges as a boat across open water were scuppered.

One of the main reasons for going with the two big sledges was for this purpose. We knew that we would, almost certainly, face open water at some point during the expedition, and had trained for this accordingly. Rune had tried it out back in Norway, while I used my outdoor swimming pool back home at Lacock, lying across the water on a couple of makeshift sledges.

We sat down to analyse the situation. I knew that we were in trouble. The last thing I wanted was to travel a further sixty, eighty or one hundred miles before the sledge gave way completely and the trip was aborted. I didn't see the point in that at all. I would have preferred to stop and return for a fresh assault in 1998 the wiser for our experience.

Rune, as was his fashion, rolled a cigarette, took a couple of puffs, and then gave his view. 'We must carry on,' he announced, finally. 'We'd be stupid to stop because of a maybe. We've got to continue until the tank's empty.' I gave this a moment's consideration and replied. 'Fine. I've got no problem with that.' I thought about the concept of the Prince's Trust. It was all about achieving success through initial adversity. The Trust tells people to keep on plugging away because, despite the hardship, you may well emerge successful. After Rune's reaction, and my own thoughts, all ideas about aborting the mission were over. The expedition would continue.

Each night after this we would carry out a salvage operation on Rune's sledge. This meant strengthening the side with the hole by using bits of wire. This seemed to do the trick and, as we entered our second week, we began to find our rhythm. The going was, of course, still slow, but we were now growing used to the conditions and to each other.

Rune found some of my English sayings a little strange, to say the least. I remember shouting out to him, 'Bloody hell, Rune, it's cold enough to freeze the balls off a brass monkey.' He stopped skiing for a moment and slowly repeated my words. 'Cold ... enough ... to ... freeze ... the ... balls ... off ... a ... brass ... monkey? What do you mean?' I spent half an hour trying to explain myself.

Each night I would put up the tent and Rune would get on with the cooking. It was dehydrated stuff, of course, but still not bad. Rune would serve up a whole range of dishes, from spaghetti bolognese to Irish stew, mushrooms and chicken to cod in sour cream. Once, after dinner, Rune asked me if I wanted some more. I replied, 'Do men like sex?' Again, he'd repeat my sentence very slowly, and with a quizzical look on his face. 'Do ... men ... like ... sex? I asked you if you wanted some more food, David. You'll have to explain that one to me.'

After a while Rune began to resemble a housewife on ice. We would be trudging along and he would suddenly ask, 'What do you fancy for dinner tonight, David? Chicken and mushrooms, or maybe some fish?' I used to take the mickey. 'Are we talking before or after the hors d'oeuvres?' Rune would ask, 'Hors d'oeuvres?' I would then ask for some caviar. And so this banter went on as we hauled our sledges across the ice.

After dinner we would talk. During the course of our trip we did not have one disagreement which, bearing in mind the conditions we were facing, was some achievement. Rune would speak of his childhood in the mountains and, often, he would describe his experiences in the marines. He would explain how to attack and enter a submarine, for example. I would sit there listening and watching him as he would go into some detail about entering from the torpedo chute. 'You'd have to make sure that the door would not squash you as you made your way inside the sub,' he would point out, helpfully, just in case I was thinking of trying it out for myself.

Another time he talked about saving hostages from a boat. 'You would arrive by helicopter, coming out of the sun to make it difficult for the terrorists. You would then abseil down firing at the protagonists.'

Rune is probably the toughest guy I've ever met. We would often be out in minus fifty temperatures sorting out our equipment. I would be covered from head to foot in thermals, but Rune would sit on a sledge with his face completely exposed to the winds, rolling up a cigarette and looking completely at home. His skiing technique was far superior to mine but he would always ensure that he would never forge too far ahead. Mind you, he was also capable of getting his own back on me. Once he watched me skiing up to him, smiled and said, 'David, your skiing technique's getting better.' I said, 'Thank you, Rune,' really pleased by the compliment. Then, after a short pause, he added, 'Well, better than a two-year-old.'

The English word Rune took to immediately was 'bugger'. I'm afraid it is a commonly used word in the Hempleman-Adams vocabulary and, as you can imagine, one uttered frequently while walking across the Arctic Ocean. Within a few days Rune was as bad as me. Every so often the word 'bugger' would float back to me as I ski'd behind Rune. It always lightened the moment and brought a much-needed smile to my face.

Midway through the second week Rune's sledge was deteriorating. The hole had widened and in the same position on the other side a new hole had appeared. We kept on strengthening the damaged areas using wire, and still believed that the sledge would hold out. It might have given us more cause for concern had an extraordinary incident not taken our minds off the problem.

We knew that a twenty-one-year-old Englishman called Alan Bywater was close by. We had met him at Resolute. He had reminded me of myself when on my first attempt at cracking the North Pole. He, too, was trying it both solo and unsupported. A computer studies student based in Vancouver, he had done his homework, and sought advice on all aspects of the trip from Richard Webber, one of the foremost experienced Arctic explorers in the world. The only thing he lacked was experience, and the only way of getting experience of real Arctic conditions is to be in the Arctic. During the course of the first week we could, occasionally, hear the click-clacking of Bywater's ski poles on the ice and boulders. Sound carries a long way on the frozen Arctic Ocean, so even though he was some distance behind us, we knew he was following our tracks.

On 21 March, having reached 83°15', we were eight miles from Ward Hunt Island and more or less on schedule. We had just eaten our dinner and were settling into our sleeping bags when we heard someone shout hello from outside. We looked at each other in amazement. I think I said, 'Who the hell is that?' It turned out to be a severely frostbitten and hungry Alan Bywater. The lad had had enough sense to shout out instead of just entering our tent. The chances are that if Rune had just heard the sound of crunching on ice, he would have assumed it was a polar bear and started blasting his rifle. Instead, he opened up the door and Bywater tumbled in and said, 'Thank God you guys are here!' Neither Rune nor I spoke for a few seconds. We just blinked and stared at him. Eventually we got to our feet. 'Bloody hell,' I said. 'You'd better come in.'

It turned out that he had fallen through the ice into freezing water and had lost one of his two sledges. Unfortunately, the lost sledge carried his Argos, his radio, his fuel and his stove. Alan was lucky to haul himself out of the water in the first place, but even more fortunate to find our tracks and discover us in time. 'I've been walking for six hours,' he told us as he shivered and spluttered. I am certain that if he had not found us he would have succumbed out on the ice to a pretty horrible death, brought on by hypothermia. I peered outside and noticed that conditions were fast deteriorating. Within half an hour we had another white-out. Alan had no base manager back at Resolute, which meant that he could have gone five days without sending a radio report and nobody would have batted an eyelid.

He already had frostbite on his fingers and toes. He was extremely cold, extremely grateful, and extremely hungry. 'I can't thank you guys enough,' he kept on saying. We put some of Rune's food down him, as well as plenty of fluids, and gave him all of our warm clothing. Rune seemed pleased that his food was so gratefully accepted and gobbled up, even if Alan happened to be starving and desperate. We even placed him between us to warm him up. The result was that we saved his life, but we also knew that Alan still needed to be airlifted out as soon as possible. He was in a bad way and needed treatment. He was also eating into our food and fuel supplies, as well as our radio batteries. Although this was, from a selfish viewpoint, a concern, we did not feel aggrieved about this. He was, after all, a fellow adventurer, and I was well aware that I too had cocked up when I was young. It is, like mountaineering, an unwritten rule that you must always help out any explorer in distress, and we were delighted to do so.

Rune and I had to get out of the tent in a minus eighty with windchill temperature to put up the radio antennae and contact the Bradley radio crew back at Resolute to ask for an emergency medivac, a special airlift. Each hour after this I had to radio giving updates on the weather conditions. It was just our bad luck that the weather closed in, rendering it impossible for any plane to land.

While I took care of the radio and Alan, Rune spent four hours out on the ice flattening the larger bumps with a shovel and creating an area big enough for a plane to land on, marking out the strip with plastic rubbish bags.

The atrocious conditions meant that the plane had to land sixty miles north of our position and sit out the storm. 'You've got another day stuck with us,' I told Alan. He smiled, weakly, but he was desperate to get out of this hell. Luckily, the next day the weather finally cleared. We were now into our eleventh day since leaving the ice shelf at Ward Hunt Island. The Twin Otter landed at the strip Rune had created, half a mile from our tent. Rune and I then placed Bywater, who was unable to walk any more because of his frostbite, on to one of our sledges, and dragged him across to the plane. I made both Alan and the two pilots sign my book confirming that we had received no aid from any of them. If we had it would have made our trip supported.

Rune and I stood at the end of the makeshift runway created on the ice, marking the pressure ridges which jutted up. As I watched the Twin Otter take off my heart was in my mouth. I even said out loud to Rune, 'It's going to be close.' The visibility was still awful and the plane must have missed the ridge by no more than three feet. My guts were really churning because it occurred to me that, in trying to save one person, we might have ended up killing three. In the end, however, Alan made it back to Resolute, where he was immediately given medical treatment. He knows, more than anyone, how lucky he was to survive the ordeal.

It was a strange feeling watching the plane disappear. We had no choice, of course, but to help Alan as much as we could, but the incident undoubtedly disrupted our flow, as well as used up what could have been vital supplies. Rune and I had built up a fantastic rapport, and when a third party suddenly appears, no matter who or what he or she may be, it can suddenly feel a bit like a crowd. Polar conditions do this to people. They strip away all niceties, exposing every conceivable wart.

We also took a breather the next day, partly because of more bad weather conditions but also because we felt exhausted, both physically and mentally, by the Bywater incident. After that we started to motor again. The size of the ice rubble began to lessen and the flat ice pans grew larger. We still had problems with Rune's sledge, of course, but we remained confident that we would still reach the Pole. After seventeen days we had travelled twenty-five miles, and after twenty-seven days we had passed the fifty-mile mark. Although in terms of mileage we had a long, long way to go, the conditions were fast becoming more favourable, we were getting stronger, and our sledges were getting lighter. The darkness of Ward Hunt Island had already been transformed to almost total daylight as we ventured further and further out into the Arctic Ocean.

My mood was improved even further when I received news over the radio that the Royal Scottish Geographical Society had decided to award me with the prestigious Livingstone Medal. I was to join a list of former recipients which included the likes of Chris Bonington, Neil Armstrong, Sir Francis Chichester, Sir Edmund Hillary, Roald Amundsen, Robert Scott, and Lord Kitchener of Khartoum. I was told that the RSGS had agreed to a recommendation from its awards committee at a meeting held on 20 March. I was to be offered the medal for my 'distinguished contribution to the advancement of geography'. I was to receive it from the President of the Society, Lord Younger of Prestwick, the former Secretary of State for Scotland and Defence Minister, at the annual President's Awards ceremony held in Glasgow later in the year.

To say that I was absolutely gobsmacked by the news is almost an understatement. I was told my achievements had been recognised, not only because of my success with the seven summits and the poles, but also because I was a lay explorer who had contributed to the advancement of science. I was also being honoured for my work with the Prince's Trust, which encouraged the future explorers of the world. I must admit I felt genuinely honoured and humbled when I was told all this. It should have been a massive morale-booster for me. From this point Rune, who had previously referred to me as 'old man', started calling me Mr Livingstone instead. In return I stopped calling him 'the kid' and resorted to 'Nansen', after Fridtjof Nansen, the Norwegian polar explorer and politician. This became a running joke throughout the remainder of the trip.

I did not have that long, however, to enjoy the news. As the days went by, and as the weather began to warm up a little, so more storms and drifts occurred. With drifts you tend to get open water, and also pressure ridges forming when two pans of ice push against each other. On one day I actually felt a ridge forming under my feet, and I had to run, hauling a sledge at that time weighing around 200lb, in order to avoid ending up sitting on top of a newly formed ridge. That was a very dangerous moment, and one that left me shaking for a moment or two afterwards. Rune, however, found the whole episode amusing. 'I've never seen a man run so fast with a 200lb sledge behind him,' he shouted as I shot by. 'I didn't know I could do this either,' I replied. I made my way back to Rune who was laughing. 'I never want to do that again,' I added. 'I reckon we've got more of that to come yet,' he said, just to cheer me up.

On our thirty-sixth day we came to open water. Rune and I went our separate ways to see if we could discover a crossing point. After looking for three miles each side of the lead, we came to the conclusion that our best bet was to attempt to cross where we were. Although Rune's sledge had holes in both sides we felt that, by giving it some stability, we could still tie the sledges together to make a boat. I was filming Rune kneeling on the makeshift boat as he tried it out; seconds later I was dropping the camcorder and running to grab the rope to help Rune haul the sledges back out of the water. Rune's sledge was filling up quickly with water and lurching over to one side. If we had not reacted quickly, we would have lost the lot in the water. If nothing else, we knew that a boat was now out of the question. We had no option but to walk five miles and find a suitable crossing.

Despite our obvious problems we were making increasingly good progress. Even in storm conditions we were now reaching nine miles a day and knew, within a week, we would be up to twelve miles. We fully expected to be recording fifteen-mile days as we drew closer to the Pole. By my reckoning we were just one day behind schedule, and with the terrain becoming ever easier to deal with, we expected to reach the North Pole by around 20 May.

On our forty-fifth day since leaving the ice shelf at Ward Hunt Island disaster struck. I didn't say anything to Rune at the time, but I noticed that morning that my wooden cross had snapped. I tried not to let it bother me, but I took it as an omen. Midway through the day I suddenly came across a huge piece of fibreglass. It was not unusual to see small slithers of Rune's sledge lying on the ice because of the terrain, but it was clear, on picking up the fibreglass, that this time a large portion of Rune's sledge had broken away. It made me think instantly of the *Apollo 13* film I had watched before leaving for the Arctic. When the first signs of trouble were apparent on board the Apollo craft Jim Lovell, who dreamed of walking on the moon, said, 'We've just lost the moon.' It was at that moment that I knew what he meant. We had just lost the North Pole.

Looking ahead I noticed that Rune's supplies were tumbling through the hole and on to the ice. He was oblivious to all this, merrily strutting along the ice and no doubt wondering why the sledge was beginning to seem lighter. I ski'd the thirty feet between us and handed him the fibreglass. We turned his sledge over to reveal a large, gaping hole. The two holes on the sides had joined together and the bottom of his sledge had given way.

We sat down to consider our options. As far as Rune was concerned, it was time for another cigarette. After a few experiments we discovered that we could not even place our light supplies around the hole in the middle of the sledge. They were still falling on to the ice, and we knew that we still faced a few ridges and rubble ahead. We couldn't make a rucksack because we didn't have the material, and one of us could not carry 200lb on his back. Neither of us could pull one sledge with all the equipment on it, so we tried to have both of us pulling the one sledge but, after trying to load up, we realised that we could not squeeze everything on. A fortnight later it might have worked, but not now.

The last thing we wanted to do was to make a rash decision but, having put up our tent, we came to the painful conclusion that all our options had just run out. It would have taken at least a week to find a suitable sledge and have it flown out to us, a time in which we would have drifted so far off course we might never be able to regain the lost ground. Besides, by obtaining a new sledge it would have made the trip supported, something neither of us wanted. Back in Bergen we had agreed that if one of us was injured, going solo was not an option. We had become a very close team, and we were either going to reach the North Pole together or not at all.

My eyes began to well up as it finally dawned on me that the expedition was over. The North Pole had, yet again, beaten me. I asked Rune, 'Have you ever seen a grown man cry before?' He just looked at me and said how sorry he was. This immediately made me feel bad, because it was not my intention to make Rune feel guilty. None of this was his fault. It was just bad luck. I said, 'If I am about to call for a plane to pick us up you have to promise that you will return with me in 1998 to finish off the job.' He took off his glove, looked me in the eye, and shook my hand. That was that. After thirty-seven days' walking we had managed 120 miles. There would be no more.

While we waited to be transported home we made separate lists in our diaries about what could be improved for the return next year. We decided to put bigger tape around the ski poles, a lighter weight canopy on the sledge, and not to take so much maintenance kit. As soon as the pilot saw Rune's sledge he shook his head and just said, 'Next year, then?' Nothing more needed to be said.

On the flight home to England I consoled myself. Last time I returned from a trip to the North Pole I was a beaten man, scared, in pain from my cracked ribs, and naive. This time I knew that Rune and I would have reached the Pole if only his sledge had not given up on us. We felt fit, confident, and were suffering from no injuries or frostbite. I knew that there would have been a couple of rough patches ahead of us, but we had covered the worst terrain by far, and with the sledges getting lighter the odds were beginning to be stacked in our favour. It was frustrating to realise all this, but also comforting.

We arrived home on Friday, 2 May. During the course of the last few hours a Labour government had been given an overwhelming vote of confidence by the British people.

It was all change back home, with a new dawn and a new mood. For me, however, nothing has changed. The North Pole has got to me. My personal history book still needs that Grand Slam, and there is absolutely no question that I will be returning to the High Arctic for another attempt. Will I be third time lucky? I certainly hope so, and I certainly expect to be. But as the Arctic proved, you can never take anything for granted when you pit yourself against the elements.

I cannot see myself ending all this. Not, at least, for the foreseeable future. I have the Geomagnetic South Pole to think about for a start, as well as other trips with novices. But the one glaring omission remains the North Pole, not only for myself but for Britain. The danger, the cold, and the worst conditions on the planet remain, for me, a drug, and there seems little chance of ending this addiction.

The boy who breathed the sharp, clean air on top of the Brecon Beacons and gazed at the stars from its summit has never looked back, and probably never will.

Afterword

On 29 April 1998 David Hempleman-Adams reached the North Pole, achieving his ambition to complete the Adventurers' Grand Slam. He enters the record books as the first person to reach the four poles and to climb the highest summit in each of seven continents.

This feat confirms him as one of the world's greatest living explorers.

MAPS

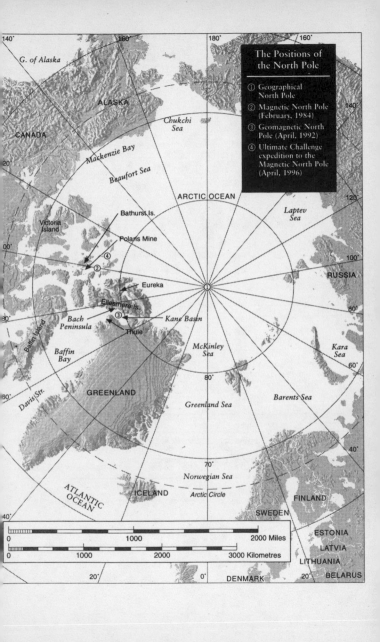

The Positions of
the North Pole

① Geographical
    North Pole
② Magnetic North Pole
    (February, 1984)
③ Geomagnetic North
    Pole (April, 1992)
④ Ultimate Challenge
    expedition to the
    Magnetic North Pole
    (April, 1996)

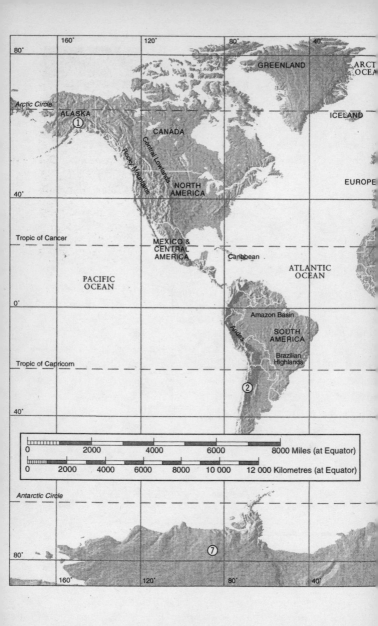

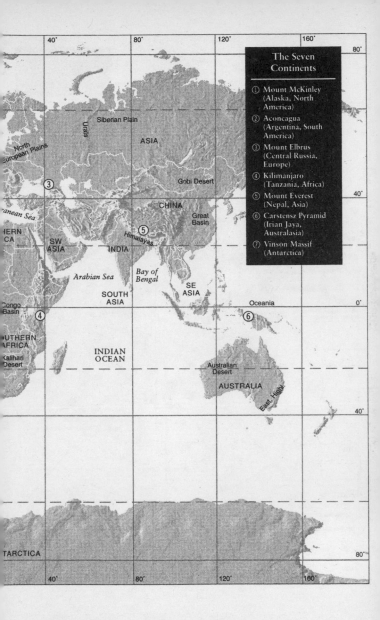

40°   80°   120°   160°
                                                                80°

The Seven
Continents

① Mount McKinley
   (Alaska, North
   America)
② Aconcagua
   (Argentina, South
   America)
③ Mount Elbrus
   (Central Russia,
   Europe)
④ Kilimanjaro
   (Tanzania, Africa)
⑤ Mount Everest
   (Nepal, Asia)
⑥ Carstensz Pyramid
   (Irian Jaya,
   Australasia)
⑦ Vinson Massif
   (Antarctica)

Urals   Siberian Plain

ASIA

North
European Plains

③   40°

Gobi Desert

CHINA   Great
                Basin

…ranean Sea

…ERN
…CA   SW   Himalayas
            ASIA   INDIA

Arabian Sea   Bay of
               Bengal   SE
                         ASIA

…Congo   SOUTH   Oceania   0°
Basin   ASIA

④   ⑥

…OUTHERN
AFRICA   INDIAN
                OCEAN
…Kalihari
Desert   Australian
                          Desert

                          AUSTRALIA   East High…

                                                    40°

…TARCTICA   80°

40°   80°   120°   160°

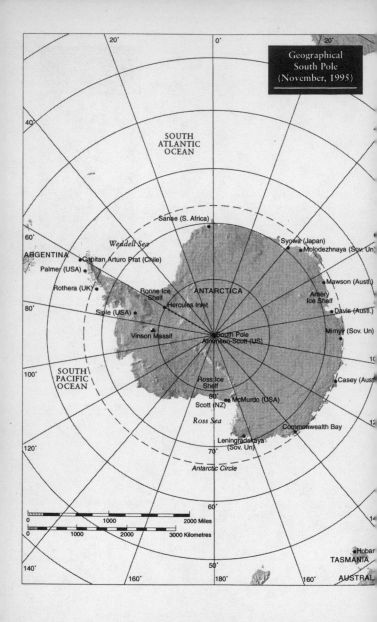

Geographical
South Pole
(November, 1995)

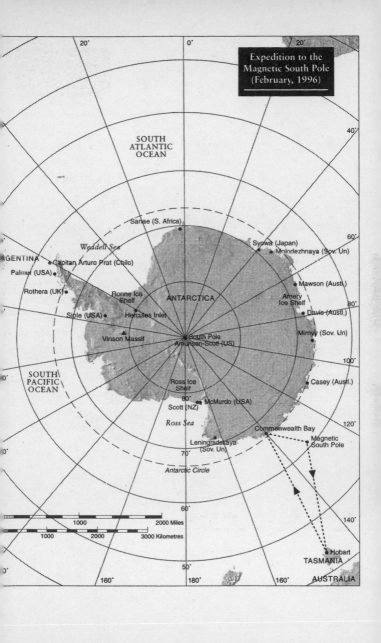

SOUTH
ATLANTIC
OCEAN

Sanae (S. Africa)

Syowa (Japan)
Molodezhnaya (Sov. Un)

Weddell Sea

GENTINA
Capitan Arturo Prat (Chile)

Palmer (USA)

Mawson (Austl.)

Rothera (UK)

Ronne Ice
Shelf

ANTARCTICA

Amery
Ice Shelf

Davis (Austl.)

Siple (USA)

Hercules Inlet

Mirnyy (Sov. Un)

Vinson Massif

South Pole
Amundsen-Scott (US)

SOUTH
PACIFIC
OCEAN

Casey (Austl.)

Ross Ice
Shelf

McMurdo (USA)

Scott (NZ)

Commonwealth Bay

Ross Sea

Magnetic
South Pole

Leningradskaya
(Sov. Un)

Antarctic Circle

1000   2000 Miles
1000   2000   3000 Kilometres

Hobart

TASMANIA

AUSTRALIA

INDEX

Aconcagua, see Andes
Across the Top of the World (Wally Herbert) 57, 65
Advantek (Robnor's agents) 61
Adventure Network 127, 132, 135, 150, 180, 193
Allcock, Dave 12
Allen Bay, Arctic 244
Alps 8, 10–11, 167
   Breithorn 12
   Eiger 11
   Matterhorn 10
   Mont Blanc 11, 16, 86
   Monta Rosa 10, 11
   Weisshorn 11, 15
Amundsen, Roald 146, 184–5, 273, 289
Anchorage, Alaska 13
Andes 16, 107, 109, 124
   Aconcagua 107, 109–13, 124–5, 139, Condor's Nest 110, Berlin Hut 111, 112
Armstrong, Neil 22, 289
Arnesson, Liv 127

Bach Peninsula, Arctic 71, 78
Balium Valley, Irian Jaya 115
Barnicott, Martin 84, 85, 95, 96, 97, 100–1, 124
Barry, John 124
Bathurst Island, Arctic 48, 249, 253, 257, 258; Black Point 249

BBC 23, 28, 29, 39, 42, 84, 85, 125, 131, 191, 200, 238, 240, 241, 243, 248, 261, 268, 277
Bearkner Island, Antarctic 133
Bell, Steve 80, 81, 83, 85, 88, 92, 93, 95, 96, 98, 102, 114, 121, 124
Bergen, Norway 275, 292
Berry, 'Delilah' (Inuit helper) 241, 242, 252, 262, 264, 268
Biak Island, Indonesia 115
Biggs, Ronnie 16
Blanco, Ramon 79, 84, 95, 98
Bland, Pete 203, 204, 214–5, 219, 224, 229, 231
Blessed, Brian 84, 85, 87, 92, 95, 97, 98, 100, 102
Boardman, Pete 83
Boat Harbour, Antarctic 213, 217
Bond, Glen 60
Bonington, Chris 8–9, 83, 92, 100, 289
Boothia Peninsula, Arctic 259
Brecon Beacons, Wales 5–6, 71, 294
Brezhnev, Leonid 105
Broad Peak, the Karakorams 79
Brunel Peninsula, Arctic 257
Buchanan Bay, Arctic 72
Burgess, John 42, 50, 54
Bywater, Alan 285–8

Cairo, Egypt 17
Calgary, Canada 278

Callaway, Dave 84, 87, 89, 91–2, 95, 96, 97
Cambridge Bay, Arctic 239
Camp Hazy, Arctic 268
Camp Ranger, New York State 9
Cape Camperdown, Arctic 71, 72, 78
Cape Columbia, Arctic 23–4, 30
Cape Kitson, Arctic 49, 256, 257
Cape Lady Franklin, Arctic 259
Carstensz Pyramid, Irian Jaya 113–16, 129, 197
Casey, Antarctic 201
Catskill Mountains, New York State 10
Caucasus Mountains 104
 Elbrus 104–6, 113, 200; Pastuhov Rocks 106; Priutt Refuge 106
Champkin, Julian 104–5, 200, 204, 209, 220, 229
Chenoweth, Shirley 61
Chichester, Sir Francis 198, 289
Colston Hall, Bristol 8
Coombs, Simon 79
Cornwallis Island, Arctic 45, 234, 239
Corrigan, Steve 'Nig' 202, 204, 205–6, 207, 210, 212–13, 217–18, 220, 223, 227, 228–9, 231
Crozier Strait, Arctic 248

Daily Mail 104
Daily Telegraph 79
Devon Island, Arctic 257
Downing Street Years, The (Margaret Thatcher) 145, 151, 155, 162
Duke of Edinburgh Award 5–6, 8, 71

Edmonton, Canada 238, 262, 278
Elbrus, see Caucasus Mountains
Elephant Island, South Shetlands 206
Ellesmere Island, Arctic 29, 57, 65, 70

Ellesworth Mountains, Antarctic 107
Endurance (ship) 206
Entebbe, Uganda 17
Eureka (weather station), Arctic 23, 28, 30, 34, 36, 37, 38, 43, 57, 62, 63, 66, 71, 279
Everest, see Himalayas

Far Rockaway, Long Island, New York 19
Ferguson, Clive 28, 30
Fiennes, Sir Ranulph 19, 21–2, 24, 121–3, 165, 272, 276
Flagler Bay, Arctic 68, 70
Flowers, Pam 279
Franklin, Lady 259
Franklin, Sir John 82, 259
Frobisher Bay, Canada 27
Fuchs, Arved 165
Fuchs, Sir Vivian 128
Fuller, Colin 13

Geological Survey 52, 57
Gjeldnes, Rune 274–94
Gorak Shep, Nepal 88
Gorbachev, Mikhail 105
Greenwich Hills, Arctic 257
Grise Fjord, Arctic 57

Haddow, Rupert 'Pen' 238, 272
Halton, Dave 107, 124
Hamilton, Archie 79
Hargreaves, Alison 124
Harman, Paul 114–7, 129, 197
Harrison, Ginette 84, 87, 88–9, 92, 95, 98, 124
Haston, Dougal 8, 83
Hattersley-Smith, Dr Geoffrey 57
Hempleman-Adams family
David Kim Hempleman-Adams:
 birth and education 4–5, 9, 13;
 Duke of Edinburgh Award 6,
 7; climbing in Alps 10–11; first
 visit to Everest 12; climbs
 McKinley 13–16; meets Claire

16; climbs Kilimanjaro 17–18; and Vascon 19; and Global Resins 130, 132; and Robnor 58, 61, 79, 80, 121, 130, 132, 199, 280; and sponsorship 22–3, 61, 129–30; attempt to canoe around Cape Horn 56; illness and death of father 58, 81; marriage and children 58–9, 81, 116, 117, 139, 152, 179, 200; climbs Everest 79–80, 81–103; climbs Elbrus 104–6; climbs Aconcagua 107, 109–13, 124–5; climbs Vinson 107, 107–8, 125; climbs Carstensz Pyramid 113–16; Geographical North Pole, 1983 21–39; Magnetic North Pole, 1984 40–55; Geomagnetic North Pole, 1992 56–7, 59–78; South Pole, 1995–6 121–2, 126–7, 132–92; sails to Magnetic South Pole, 1996, 129, 197–230; Ultimate Challenge trip, 1996 128–9, 233–71; North Pole, 1997 3–4, 272–94; injury and dangers 24–5, 32–3, 35–6, 45–8, 49–50, 51, 64, 65, 71, 73–4, 91, 92, 102, 142, 149–50, 163–4, 168, 174–6, 182, 187, 211, 250–3, 261; family farewells 26, 131–2, 200–1, 236, 278; awarded Livingstone Medal by RSGS 289; and the Prince's Trust 277, 283, 290

David Hempleman (father) 4, 58, 81 (mother) 4

Mark (brother) 4, 81, 139, 194, 201, 270

Peter (uncle) 8

Nick (cousin) 135

Claire, née Brooks (wife) 36, 39, 55, 81, 96, 103, 131–2, 155, 166, 179, 188–9, 193–4, 197, 200–1, 223, 225, 228, 235–6, 276; courtship 16, 18, 20; studies

law 21, 23, 26, 36; marriage and children 58, 114, 116, 117

Alicia (daughter) 59, 132, 139, 152, 193–4, 236

Camilla (daughter) 81, 132, 193–4

Amelia (daughter) 117, 131, 193–4

Ron Brooks (father-in-law) 199, 201, 204, 208–9, 211, 221, 229

Herbert, Wally 22, 25, 57, 65, 67, 70

Hercules Inlet, Antarctic 136–7, 138, 139, 159, 160, 163, 170, 183

Higgs, Andy 242, 245, 248, 260, 263, 264, 266, 268

High Arctic International 60, 240, 278, 279

Hillary, Sir Edmund 83, 101, 289

Himalayan Kingdoms 79–80, 114, 121, 124

Himalayas 60, 82, 86, 101, 206, 207, 228; Everest 8, 9, 12, 19, 79–103, 104, 105, 107, 113, 121, 124, 159, 182, 200, 207, 212, 222, 225; South Col 85, 94, 97, 99, 102; Western Cwm 91, 96; Hillary Step 94, 101; Geneva Square 98; the summit 101; Lhotse 85, 93, 98, 100

Hobart, Tasmania 198–9, 201, 203–4, 209, 214, 216, 219, 230, 232

Hollings College, Manchester 9

Houseman, Oliver 'Ollie' 199, 202, 204, 209, 211, 218, 219, 222

Howells, Ian 240, 241, 243, 248, 255, 261

Hoyland, Graham 84, 92, 95, 98, 114, 200, 204, 205, 222, 228, 231

Hughes, Michael 242, 245, 247, 260, 264

Hunt, Lord (John) 83

Hunt, Rikki 129, 241, 245, 251, 255, 257, 258, 260, 264, 265

Ice Climatology Unit, Ottawa 61
Isaachsen, Arctic 268

Jakarta, Indonesia 114, 232
James, Mansell 'Jesse' 5, 6, 41, 71
James Caird (boat) 206
Jesudason, Bezal 60, 240
Jesudason, Terry 240, 268, 278
Johnson, Julian 239, 241, 245
Jonasson, Bruce 47
Jones, Chris 131

Kahilitna Glacier, Alaska 13
Kane Basin, Arctic 57, 61, 64, 65,
    71, 72, 77, 78
Kathmandu, Nepal 83, 85, 86
Kavalik Island, Arctic 248
Kearton, Mark 242, 244
Kenya, Mt 17
Kershaw, Annie 127, 132-3, 134,
    180, 193
Kershaw, Giles 127
Kew Bay, Arctic 51
Khumbi icefall, Nepal 88, 90, 96
Kilimanjaro, Mt 16-18, 113
King Christian Island, Arctic 262
Kiss, Paul 239, 242, 253, 259, 261,
    264
Knud Peninsula, Arctic 72
Kragge, Erling 273
Konikov, Feodore 133-4, 136-7,
    187-8, 191-2
Koran, Alex 105-6
Koran, Peter 105-6

La Rosee, Christine 268
La Rosee, Franz 268
Larsen, Torry 274, 276
Lees, Alan 84, 87, 89
Lewington, Roy 199, 202, 217-18,
    220, 222, 229
Little Cornwallis Island, Arctic 247
Lobuje, Nepal 88
Lomonosov Ridge, Arctic 27
Lonely Island, Arctic 258
Ludgrove School 56, 57

Lukla, Nepal 86
Lundgard, Leif 60

McIntyre, Don 198-9, 201-3, 211,
    221, 230
McIntyre, Marge 198-9, 201, 211,
    221, 230
McIvor, Scott 84, 95, 98
McKinley, Mt, Alaska 13-15, 18,
    87, 110, 113
McMurdo Sound, Antarctic 189,
    201
Major, John 79
Malankov, Mikal 282
Mann, Clive 129
Matranga, Giorgio 'Mac' 21, 26,
    28-30, 33, 34, 36, 37, 42
Mawson, Douglas 142
Mawson's Hut, Antarctic 199, 217,
    220-1
May, Elaine 61, 64, 66-7, 71, 73,
    75, 78
May, Jeff 78
May, Jim 61, 78, 130
Mear, Roger 84, 85, 91, 94, 95, 96,
    97-8, 107, 107-9, 121-8, 129,
    132-4, 151, 169, 177-8
Melville Peninsula, Arctic 259
Merritt, Jim 54, 60
Messner, Reinhold 19, 108, 128,
    165
Michlmayr, Simon 240, 242, 248,
    260
Mineralniye Vody, Russia 105
Mitchell, Capt Richard 'Mitch' 60,
    61, 62, 63-9, 71-8, 104-5,
    114, 126, 128, 131, 132, 235,
    262
Montreal, Canada 26-7, 39, 43
Morris, Steve 28, 42-4, 50-1, 53-4,
    60
Moscow, Russia 105

Nairobi, Kenya 17
Nanche Bazaar, Nepal 87, 94
Nansen, Fridtjof 290

INDEX

Napper, Jack 54, 60
Natemba (sherpa) 94, 99, 101–2
National Geographic 19
Nelligan, John 130
New York, USA 13, 15, 19
Newitt, Dr Larry 237, 267
Newpalz, New York State 10
Ninnis, Belgrave 142
Nobmann, Lee 84, 95, 96, 98, 100, 101, 102
Noice Peninsula, Arctic 265
Norgay, Tenzing 83, 101
Norman, Bill 28
North Pole, trips 3–4, 272–94; Geographical North Pole 21–39, 41; Magnetic North Pole 40–55, 233–71; Geomagnetic North Pole 56–78
Novak, Skip 198

Operation Caesar 27, 34, 37
Organ Heights, Arctic 256
Ottawa, Canada 237, 267
Ousland, Borge 127–8, 133–4, 181–2, 235–7, 273–4, 277, 282

Patrese, Thierry 133–4
Patriot Hills, Antarctic 124, 125, 135, 144, 146, 149, 155, 190, 192, 240
Peak Lenin, the Pamirs 80
Pelagic (boat) 198
Percy, Mt, Arctic 259
Pfisterer, Gary 84, 88, 95, 98
Pheriche, Nepal 88, 93–4, 102
Pirrit Mountains, Antarctic 160
Plas-y-Brenin, Wales 12
Polar Bear Pass, Arctic 48, 249–53
Polar Continental Shelf Project 60, 70
Polaris Mine, Arctic 45, 48, 240, 244, 245, 247
Pollock, George 104–5, 106, 130
Prince's Trust 277, 283, 290
Punta Arenas, Chile 125, 127, 133, 135, 160, 165, 193, 198

Punta de l'Inca, Chile 110, 113, 124

Resolute, Arctic 1983 expedition 27, 36, 38; 1984 expedition 43, 44, 46, 48, 51, 55; 1992 expedition 60, 66; Ultimate Challenge trip 234, 237, 238, 239–40, 243, 251, 254, 261, 262, 263, 268; 1997 expedition 278, 279, 280, 285, 287, 288; Bradley base 47, 287
Rhodes, Charles 243, 277
Rockefeller Center, New York 84
Rolls, Tony 71, 132
Royal Geographical Society 22, 57, 123, 277; Scottish 277, 289

Samson (Inuit helper) 241, 242, 252, 262, 264, 266, 268
Sandhurst military academy 131
Santiago, Chile 109, 124, 135, 193
Scott, Doug 8, 83
Scott Polar Society 57
Scott, Robert Falcon 82, 122, 146, 165, 182, 184, 237, 273, 289
Scriven, Jerry 16, 19
Shackleton, Sir Ernest 57, 122, 175, 206, 237
Shaw, Ray 59, 61
Simnett, John 234, 242, 244, 246, 248, 257, 264, 266
Smith, Norman 82
Snowdonia, Wales 7
Somers, Geoff 136, 144, 145, 148, 150–1, 156, 164, 168, 180, 181, 190–1, 240, 245, 246, 252, 254, 255, 266, 269, 270–1
South East Indian Ridge, Southern Ocean 210
South Georgia, Antarctic 206
South Pole, trips 121–94; Magnetic South Pole 197–232
Southern Lights 227–8
Spirit of Sydney (yacht) 199, 202, 208, 225, 229, 232

Spurdens, David 279
Stanley Head, Arctic 45
Stephens, Rebecca 'Becks' 84, 87, 107, 124–5, 200, 204, 212, 214, 216, 222, 231
Stockdale, Sue 240, 241, 257, 267
Stroud, Dr Michael 121–3, 165, 276
Sumardo, Djojo 115–17
Sunday Express 36
Sveen, Steiner 127
Sverdrup, Otto 57, 68
Sverdrup Pass, Arctic 58, 65, 67
Swan, Robert 91, 124
Swithinbank, Dr Charles 128

Talkeetna, Alaska 13
Tasker, Joe 83
Taunton Technical College 42
Thiel Mountains, Antarctic 167
Thule, Greenland 57, 71
Thumb Mountain, Arctic 66
Thyangboche monastery, Nepal 87
Tighe, Tony 92
Toronto, Canada 237
Trollheimen Mountains, Norway 275

Uemura, Naomi 19, 24, 25
Ultimate Challenge trip 128–9, 130, 197, 203, 206, 209, 226, 232, 233–71, 277, 278

Victoria Head, Arctic 73
Vincent, Cathy 17, 20, 29, 42
Vincent, Steve 9–20, 21, 26–30, 33, 34, 36, 38, 42, 63, 110, 114

Vinson, Mt, Antarctic 107–9, 111, 113, 123, 125, 127, 192
Vjessel Fjord, Arctic 64
Voyear, Bernard 133–4

Wahi, Rajiv 280
Wallace, Malcolm 129
Ward, Hugh 61, 62, 63, 66, 68, 69, 71, 74–5
Ward Hunt Island, Canada 277, 279, 281, 286, 288, 289, 291
Warham, Mark 84, 90, 95, 97
Webber, Richard 282, 286
White, Martin 28
Wickman, Susanna 241, 245, 247, 258, 260, 261, 267–8
Williams, Neill 104, 126, 132; and Elbrus 104, 105; and Aconcagua 109–13; and North Pole, 1992 1, 62, 63–4, 68, 71–2, 74, 75, 76, 77; and Ultimate Challenge 129, 131, 235, 238, 239, 241, 245, 246, 252, 254, 255, 258, 264, 265, 269
Wilson, Edward 237
Wishart, Jock 59, 155, 191; and North Pole, 1992 61–2, 63–7, 69, 71, 73, 75, 77; and Ultimate Challenge 128, 131, 197, 203, 209, 226, 238, 240, 241, 243–4, 247, 248, 254, 258, 260, 267, 269
Witch Mountain, Arctic 68, 69
Wood, Gareth 91

Yellowknife, Canada 60, 238
Yeltsin, Boris 105